P9-DFI-245

WHAT TO DO WHEN I'M GONE

Also by Hallie Bateman

Brave New Work:
A Journal to Help You Unleash
Your Inner Artist

Love Voltaire Us Apart:
A Philosopher's Guide to Relationships
(illustrator)

If Our Bodies Could Talk
(illustrator)

WHAT TO DO WHEN I'M GONE

I'M GONE

A MOTHER'S WISDOM TO HER DAUGHTER

SUZY HOPKINS & HALLIE BATEMAN

BLOOMSBURY

NEW YORK · LONDON · OXFORD · NEW DELHI · SYDNEY

BLOOMSBURY PUBLISHING
Bloomsbury Publishing Inc.

1385 Broadway
New York
NY 10018
USA

BLOOMSBURY, BLOOMSBURY PUBLISHING, and the Diana logo
are trademarks of Bloomsbury Publishing Plc

First published in the United States 2018

ISBN: HB: 978-1-63286-968-5
eBook: 978-1-63286-970-8

Library of Congress Cataloging-in-Publication Data is available
A catalogue record for this book is available from the British Library

2 4 6 8 10 9 7 5 3 1

Designed and typeset by Ann Bobco and Katya Mezhibovskaya
Printed and bound by RR Donnelley Asia Printing Solutions Limited

To find out more about our authors and books visit
www.bloomsbury.com and sign up for our newsletters.

Bloomsbury books may be purchased for business or promotional use.
For information on bulk purchases please contact Macmillan Corporate
and Premium Sales Department at specialmarkets@macmillan.com.

This book is dedicated to our moms.

Introduction

When I was a kid and fears of death came to me in the night, I'd wake up my mom and she would console me.

> *Am I going to die?*
> Yes, but not for a long, long, long time.
> *Are you going to die?*
> Yes, but not for a long, long time.

As I got older, death entered our casual family discourse. Over dinner, we would engage in the burial-vs.-cremation debate, or my mom would issue one of her decrees: "If I ever become a drooling mess, just shoot me." As with most things, joking about death was our way of acknowledging its inevitable presence. We spoke about it in the light of day so that when we faced it later, alone, it wouldn't be so scary.

One night, when I was twenty-two or twenty-three, I couldn't sleep: That recurrent and agonizing prospect of losing my mom slipped in again. This time I decided not to push the thoughts away. I allowed myself to vividly imagine my mom's death, to feel the pain of the moment I learned she was gone.

With sleep an ever-more-distant prospect, I went even further: I imagined the next day, and the day after that. The earth would continue to spin, and I'd be left in a world without her. My map would be gone. The ground beneath my feet would be gone.

Who could I call to ask how to cook a potato? Who would listen to me talk about my work for more than five minutes? Who would tell me everything? Who would forgive me for everything? How could I possibly navigate this world without the person who brought me into it?

I cried. Then I had an idea. The next morning, while we made breakfast, I asked my mom to write a book of step-by-step, day-by-day instructions I could follow after her death.

She laughed. Then she said yes.

Hallie Bateman

The day I die will go something like this . . .

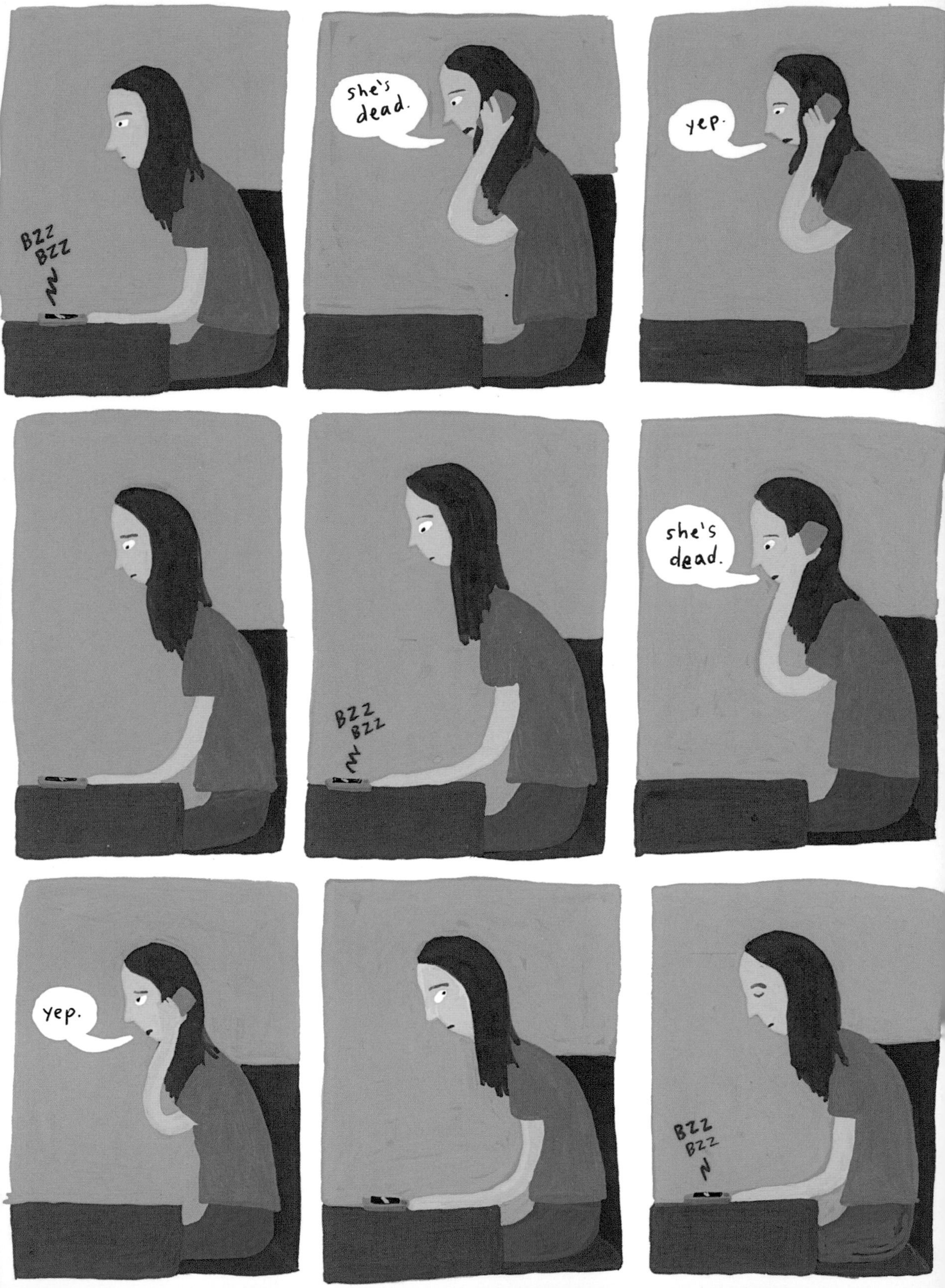
BZZ BZZ
she's dead.
yep.
BZZ BZZ
she's dead.
yep.
BZZ BZZ

This could go on for days.
Step away from the phone.

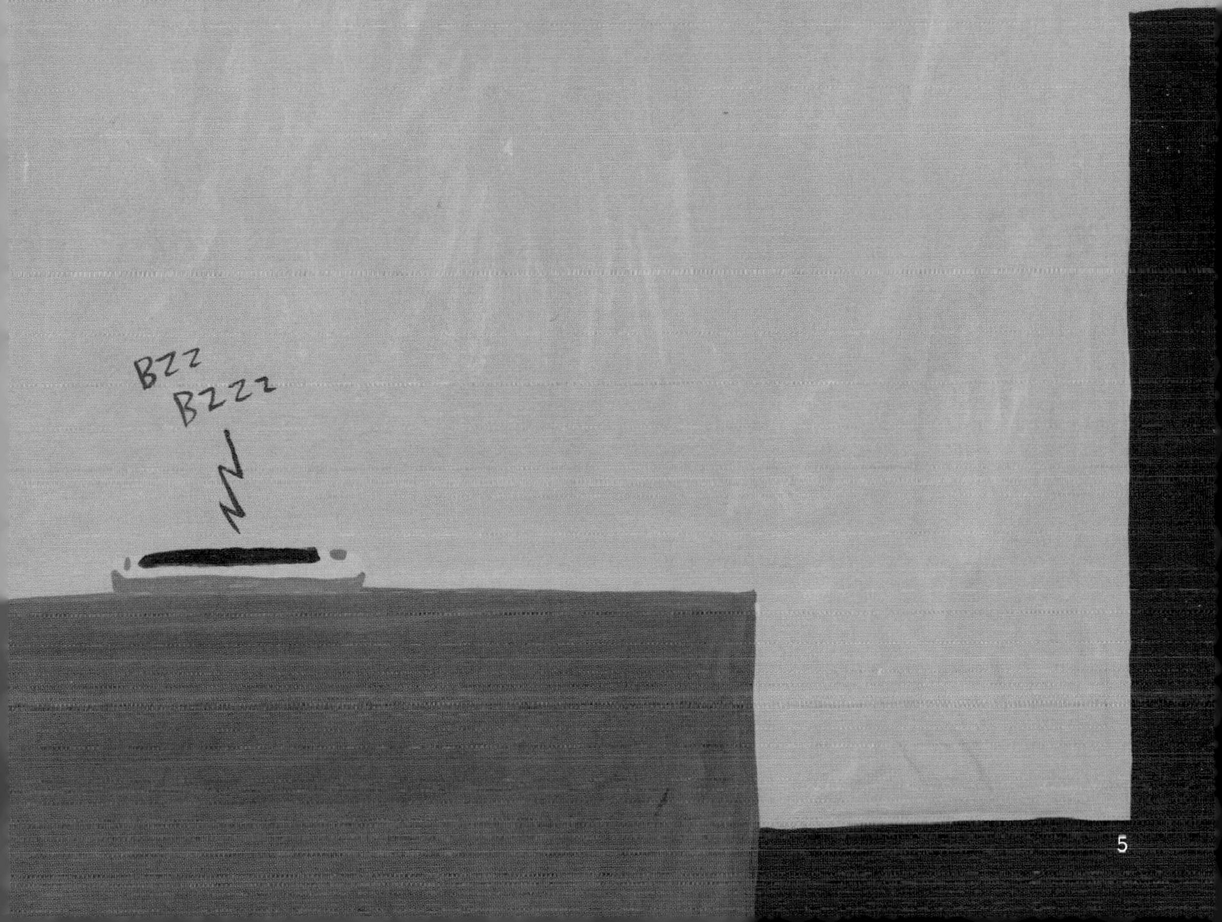
BZZ
BZZZ

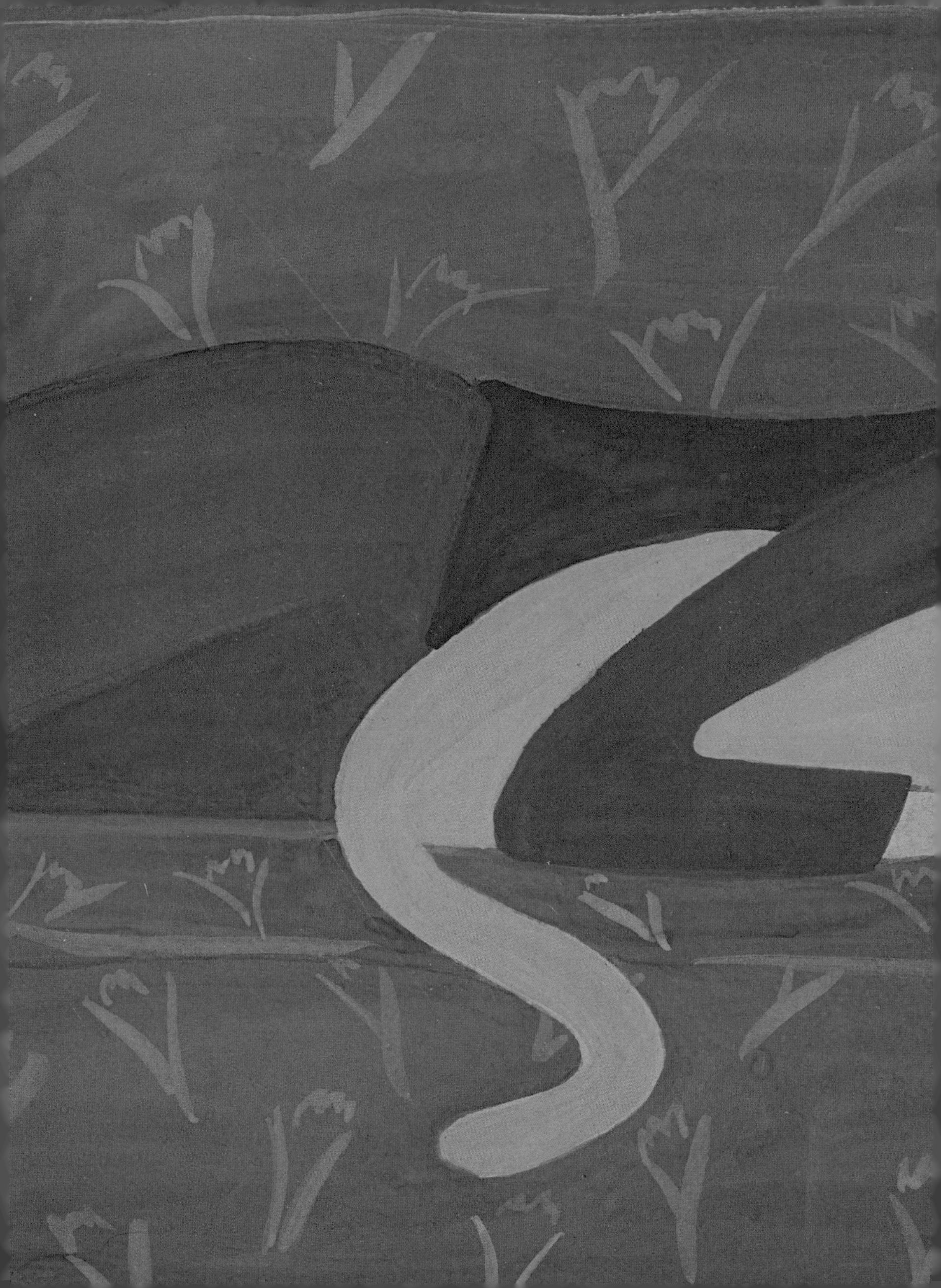

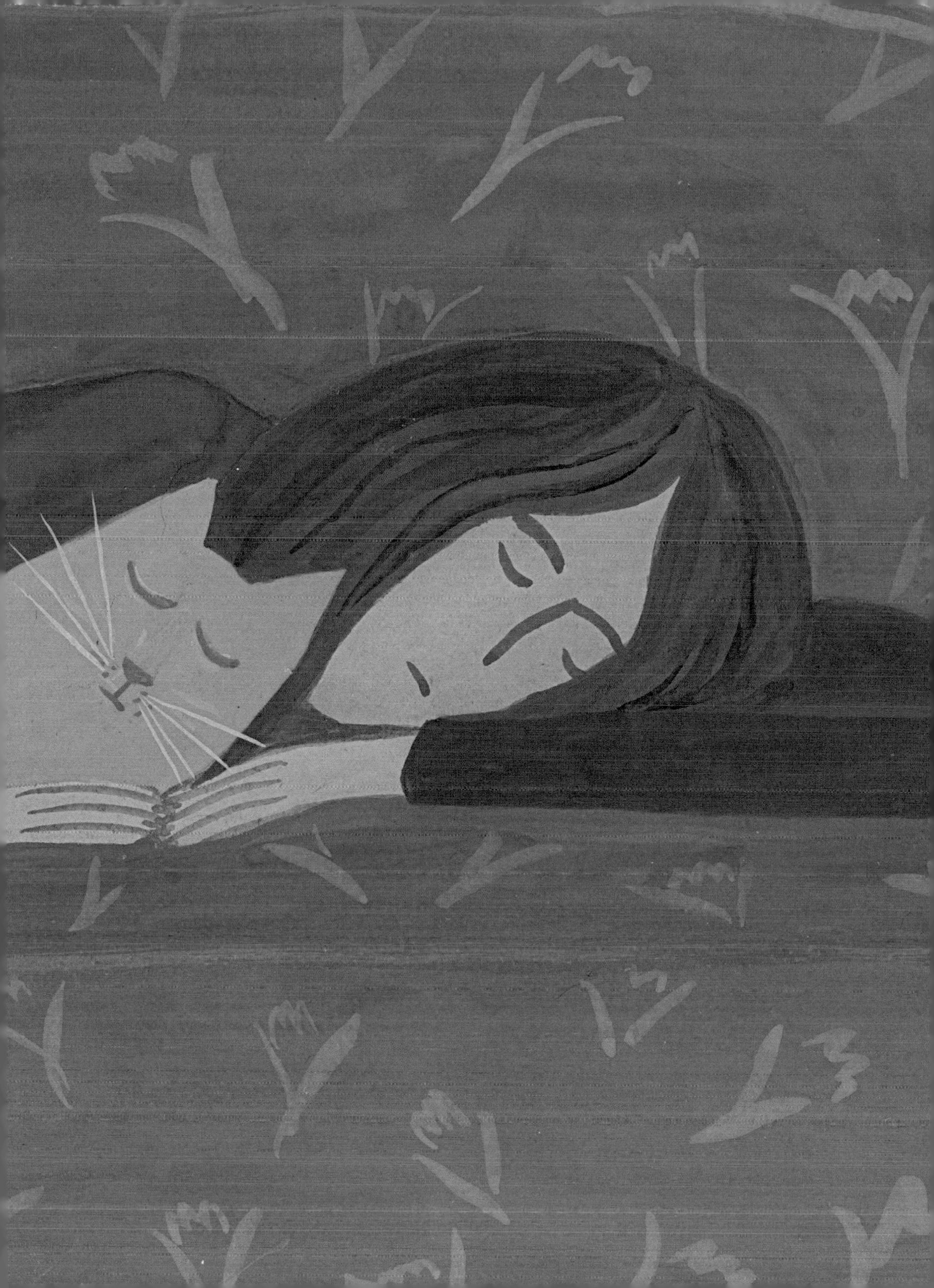

DAY 1: *Make fajitas*

Slice a giant pile of sweet onions. You'll be crying, but the dish will be worth it in the long run.

Heat equal amounts of olive oil and butter in a large sauté pan, add the diced garlic and serrano pepper, then pile the onions on top. The gym I went to always had cooking shows playing on TV while the women worked out; go figure. Anyway, I didn't get in great shape but I learned a lot, including that the weight of that onion pile will aid caramelization—the slow sweetening of the final product.

So just cook over low heat for 20 to 30 minutes, letting the onions do most of the work.

Tumble the pile now and then until it's nearly caramelized. Sprinkle the mixed chili powder, cumin, salt, pepper, and cayenne on top, stirring to distribute the spices while cooking

a bit longer. Lay thin slices of green, red, and yellow peppers on top; this will make you feel like an artistic genius and less like crying.

Next, cook a chicken breast (or firm tofu if you're a vegetarian) and add thin slices to the onion-vegetable mixture.

I like to cut the tomatoes in quarters or eighths. But hell, who cares, they're going to mash down anyway. Sprinkle with salt and pepper and stir them into the mix in the last few minutes of cooking.

Serve with fresh tortillas, chopped cilantro, good salsa, and thin slices of avocado. Great job. Now don't you feel better?

Of course you don't. Pour yourself a stiff glass of whiskey.

Vidalia onions
Olive oil, butter
Fresh garlic, diced
Serrano pepper, seeded, diced
Green, red, and yellow peppers
Chili powder, cumin, salt,
  pepper, and cayenne
Chicken breast or firm tofu
Fresh tomatoes
Flour or corn tortillas
Cilantro, salsa, avocado
Whiskey

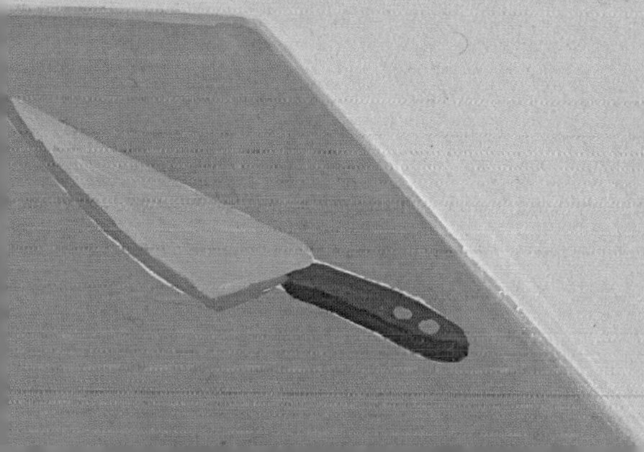

DAY 2: *Let people in*

The doorbell is going to ring and you're going to get up and open the door and greet the people and let them in. Talk. Listen. Cry. Serve them tea and toast if you're up to it.

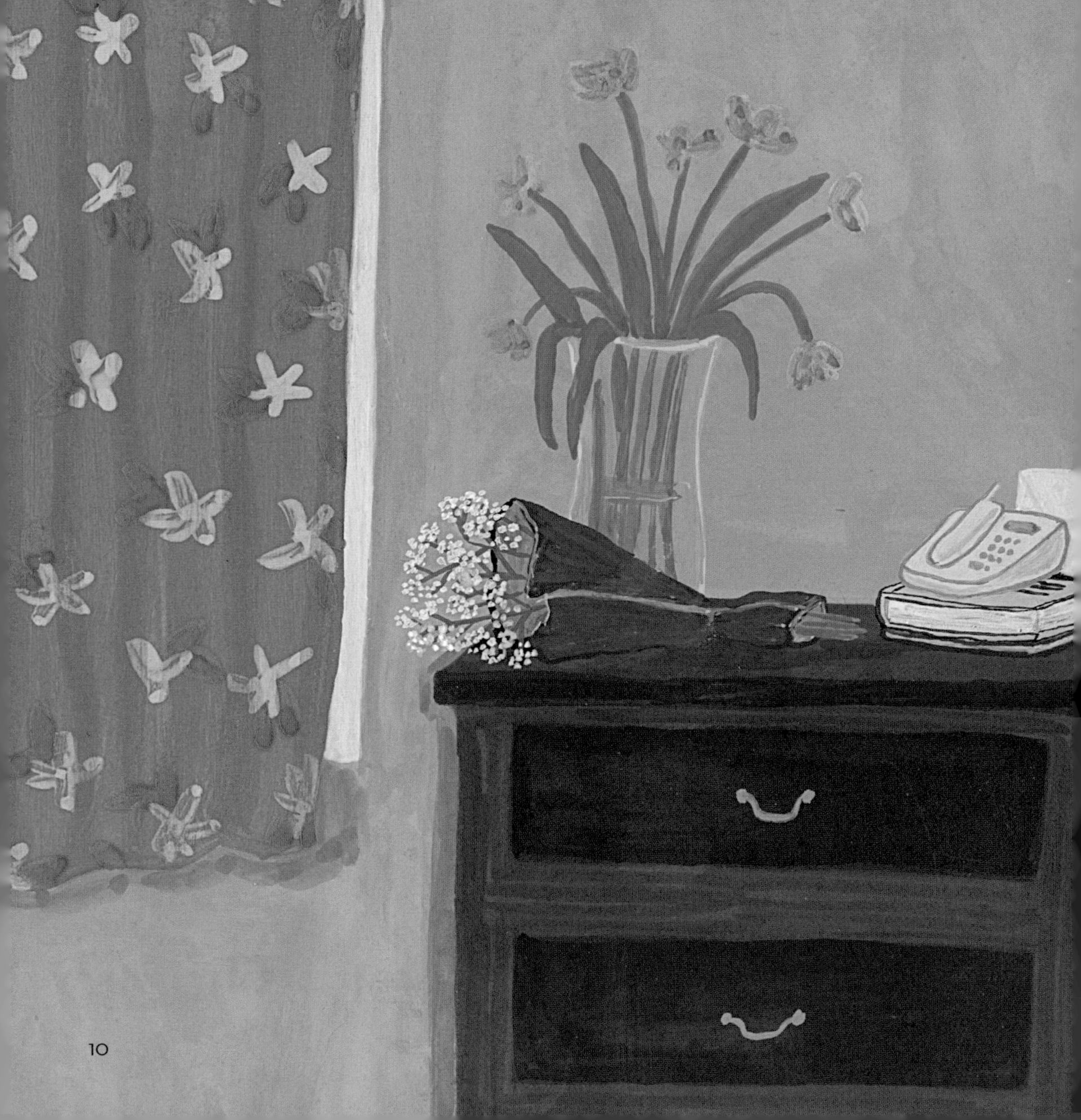

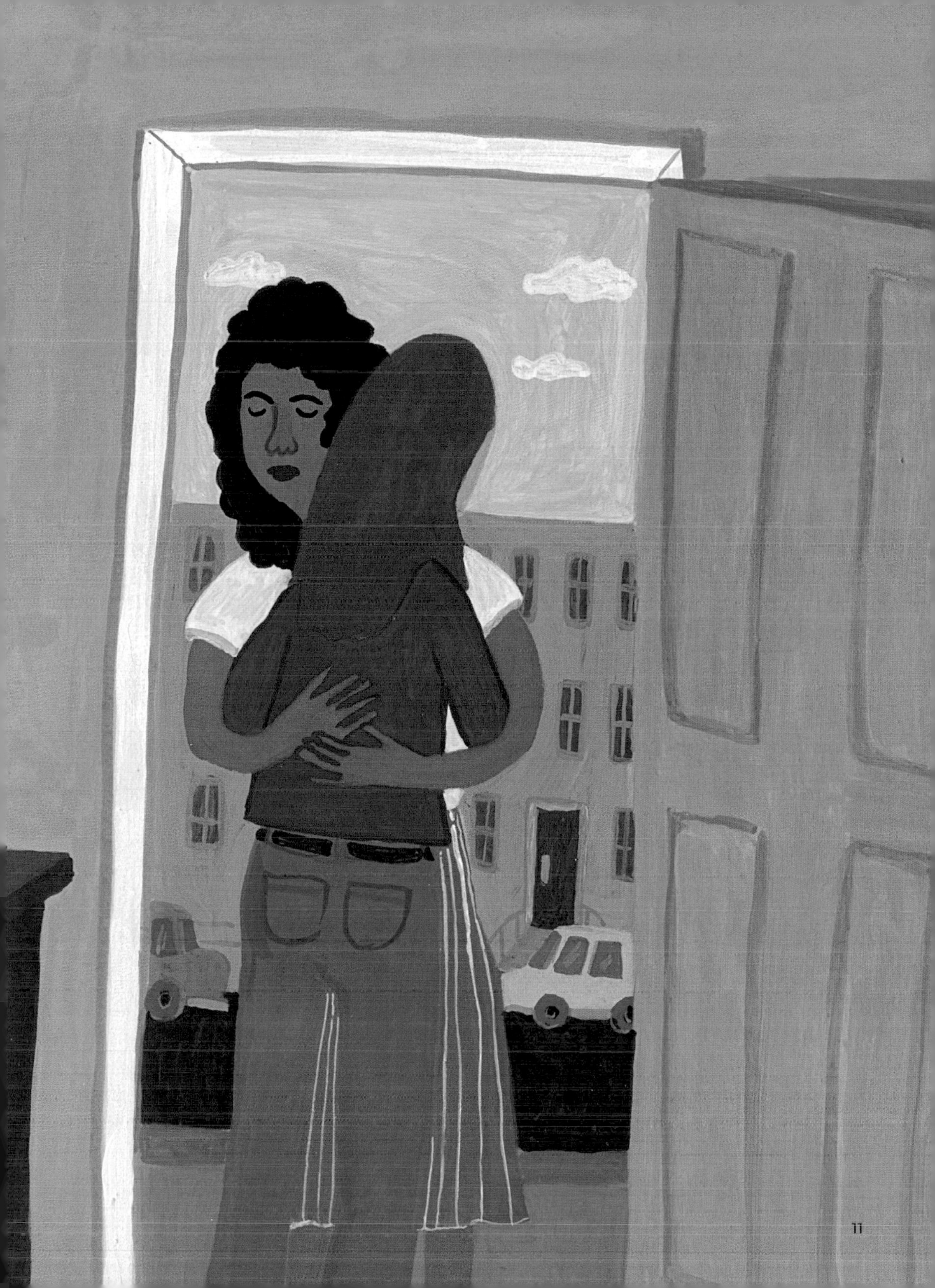

DAY 3: *Brush the dog*

Get all the tangles out of his fur. It's not the dog's fault I died.*

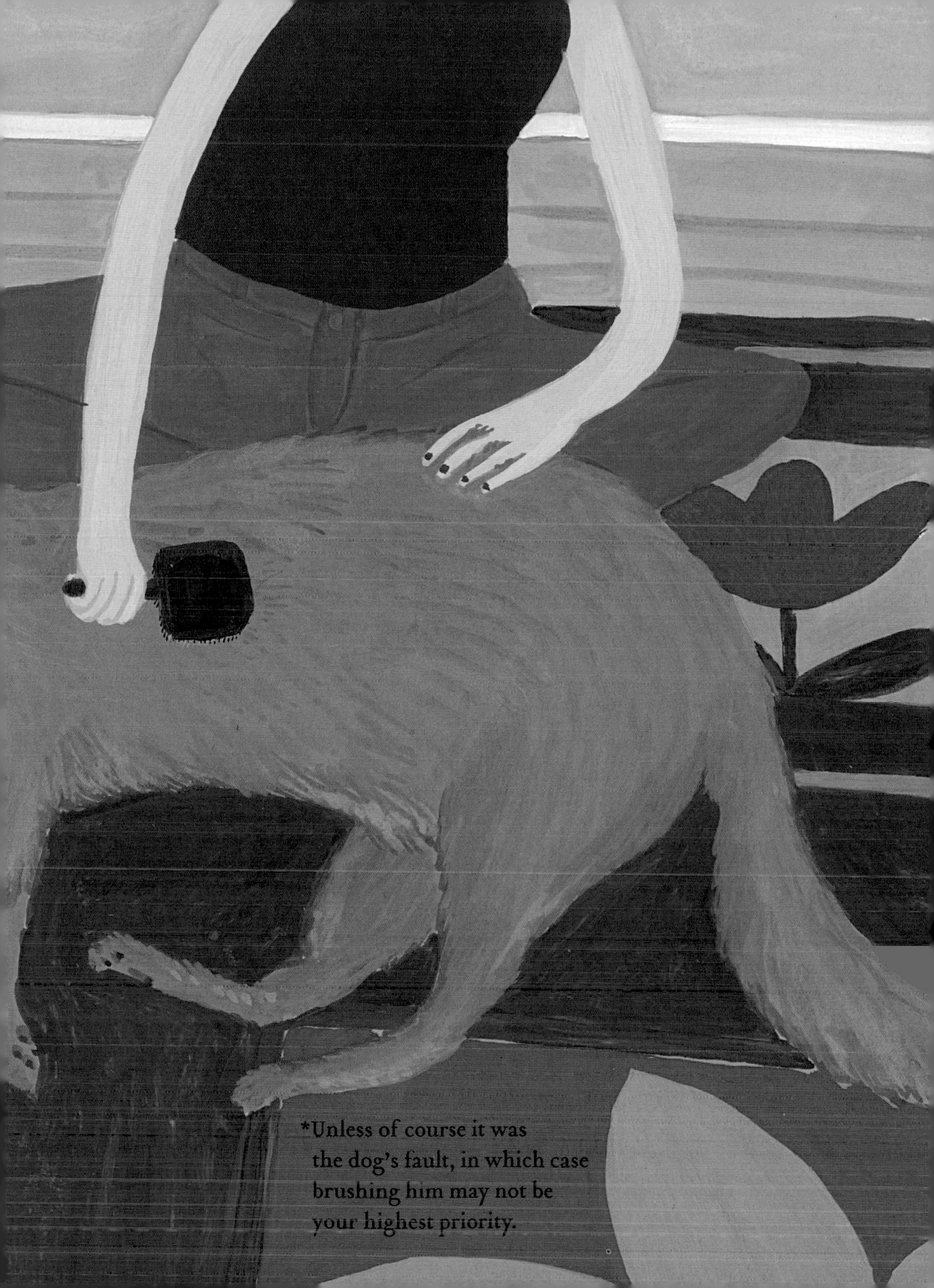

*Unless of course it was the dog's fault, in which case brushing him may not be your highest priority.

DAY 4: *Write my obituary*

It used to be that obits were free and written by journalists. They included basics about your family, schooling, career path, contributions to your community.

Now most are sent in by family members who can't write very well and focus on obscure highlights: "She was devoted to her beloved dachshund, Dinky, with whom she shared so many joyous years."

Obits are more than just a formality. They are one of the few written records of your time here. The collective memory of a person's existence fades quickly; after a generation or two you're wiped off the face of the earth.

If I had planned better, and died later, I might have written it myself. But obviously I ran out of time. So get together with the people who knew me best, talk for a while, and realize how little you actually know about my life.

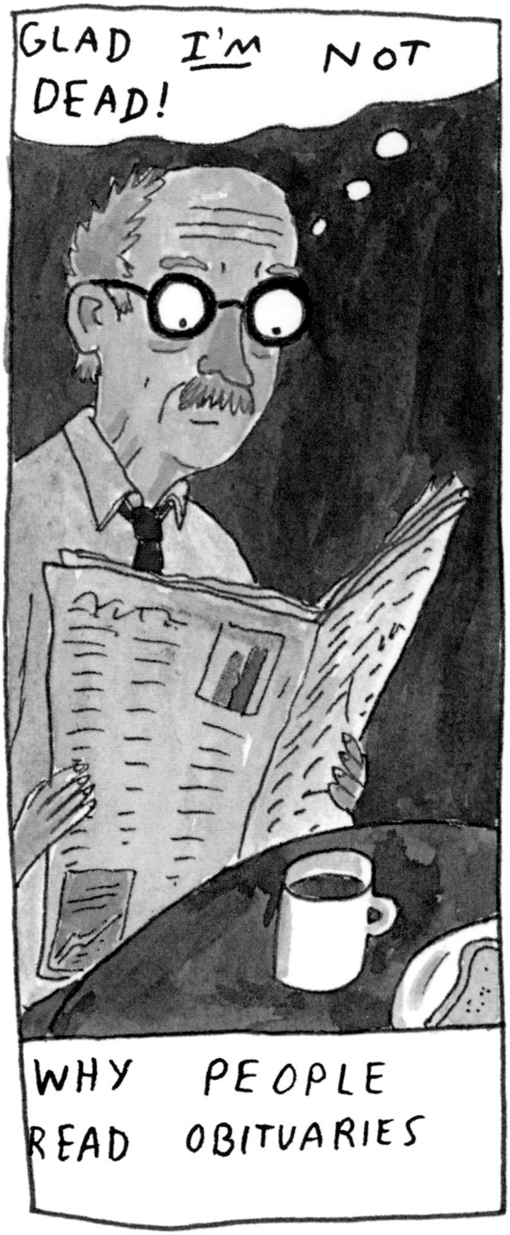
GLAD I'M NOT DEAD!
WHY PEOPLE READ OBITUARIES

What NOT to include

"She moved to Florida in 1987, to Funkville in 1993, to Cleveland in 1995, then shacked up with a man she later regretted even knowing, before settling in Tacoma."

I can't even remember all the places I've lived, and it doesn't need to be part of the permanent record.

"She loved crossword puzzles and [endless list of boring hobbies]."

Nobody but my immediate family needs to know that I made mosaic tile flower pots, played piano badly, bought season tickets but only saw two plays a year, or cooked with the same six ingredients for the past twenty-five years.

"She died peacefully with her loving family at her side."

I don't think it's possible that everyone dies peacefully. I'm guessing some people die screaming. Everyone should have access to their own gallon of morphine at the first sign of pain.

"She shared her wisdom, love, and light with everyone she met."

Oh, come on. Let's be honest. Plus I'm pretty sure there's a traffic cop near my office who would disagree.

DAY 5: *Clean your house*

You are numb. It's time
to put your home in order.
Give everything a place.
Make it make sense.
Make your room the exact
opposite of the randomness of
existence, the mercilessness
of mortality.

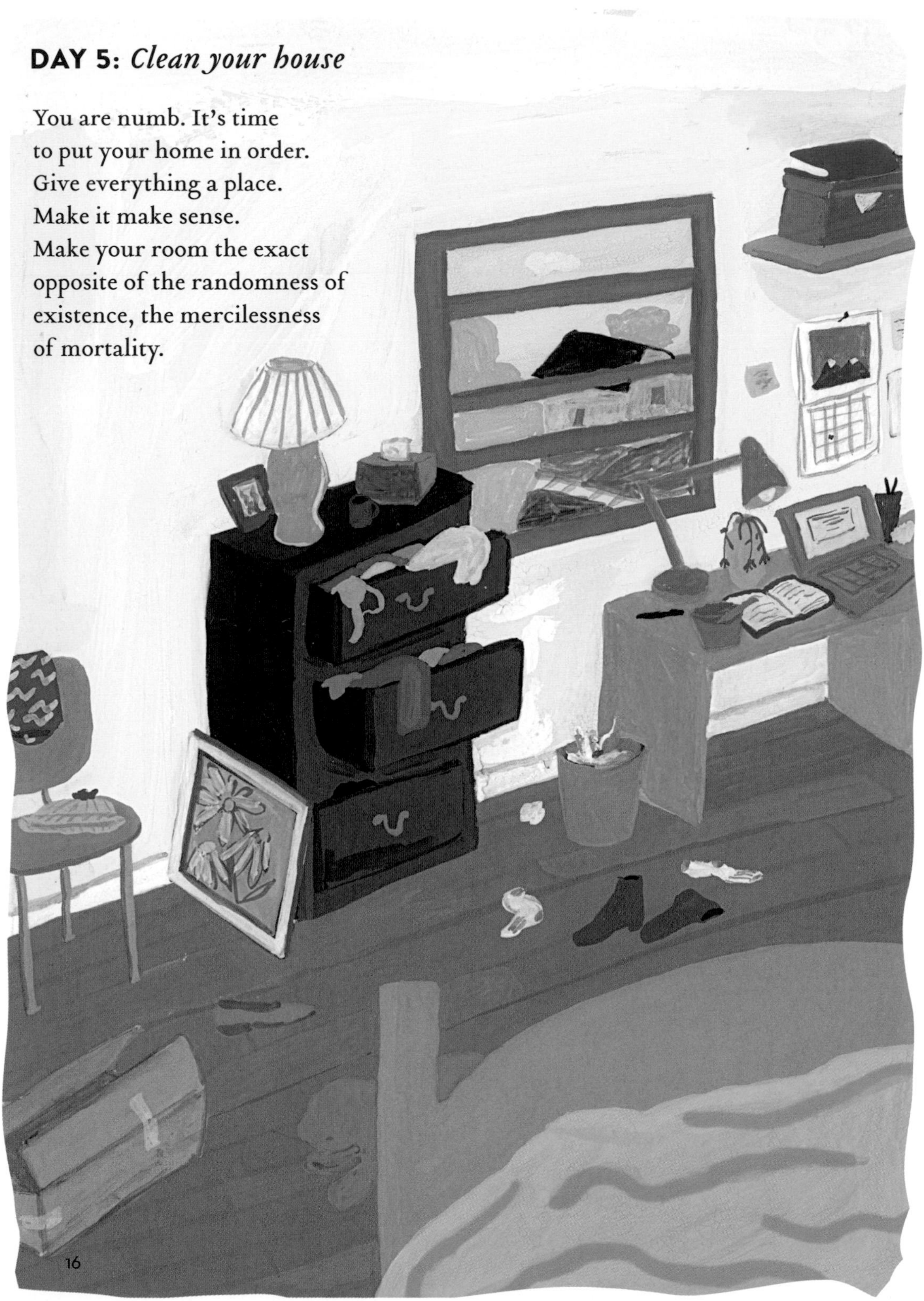

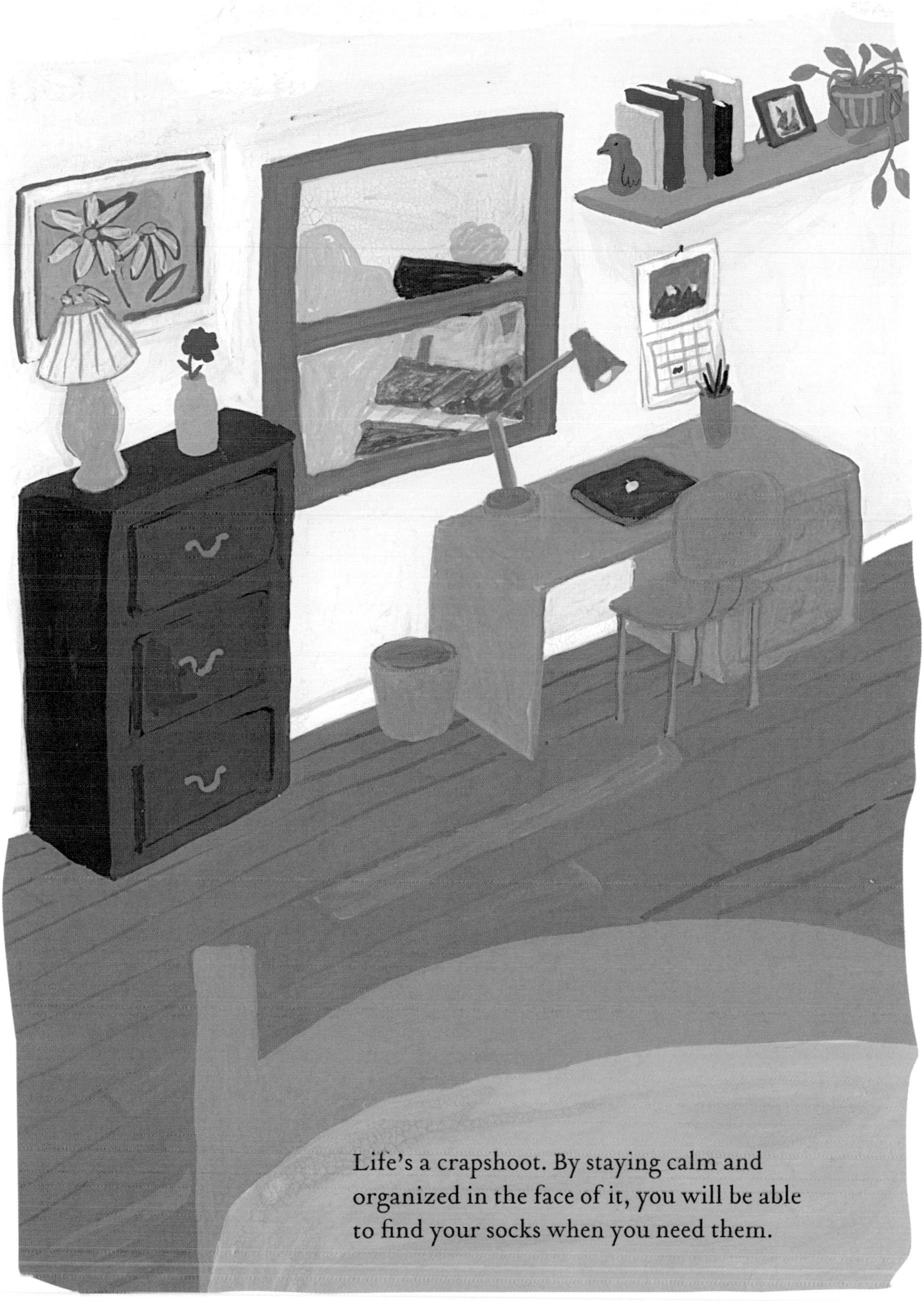

Life's a crapshoot. By staying calm and organized in the face of it, you will be able to find your socks when you need them.

DAY 6: *Visit an all-night diner*

You need a good friend right now, one who will come right over, even if that means flying across country. Tell her exactly what you need, whether you need her to listen, cry with you, chat up a storm, or sit together in silence.

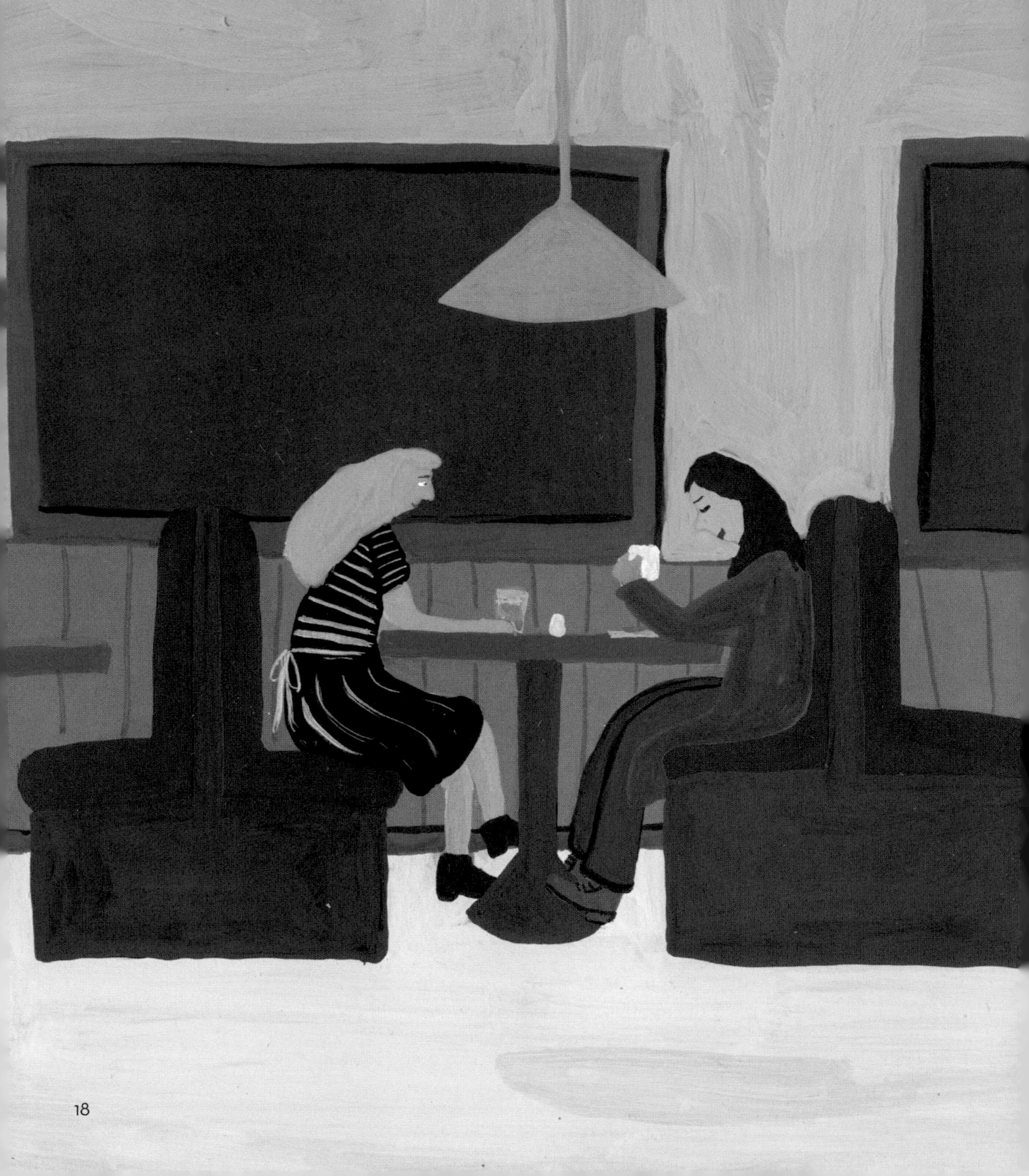

Go to your favorite all-night diner. Eat pie, drink coffee, and make small talk in which death is never mentioned. Or share what happened, how it feels to lose me. Tell her what I said that made you laugh, what I did that drove you crazy.

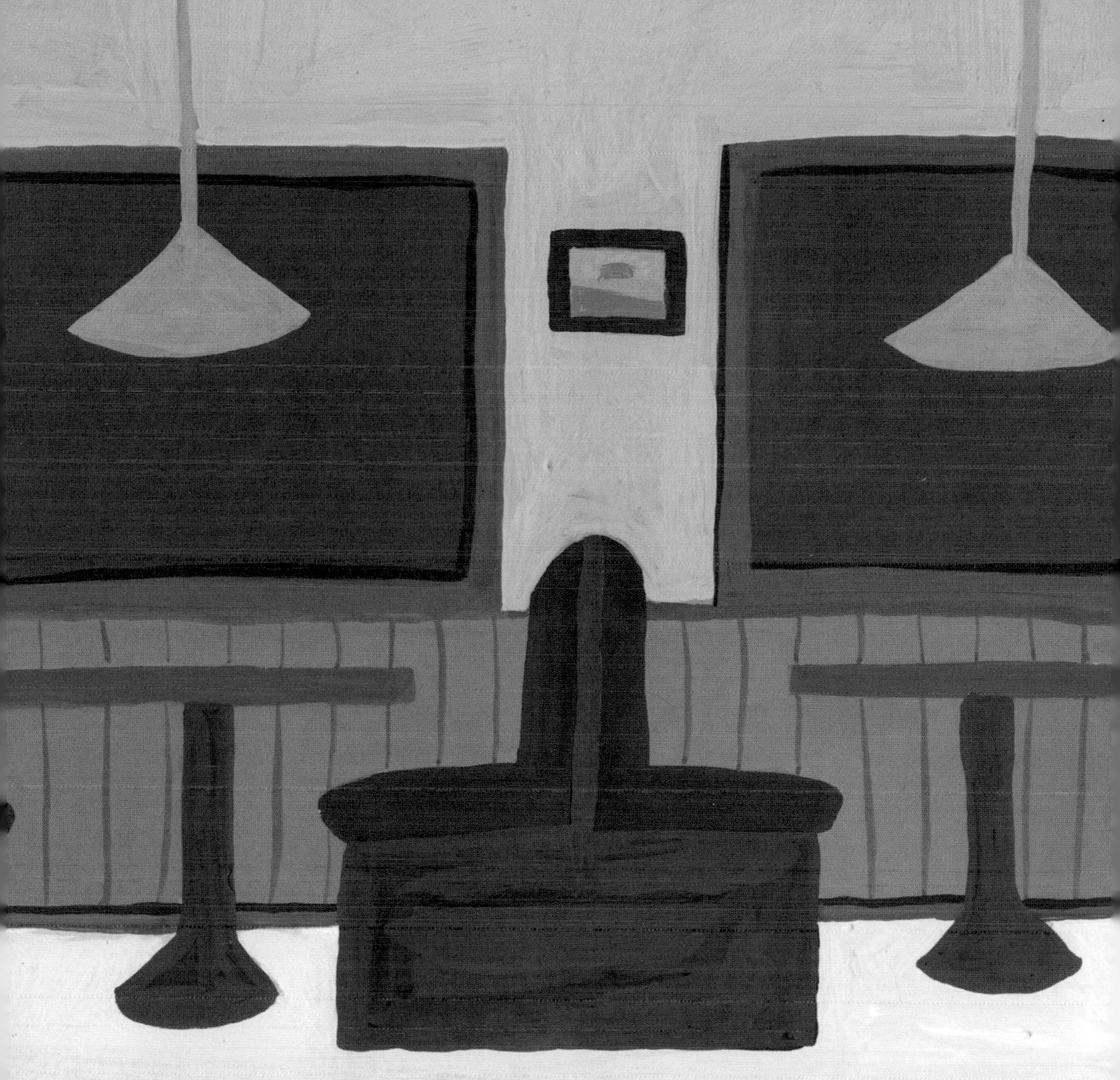

There are no rules here. A good friend will understand, and a really good friend will bring a box of tissue. You don't have to go through this alone, now or in the future.

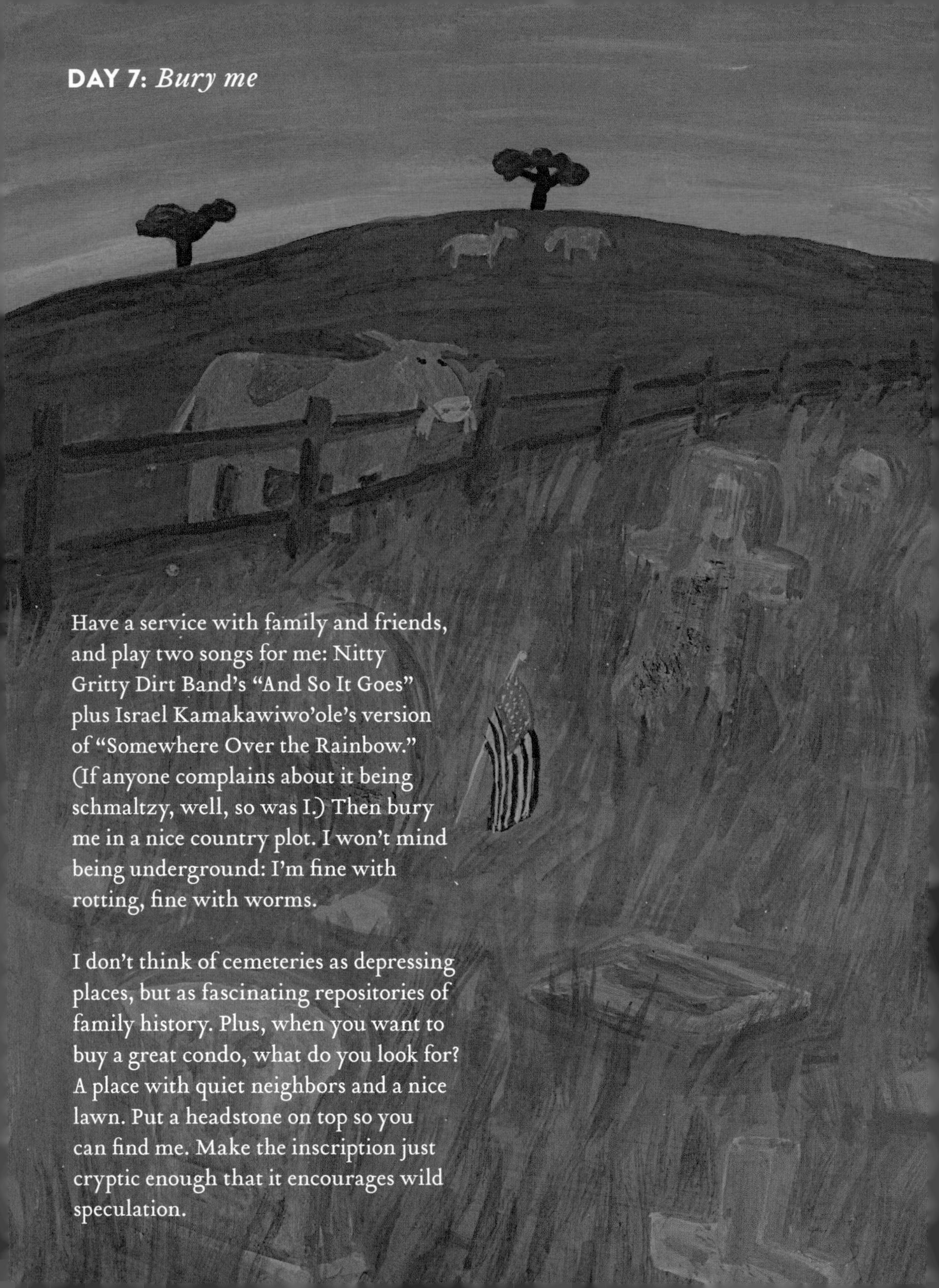

DAY 7: *Bury me*

Have a service with family and friends, and play two songs for me: Nitty Gritty Dirt Band's "And So It Goes" plus Israel Kamakawiwo'ole's version of "Somewhere Over the Rainbow." (If anyone complains about it being schmaltzy, well, so was I.) Then bury me in a nice country plot. I won't mind being underground: I'm fine with rotting, fine with worms.

I don't think of cemeteries as depressing places, but as fascinating repositories of family history. Plus, when you want to buy a great condo, what do you look for? A place with quiet neighbors and a nice lawn. Put a headstone on top so you can find me. Make the inscription just cryptic enough that it encourages wild speculation.

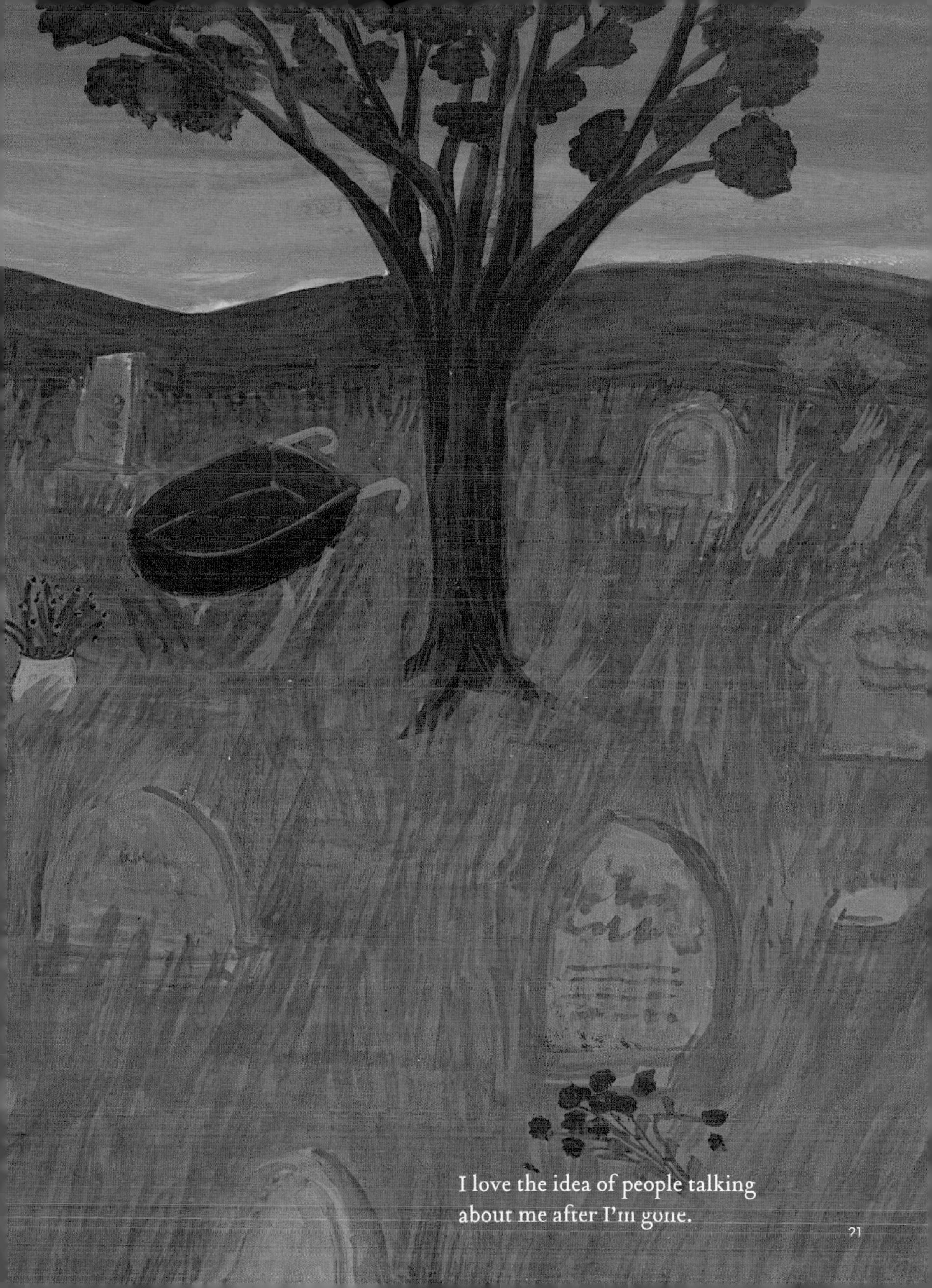

I love the idea of people talking
about me after I'm gone.

DAY 8: *Go Rollerblading*

Your job today is not to think. Just be. When you're Rollerblading, you can't think in the conventional way, unless you're a really good Rollerblader.

If you're the kind of Rollerblader I was, all you're thinking is, "I'm gonna fall I'm gonna fall I'm gonna fall!" This is good. You won't have time to dwell on real or imagined memories, sorrow, or angst. You won't have time to think, "Oh no, I yelled at my mother the last conversation we ever had."

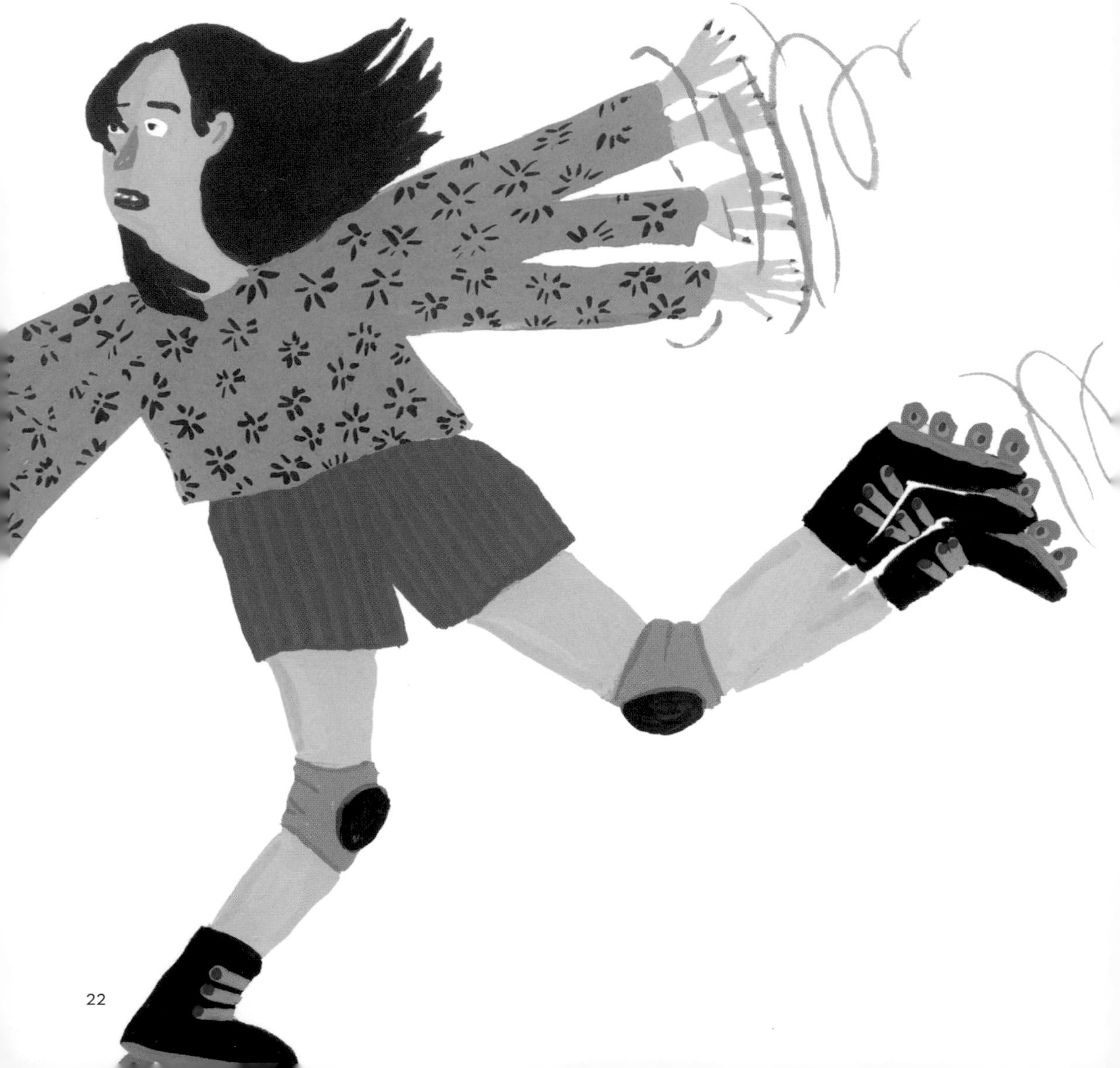

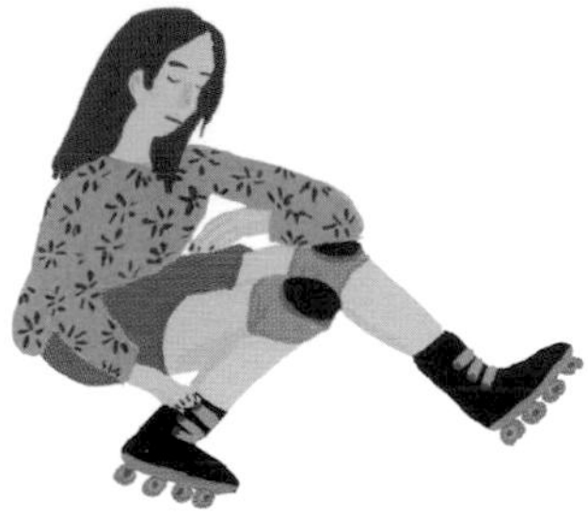

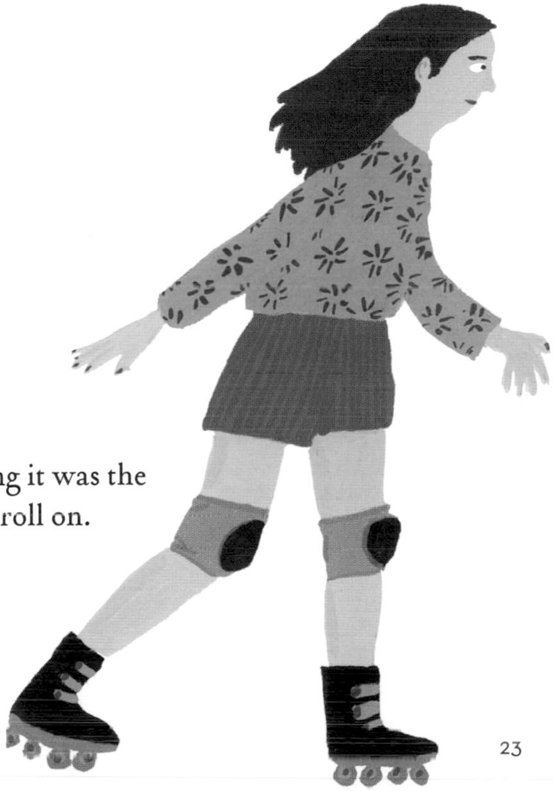

That's OK. You had no way of knowing it was the last time we'd talk. Feel bad, feel sad, roll on.

DAY 12: *See a blockbuster movie*

Why did this happen the way it did? Could it have been prevented?
Are you tempted to blame me for how I wrote my own demise: smoking, drinking, lackluster gym workouts? Go ahead, rewrite my ending. I'm not attached to it anymore. Here are a few alternatives if you need help.

Swallowed by a sinkhole

Trampled in a Black Friday sale

Directed off a cliff by Siri

Heart attack (brought on by sheer love)
while clutching a photo of you

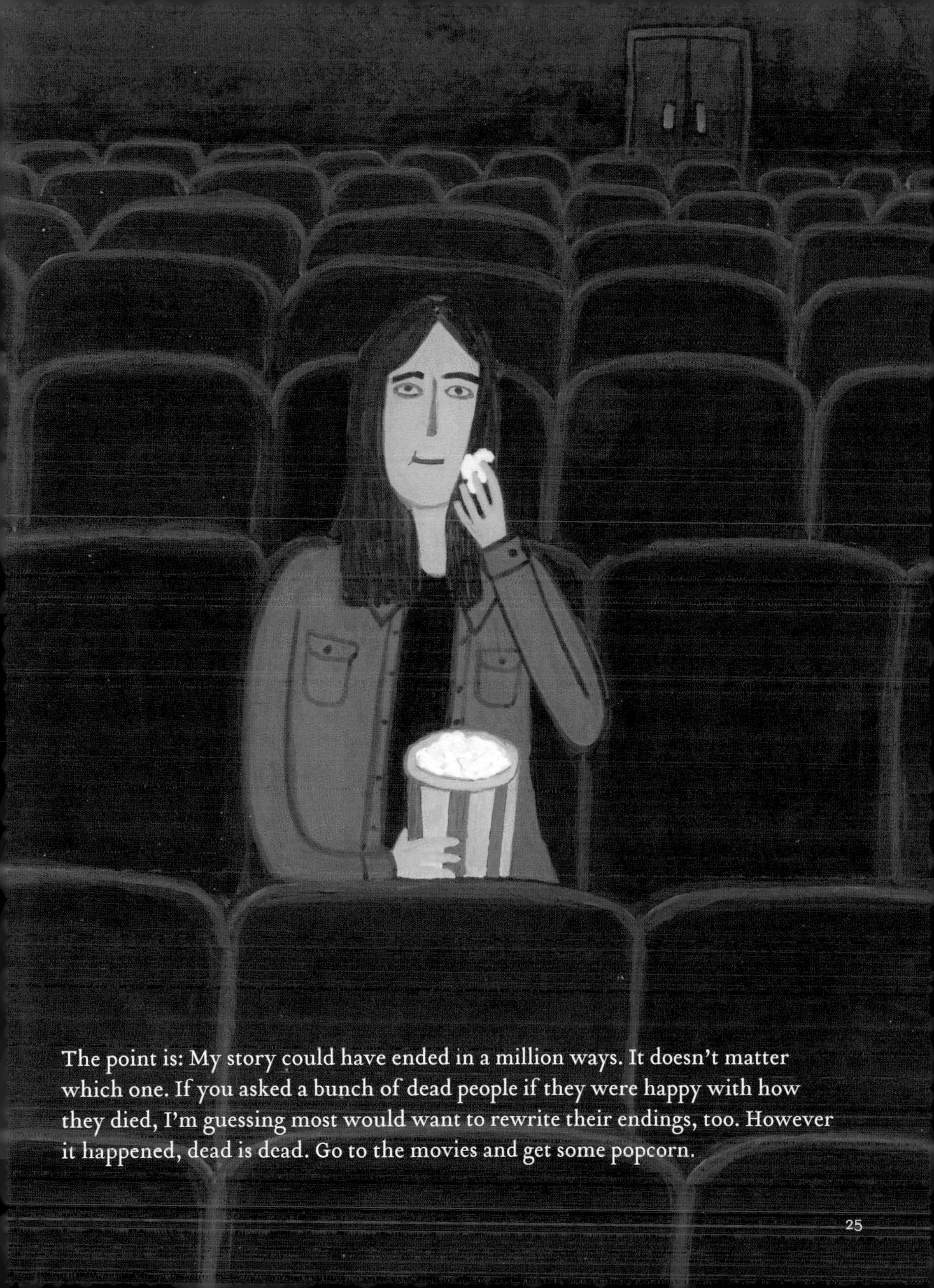

The point is: My story could have ended in a million ways. It doesn't matter which one. If you asked a bunch of dead people if they were happy with how they died, I'm guessing most would want to rewrite their endings, too. However it happened, dead is dead. Go to the movies and get some popcorn.

DAY 15: *Bake brownies*

Until now you've been so busy that you haven't had much time to think. But the forever nature of the loss is beginning to sink in. This is the new normal. You won't get over it but in time you'll get through it.

Baking brownies will help, especially if you share them. This recipe is one your grandma used for many years.

In a heavy saucepan, melt the butter and chocolate together over low heat, stirring frequently. Cool slightly. Add the sugar and vanilla, mixing well. Add the eggs one at a time, mixing after each addition.

Stir in the dry ingredients plus the nuts or peppermint bits, mixing until just combined. Grease and flour the bottom of a 13-by-9-inch baking pan and spoon in the batter, spreading evenly. Bake at 325 degrees for 35 to 40 minutes. Cool and cut into squares.

½ cup butter
4 oz. unsweetened chocolate
2 cups sugar
2 tsp. vanilla
4 eggs
1 cup oat flour
½ cup + 2 tbsp. all-purpose flour
1 tsp. baking powder
½ tsp. salt

Optional: ½ cup chopped walnuts or pecans, or 20 red peppermints broken into bits (unwrap, put in a plastic bag, and gently have at it with a hammer)

Brew a pot of good coffee while you're at it, and figure out who you'll share these brownies with.

Make sure it's not someone who's going to carp about fat and calories; that's the last thing you need. Look for a person who lights up at the mere mention of homemade brownies.

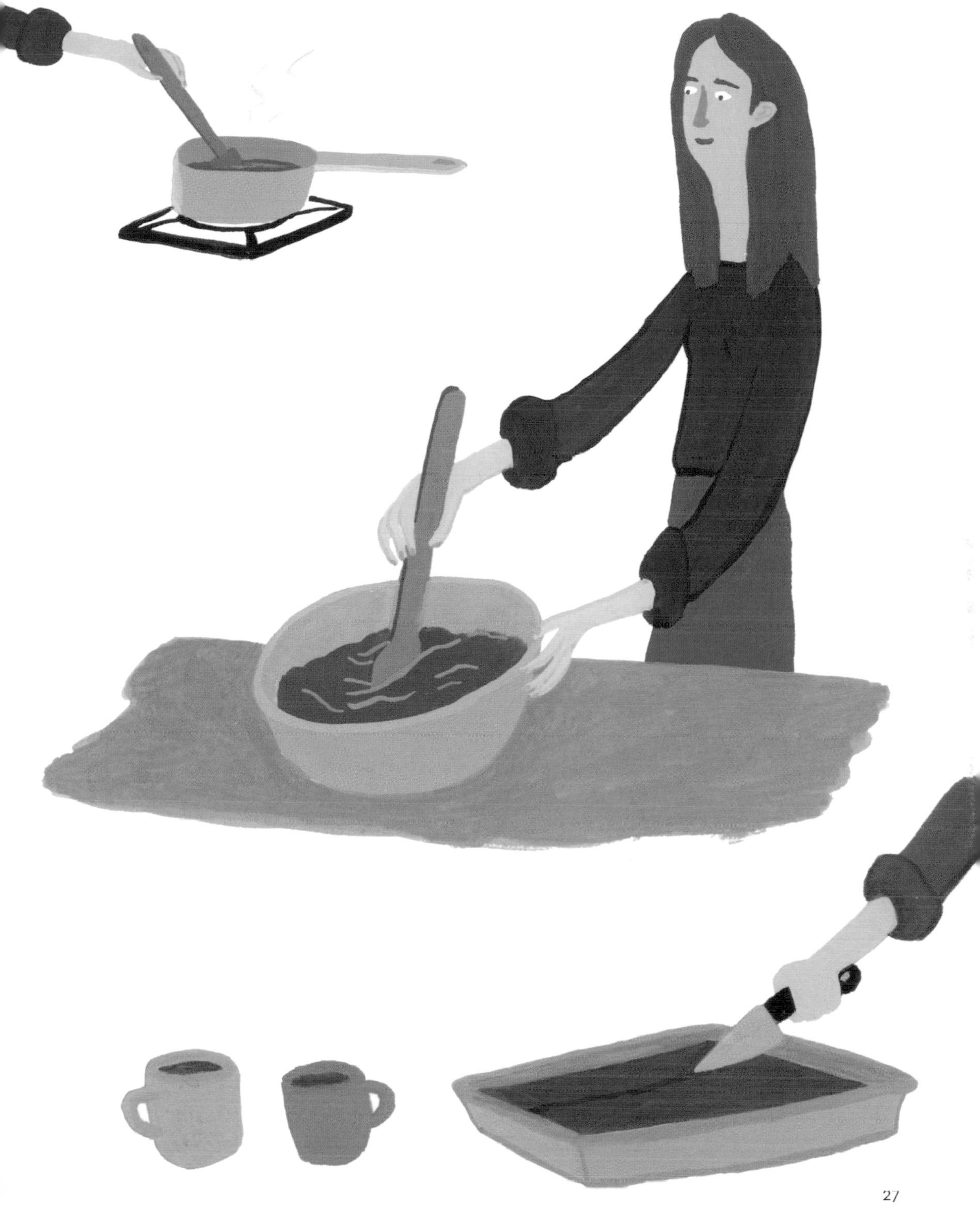

DAY 17: *Smile and nod*

WHAT PEOPLE ARE GOING TO SAY TO YOU

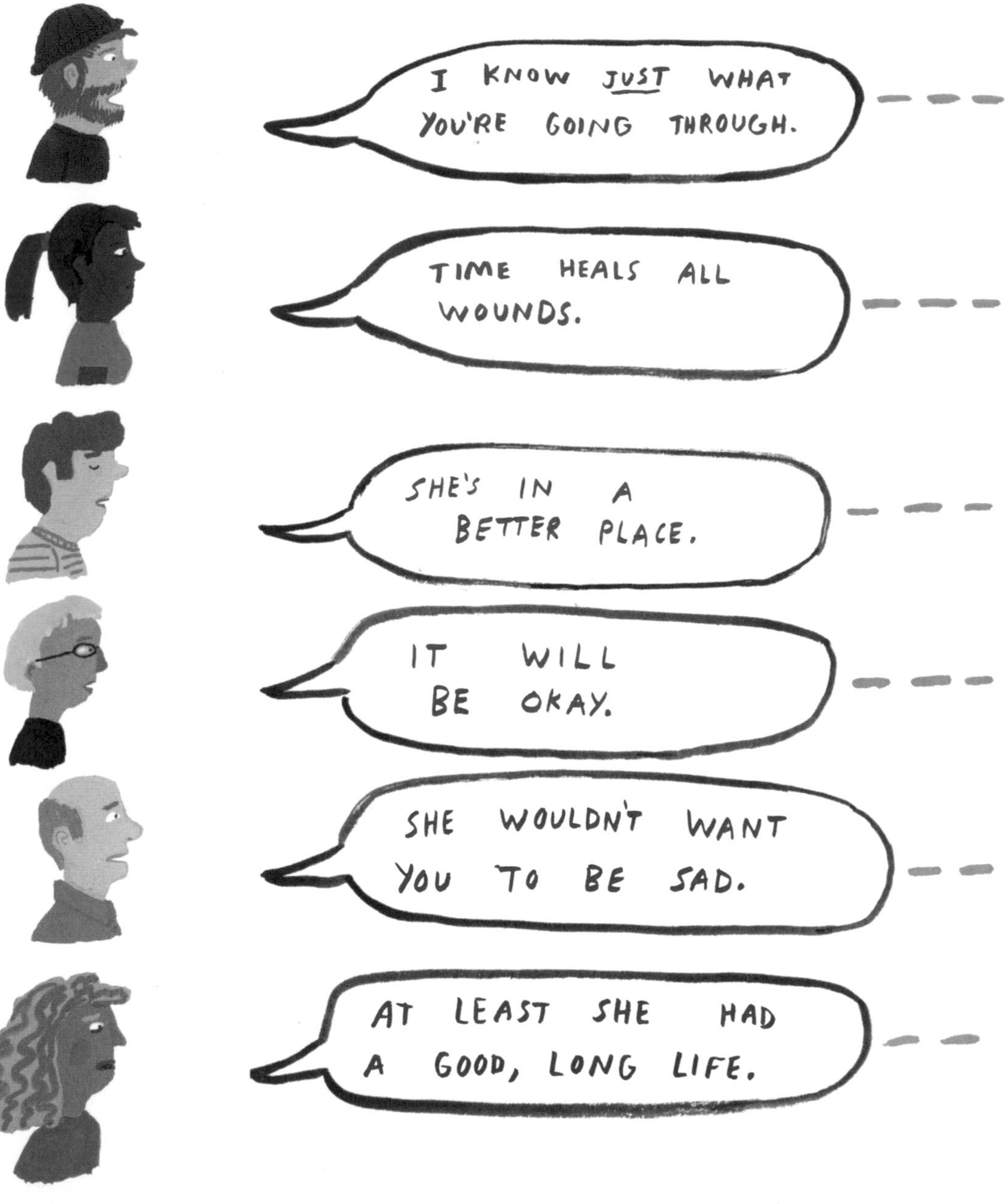
I KNOW JUST WHAT YOU'RE GOING THROUGH.
TIME HEALS ALL WOUNDS.
SHE'S IN A BETTER PLACE.
IT WILL BE OKAY.
SHE WOULDN'T WANT YOU TO BE SAD.
AT LEAST SHE HAD A GOOD, LONG LIFE.

HOW NOT TO RESPOND

(NO MATTER HOW BADLY YOU WANT TO)

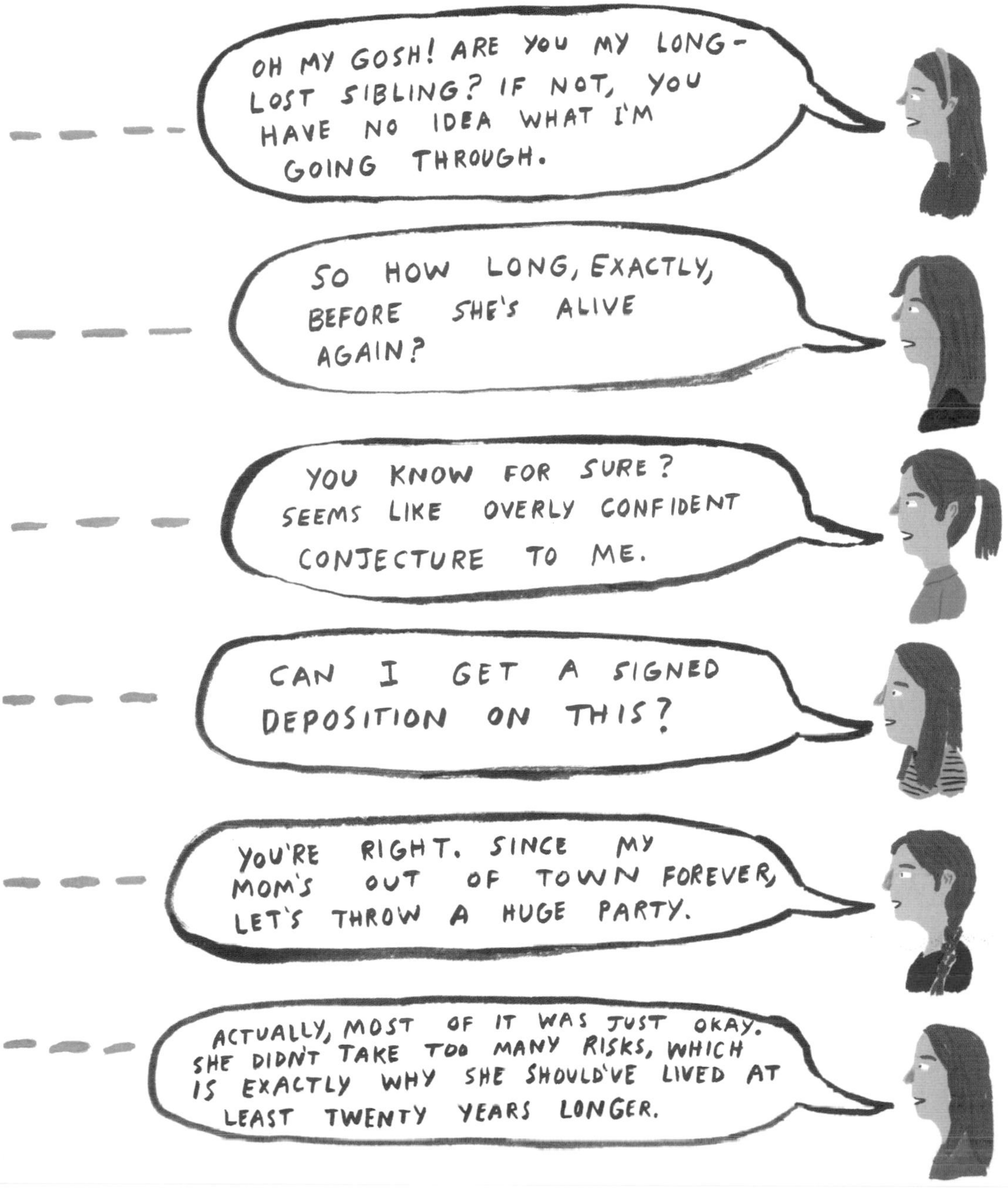
OH MY GOSH! ARE YOU MY LONG-LOST SIBLING? IF NOT, YOU HAVE NO IDEA WHAT I'M GOING THROUGH.
SO HOW LONG, EXACTLY, BEFORE SHE'S ALIVE AGAIN?
YOU KNOW FOR SURE? SEEMS LIKE OVERLY CONFIDENT CONJECTURE TO ME.
CAN I GET A SIGNED DEPOSITION ON THIS?
YOU'RE RIGHT. SINCE MY MOM'S OUT OF TOWN FOREVER, LET'S THROW A HUGE PARTY.
ACTUALLY, MOST OF IT WAS JUST OKAY. SHE DIDN'T TAKE TOO MANY RISKS, WHICH IS EXACTLY WHY SHE SHOULD'VE LIVED AT LEAST TWENTY YEARS LONGER.

DAY 18: *Throw something*

Find something breakable. Just whatever is closest to you at the moment. Don't think too hard before chucking it as hard as you can at the wall.

You make a really good point. Life isn't fair.

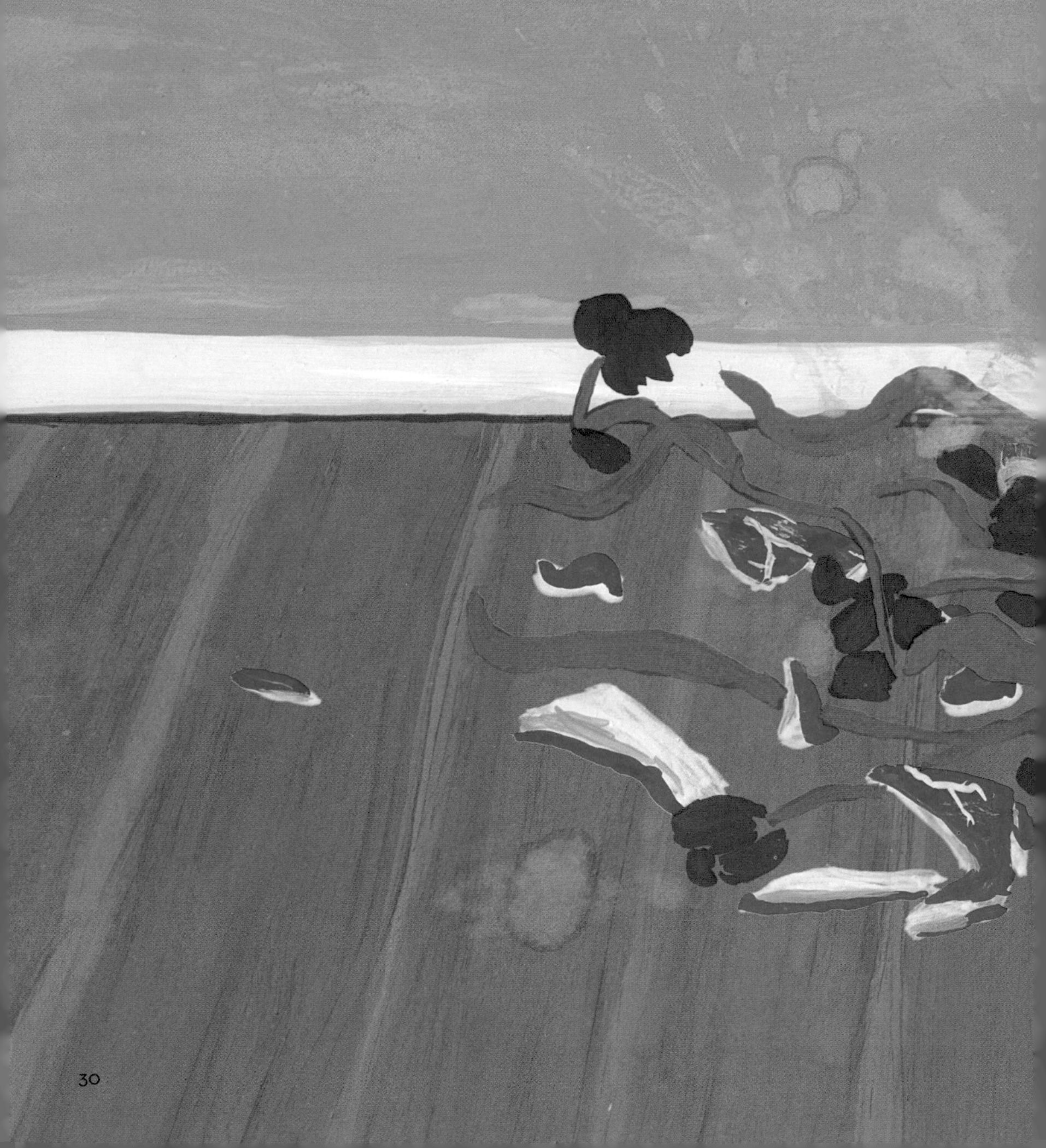

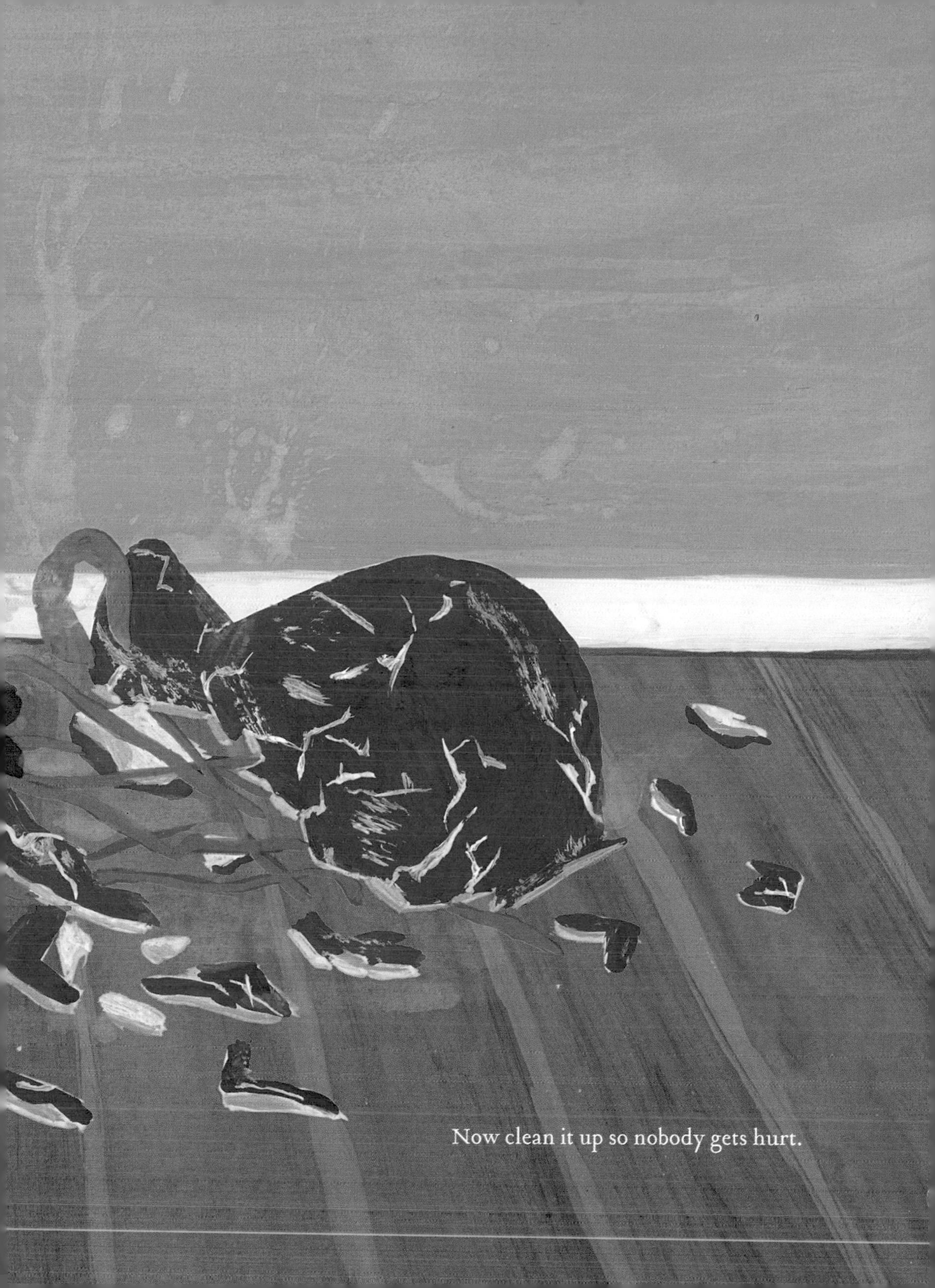
Now clean it up so nobody gets hurt.

DAY 21: *Take a hike*

Your parent's death is nature's way of breaking the shocking news that it's your turn next.

I think of it as being next up on life's diving board, preparing to jump or be pushed into a bottomless, unfathomable pool. This should not come as a surprise but somehow it does, and when you lose someone close to you, it may hit you with surprising force.

This is not a day for swimming. Go for a walk in the woods instead. Think about the raccoons and bears and foxes who live and die there. They aren't the least bit worried about life's diving board, and after a while you'll get used to the idea, too.

Why go on if we all just die in the end? There's a great reason. If you knew you were going to live forever, imagine how much time you'd waste. Amazing things can happen when there's a deadline looming.

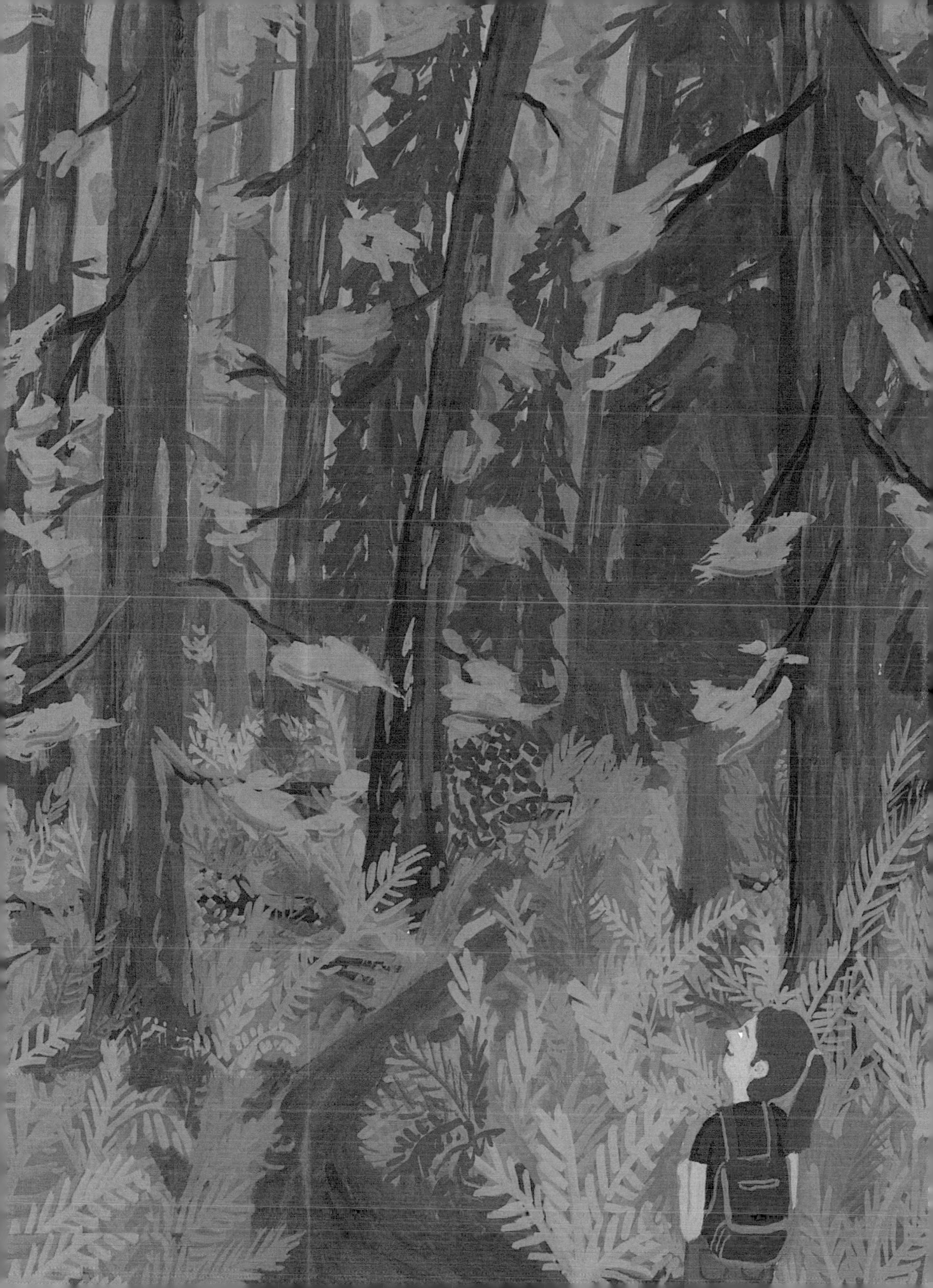

DAY 26:

Allow me to explain the stuff you found while cleaning out my house

A moldering box of candy: I hid it five years ago
so that your dad wouldn't eat it,
and then forgot about it.

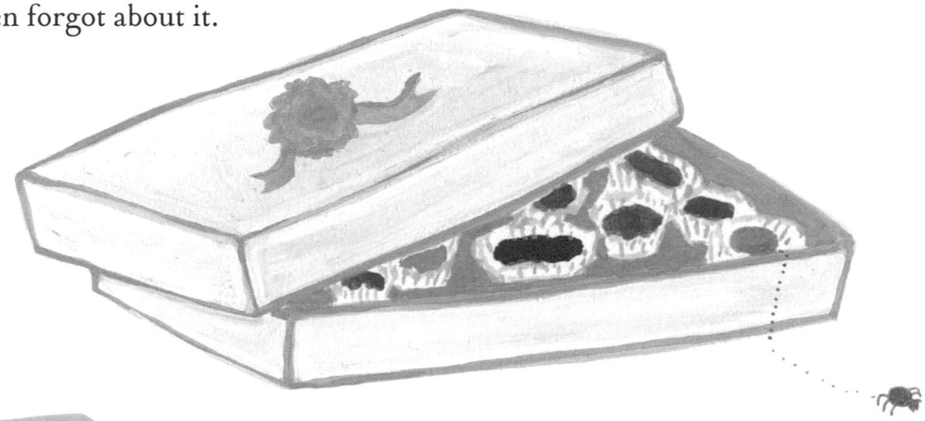

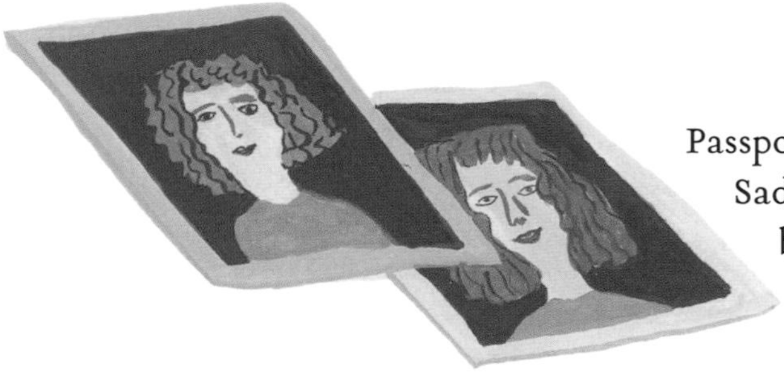

Passport photos:
Sadly, perms were the style
back then.

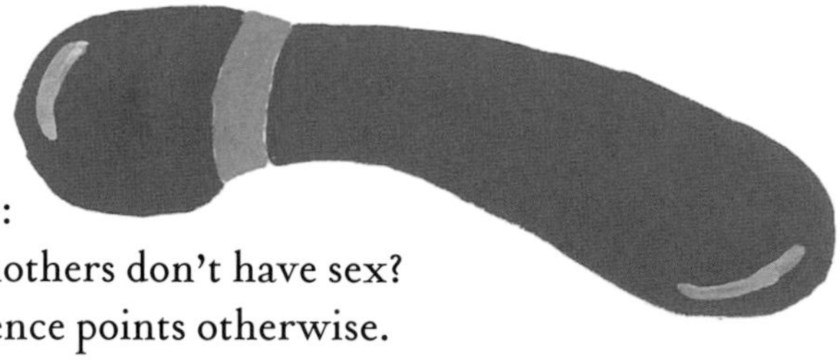

Vibrator:
What, mothers don't have sex?
All evidence points otherwise.

High school journals: I had a lot of anxiety about everything, as you will learn (yeah, like you didn't already know, right?).

Foreign coins I couldn't bear to throw out even though I can't remember what country they're from.

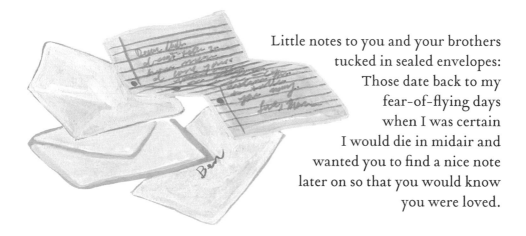

Little notes to you and your brothers tucked in sealed envelopes: Those date back to my fear-of-flying days when I was certain I would die in midair and wanted you to find a nice note later on so that you would know you were loved.

No secret affairs, no double life, no hidden keys to safety deposit boxes containing millions of dollars: I'm sorry, but I didn't really have any secrets to keep. Believe me, you're not nearly as disappointed as I am.

DAY 45: *Say thank you*

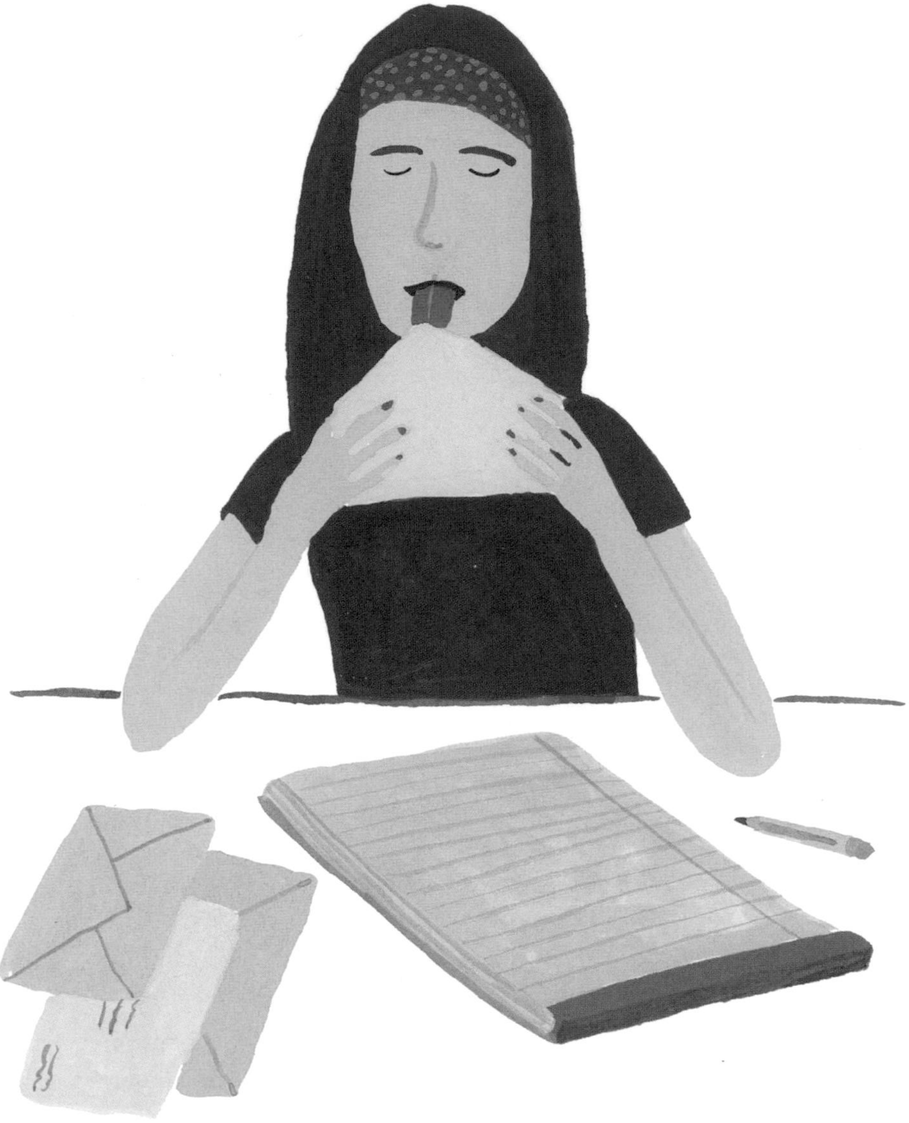

A lot of people have probably done nice things for you since I died. Write each one a thank-you note.

Death is uncivil; thank-you notes are civil. Expressing gratitude forces you to focus on living people who care about you rather than on the enormity of your loss.

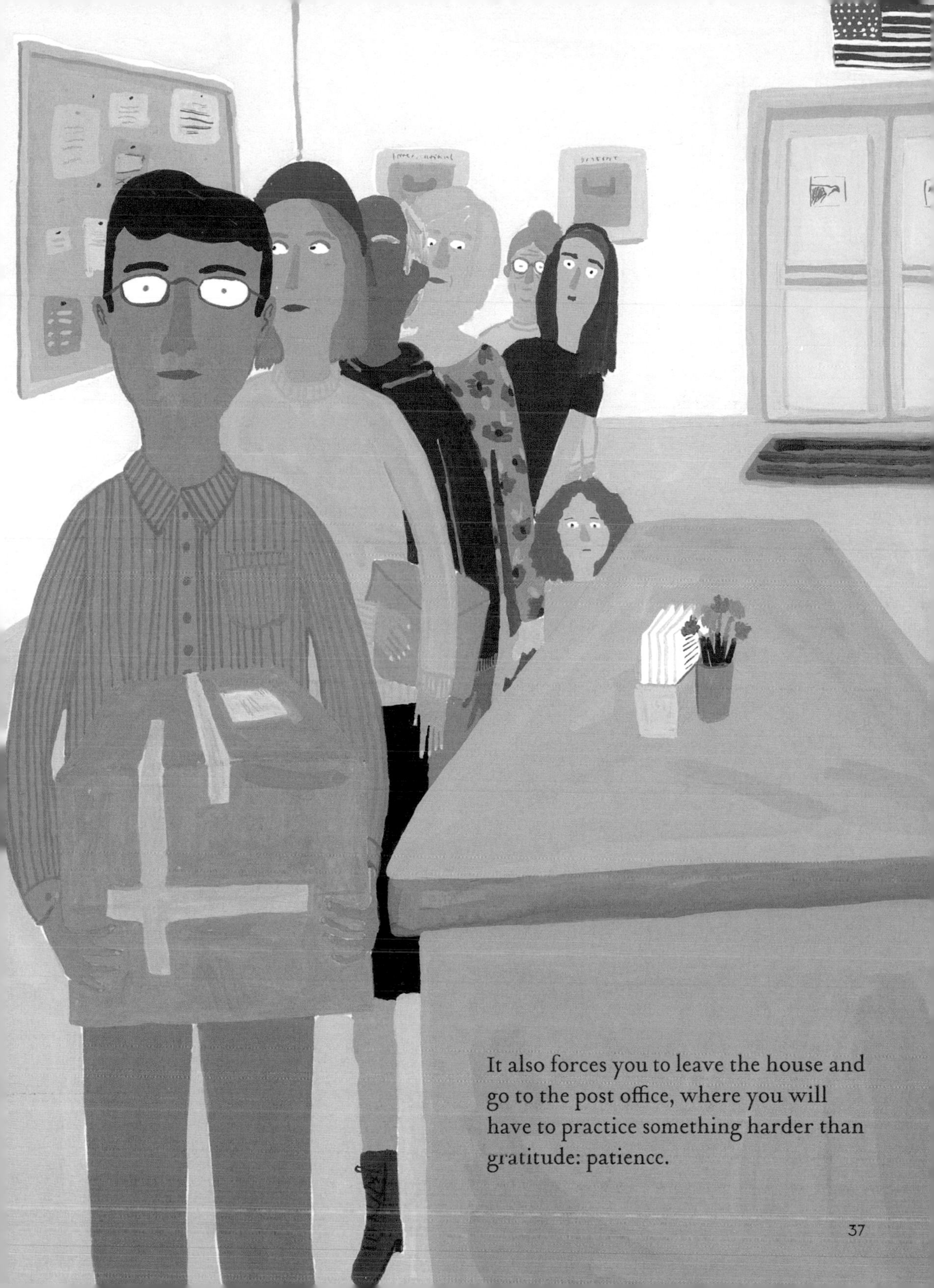

It also forces you to leave the house and go to the post office, where you will have to practice something harder than gratitude: patience.

DAY 76: *Breathe in*

Grief will suddenly send your mind racing back to a face, place, or time, or veering wildly ahead to your sad orphaned future. Your thoughts are just that: thoughts, not reality, and honestly, you can't always trust them.

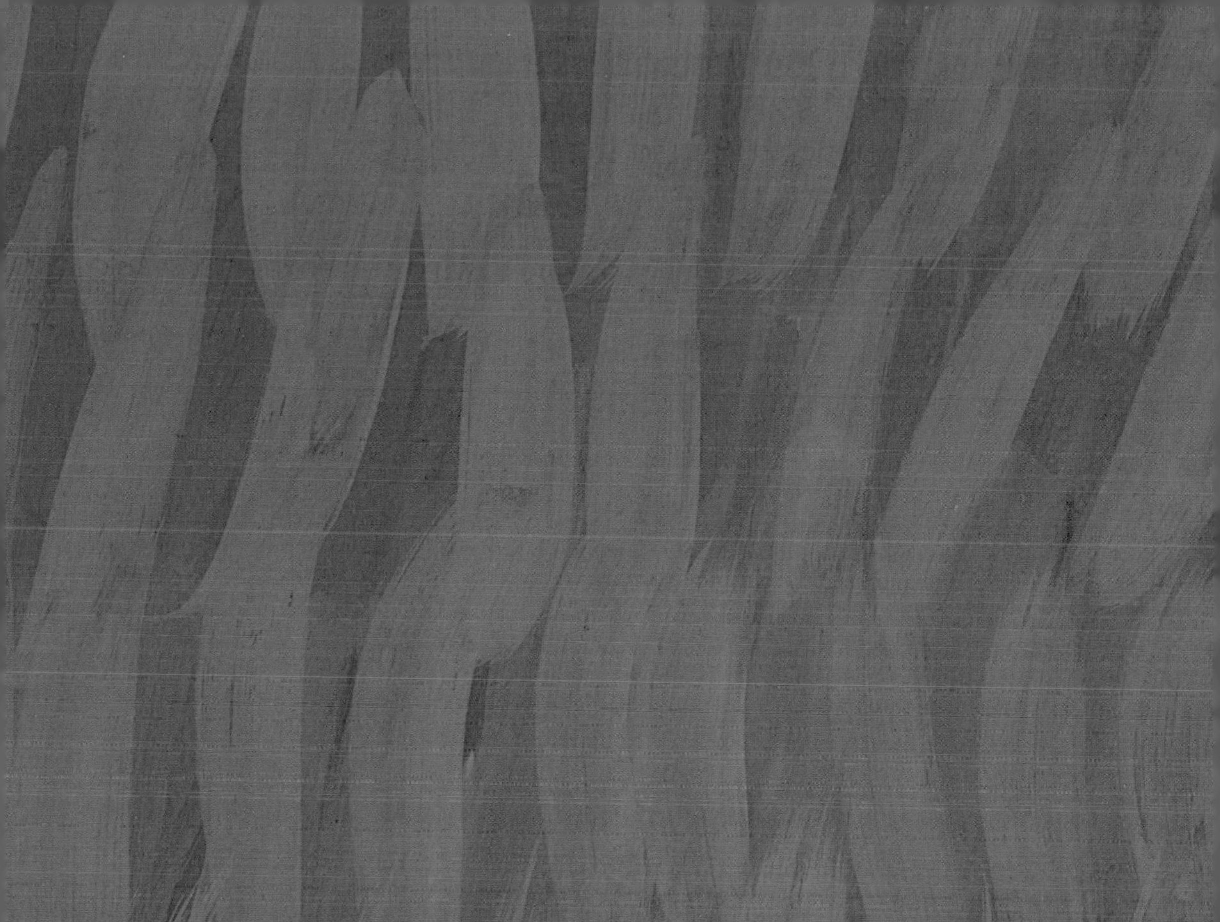

Kneel down on the greenest patch of grass you can find and peer into it. What you see—little bugs, colorful striations, the tangle of leaves—is real. Close your eyes, breathe in that earthy scent, and if you're lucky, the sprinklers won't come on.

DAY 110: *Create a new holiday tradition*

This is the first year that I'm not there and it will feel different. Don't try to do the things we've always done and watch a gaping hole appear in each one. Come up with something new to do each year, and think, offhandedly, that you wish I was there.

Watch gory horror movies together

Order pizza instead of
cooking a traditional dinner

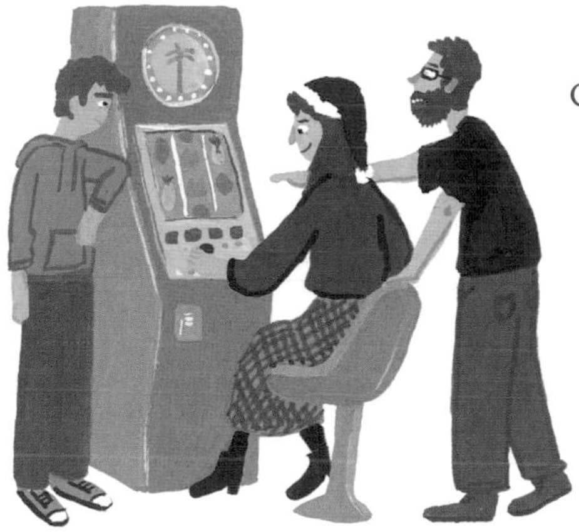

Go to the casino as a family

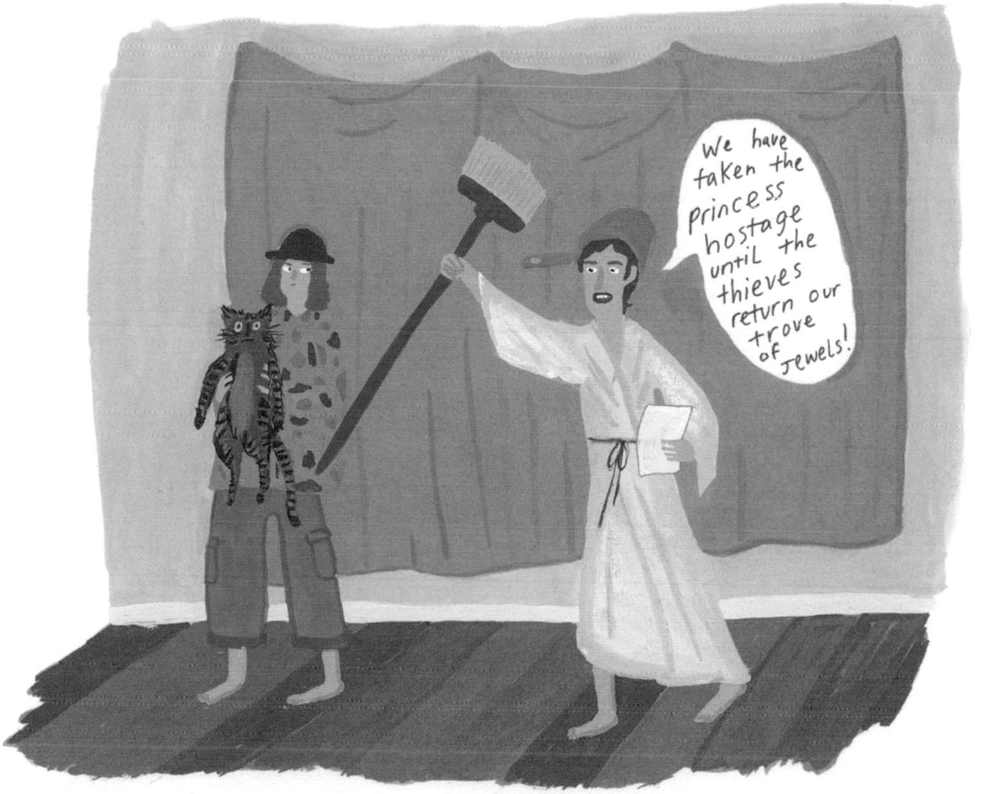
We have taken the princess hostage until the thieves return our trove of jewels!

Write a play together

DAY 144: *Bake a pecan pie*

FLOUR

My own mom always made this pie at the holidays. I never understood why I liked it so much. After she died, I made it myself to carry on the tradition and then I understood: It contains massive amounts of sugar.

First, make the crust. You could buy a frozen pie crust, but this is so much better:

SALT

4 cups sifted flour
1 tbsp. sugar
2 tsp. salt
1½ cups solid vegetable shortening (coconut oil, softened but not melted, also works great)
1 tbsp. white or cider vinegar
½ cup cold water, plus 1 tbsp. more if needed
1 large egg

VEGETABLE SHORTENING

Before you get started, know that you can't mess this up. It always turns out great, and how often in life can you say that? Dump the flour, sugar, salt, and shortening into a food processor, and give it a few whirls.

In a separate small bowl, combine the vinegar, cold water, and egg and beat it with a fork. Don't hold back. Pour the wet mix into the food processor and hit "pulse" a few times until all is combined.

Dump the mixture onto a floured counter, and separate into two portions. Wrap each separately in plastic and chill for a half

hour or more. Then roll one portion out on a floured surface and fit to a 9- or 10-inch pan, preferably deep dish. The other packet will keep for up to a week in the refrigerator, for the second pie you will inevitably make.

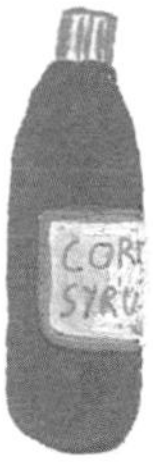

While the dough is chilling, prep the pie filling:

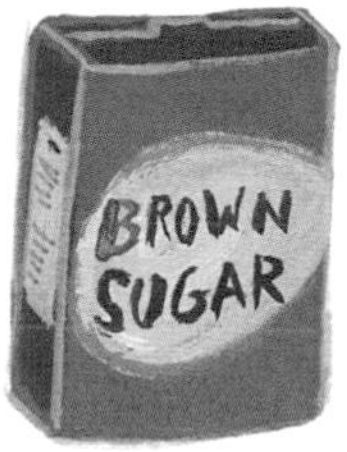
BROWN
SUGAR

¾ cup light corn syrup
1 cup firmly packed dark brown sugar
3 eggs, slightly beaten
½ cup butter, melted
½ tsp. salt
2 tsp. vanilla
2 cups pecan halves

Optional: ⅓ cup chocolate chips, chopped in food processor, and ⅓ cup shredded, unsweetened coconut

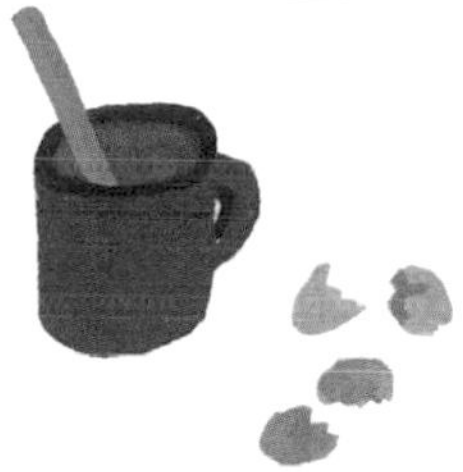

If including the chocolate and coconut, sprinkle both evenly onto the unbaked crust. Then pour the filling (all the other ingredients, mixed thoroughly) on top.

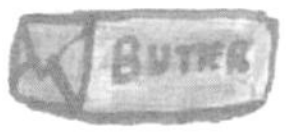

Bake at 350 degrees for 45 to 50 minutes until center is set. Let it cool. Or don't let it cool. Who's going to stop you from eating it right out of the pan?

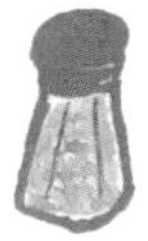

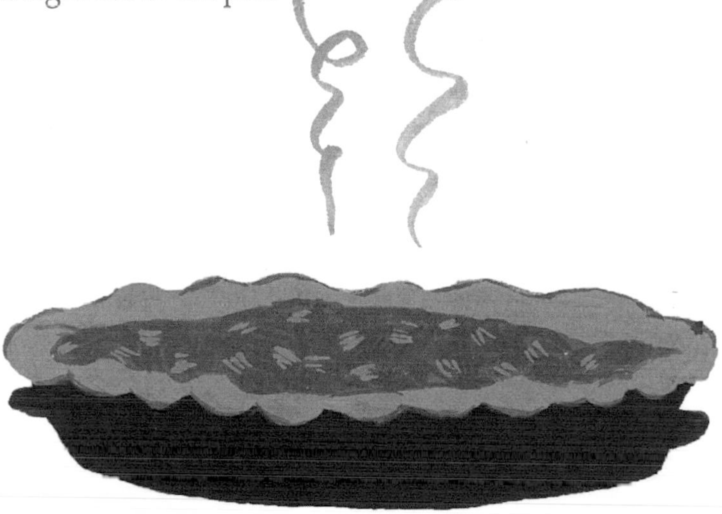

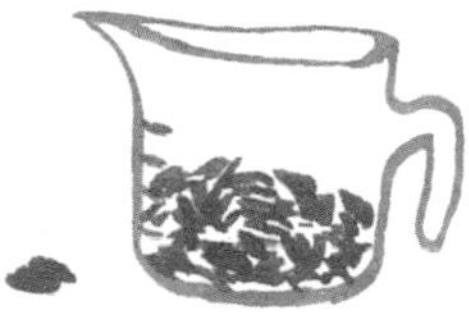

DAY 170: *Jump on the trampoline*

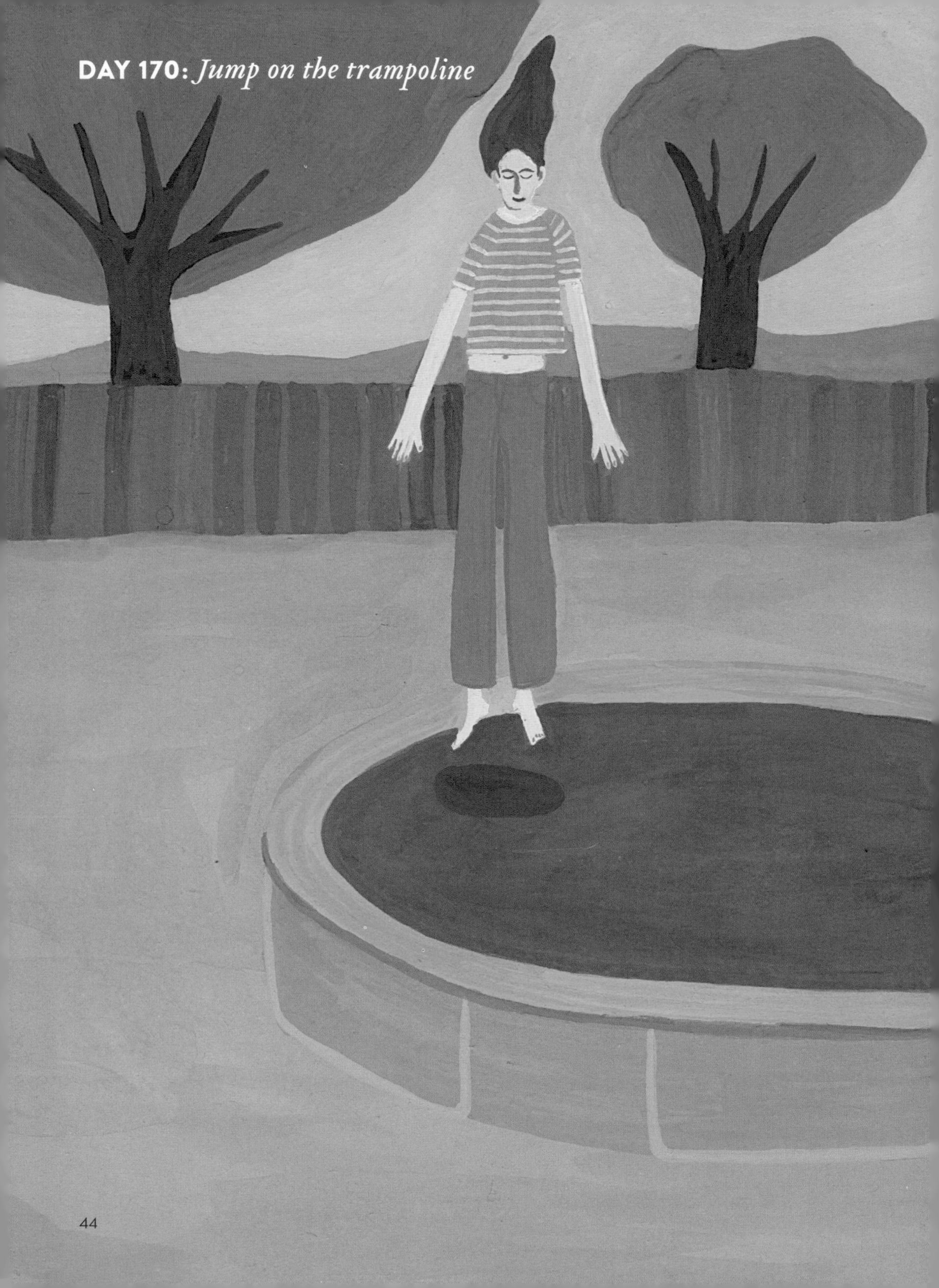

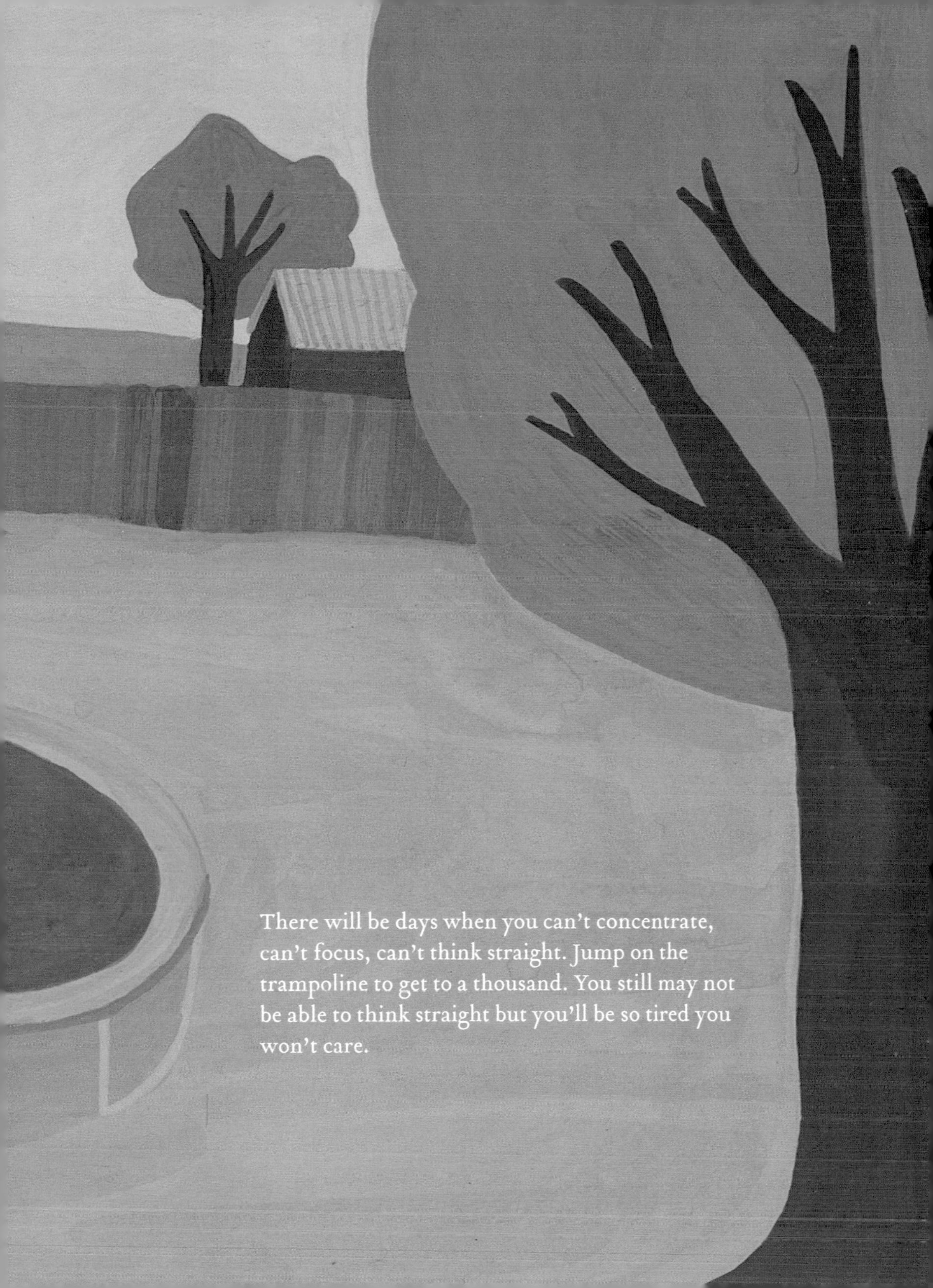

There will be days when you can't concentrate, can't focus, can't think straight. Jump on the trampoline to get to a thousand. You still may not be able to think straight but you'll be so tired you won't care.

DAY 231: *Celebrate your birthday*

For me, being dead has been really easy until now. I've been cracking jokes, making facetious comments.

But not today.

Here I am, dead instead of calling you.

Dead instead of giving you cash tucked in a greeting card with a golden retriever on the front of it.

The truth is, I feel terribly sorry for myself for being in a grave instead of hanging out in the kitchen fussing over a toppling hand-frosted cake and hugging you. So I can only imagine what you are feeling.

This is going to be a hard day for you, but don't forget—I'm the victim here. You should be feeling sorry for ME on your birthday, not yourself.

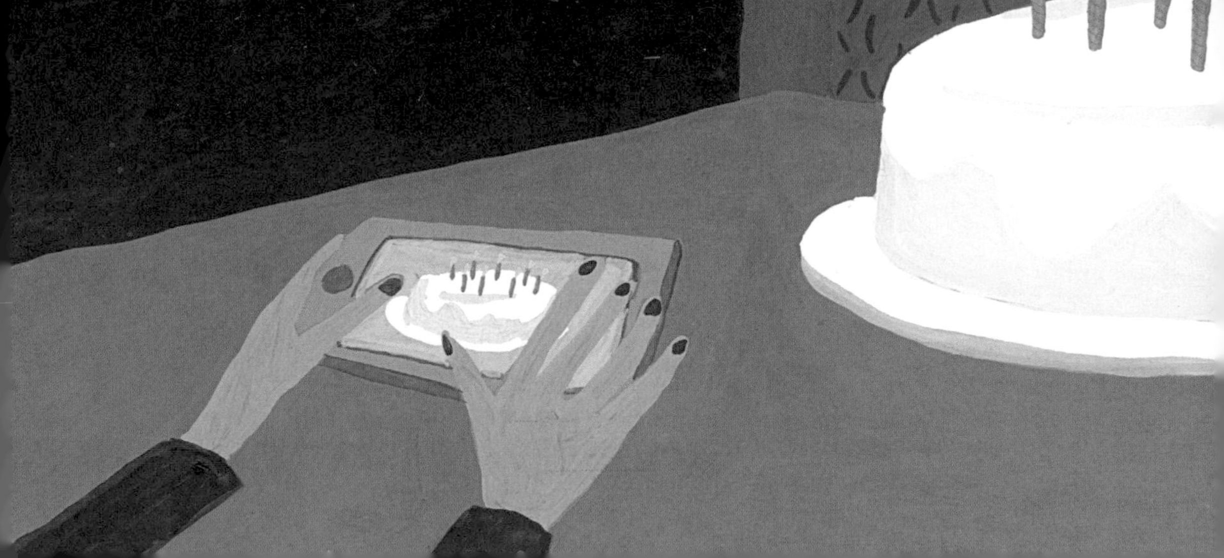

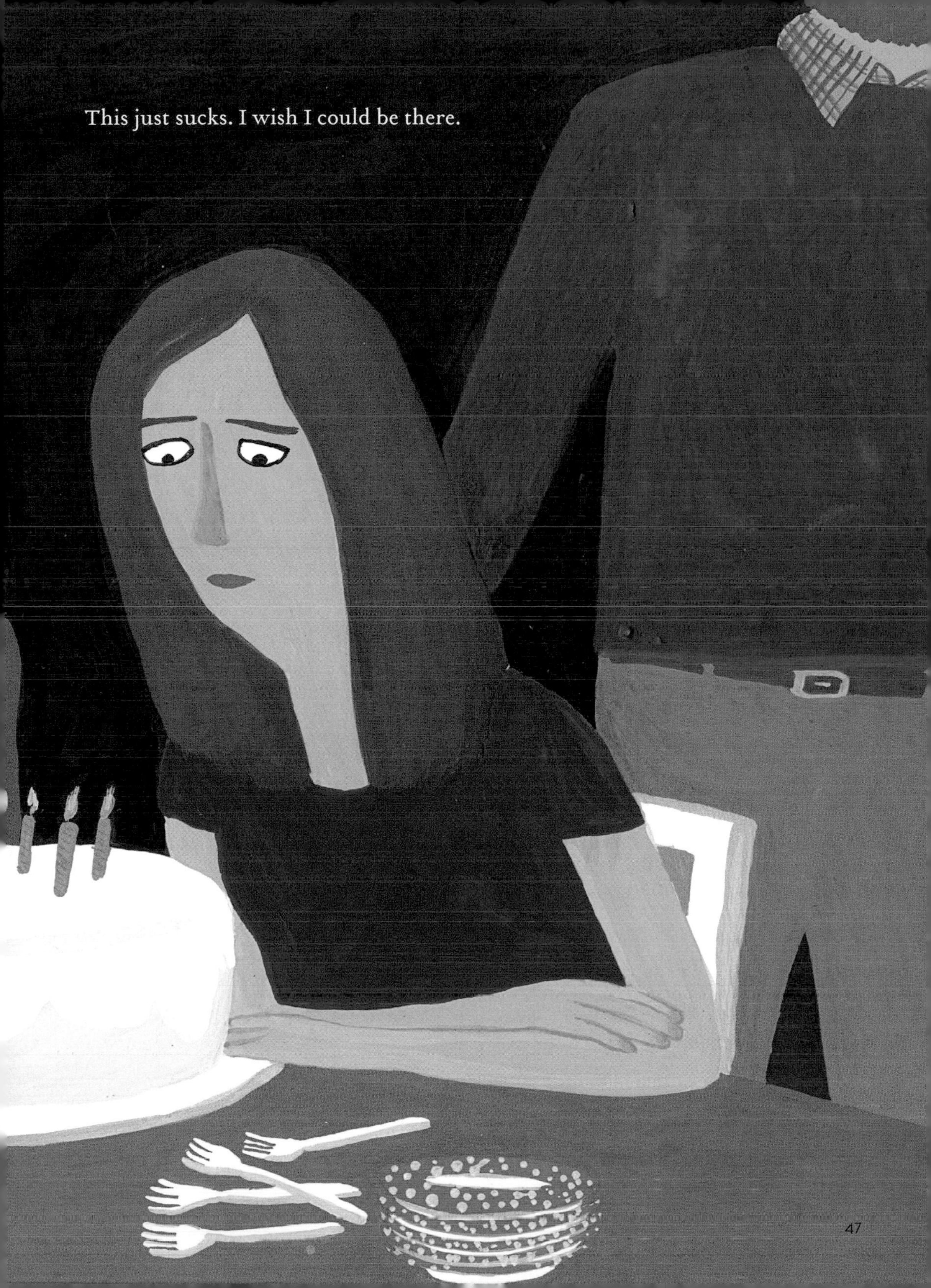
This just sucks. I wish I could be there.

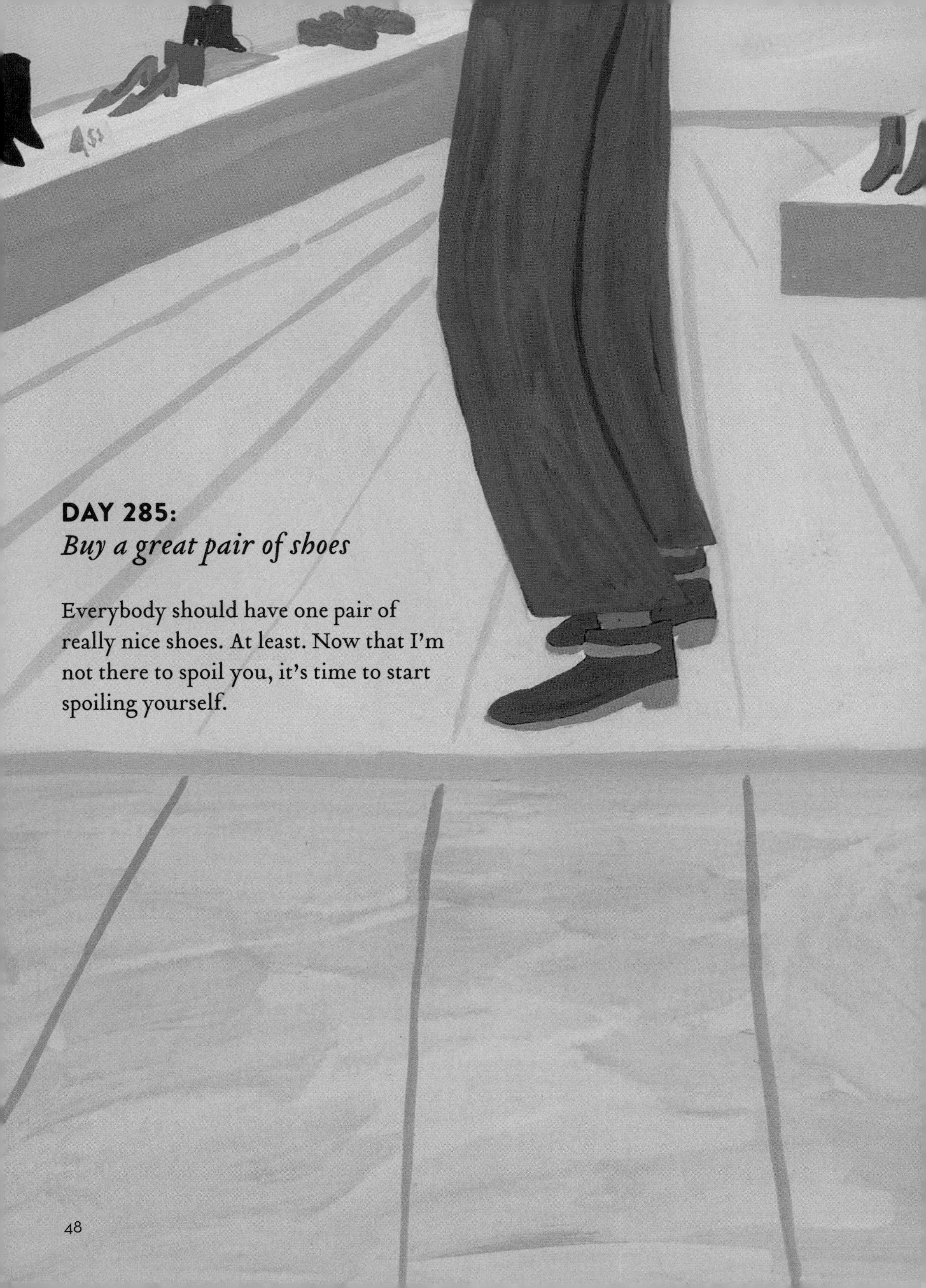

DAY 285:
Buy a great pair of shoes

Everybody should have one pair of really nice shoes. At least. Now that I'm not there to spoil you, it's time to start spoiling yourself.

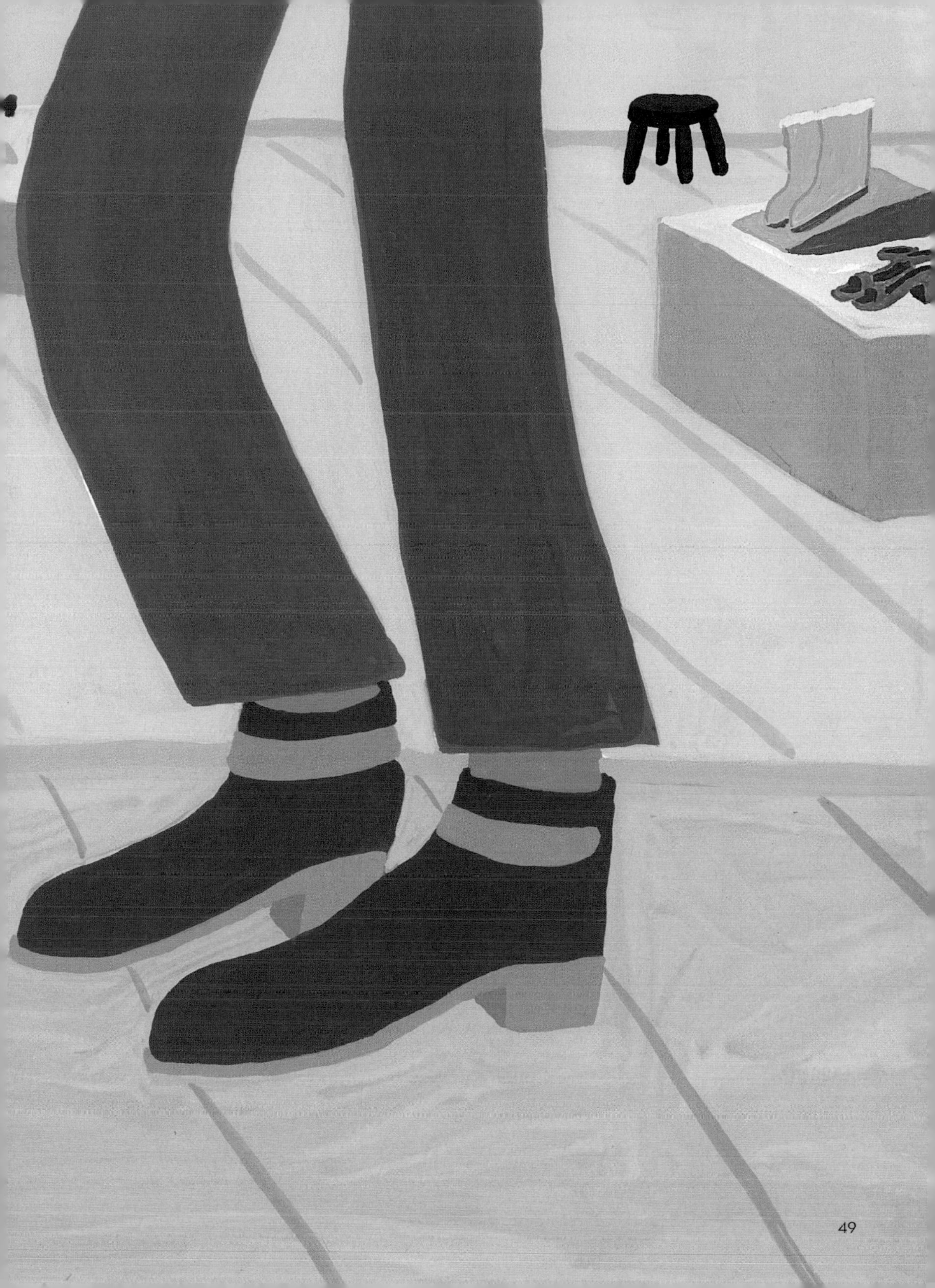

DAY 320: *Stop doing stuff you hate to do*

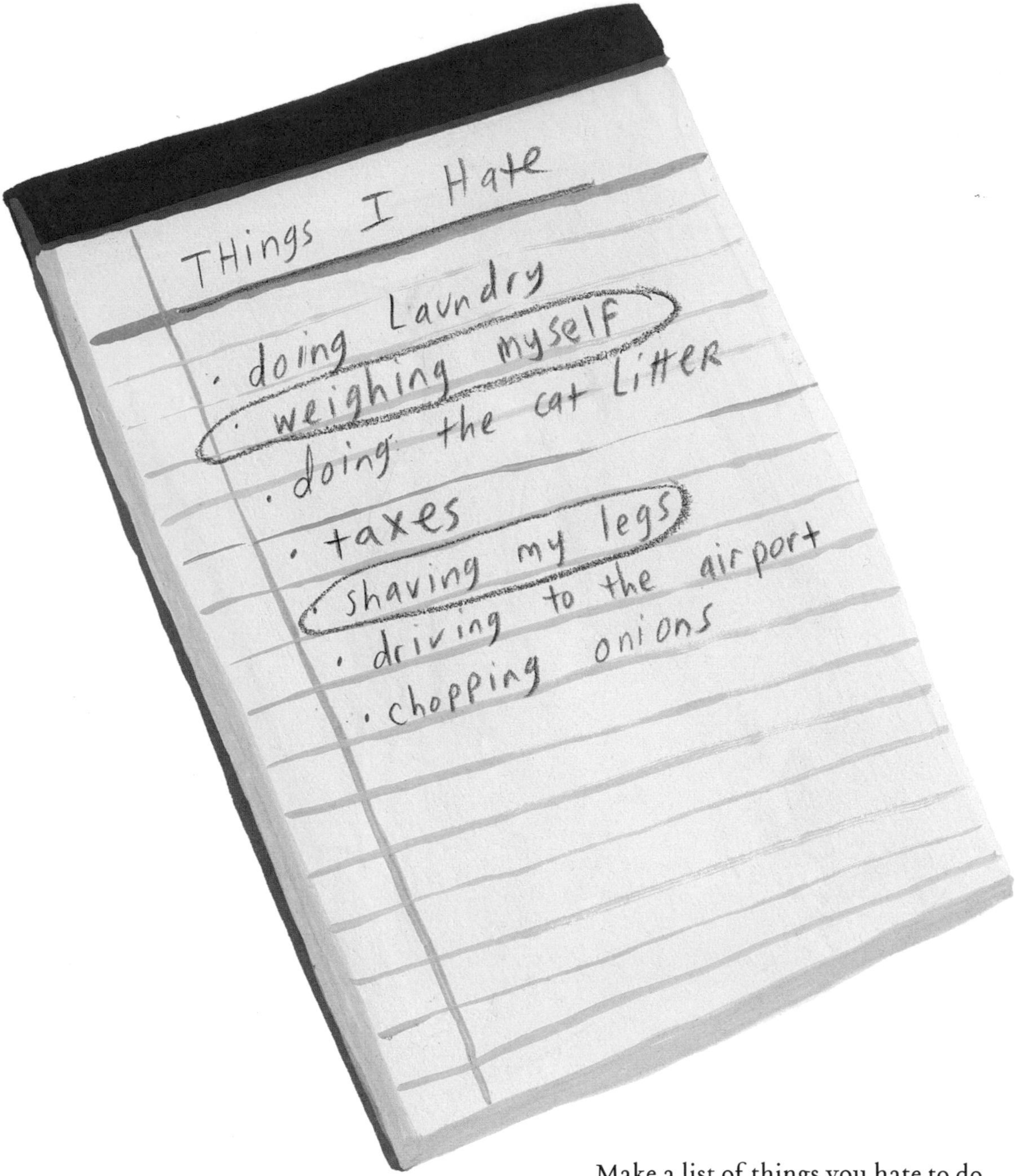
THings I Hate
· doing Laundry
· weighing myself
· doing the cat Litter
· taxes
· shaving my legs
· driving to the airport
· chopping onions

Make a list of things you hate to do.
Immediately stop doing at least two of them.

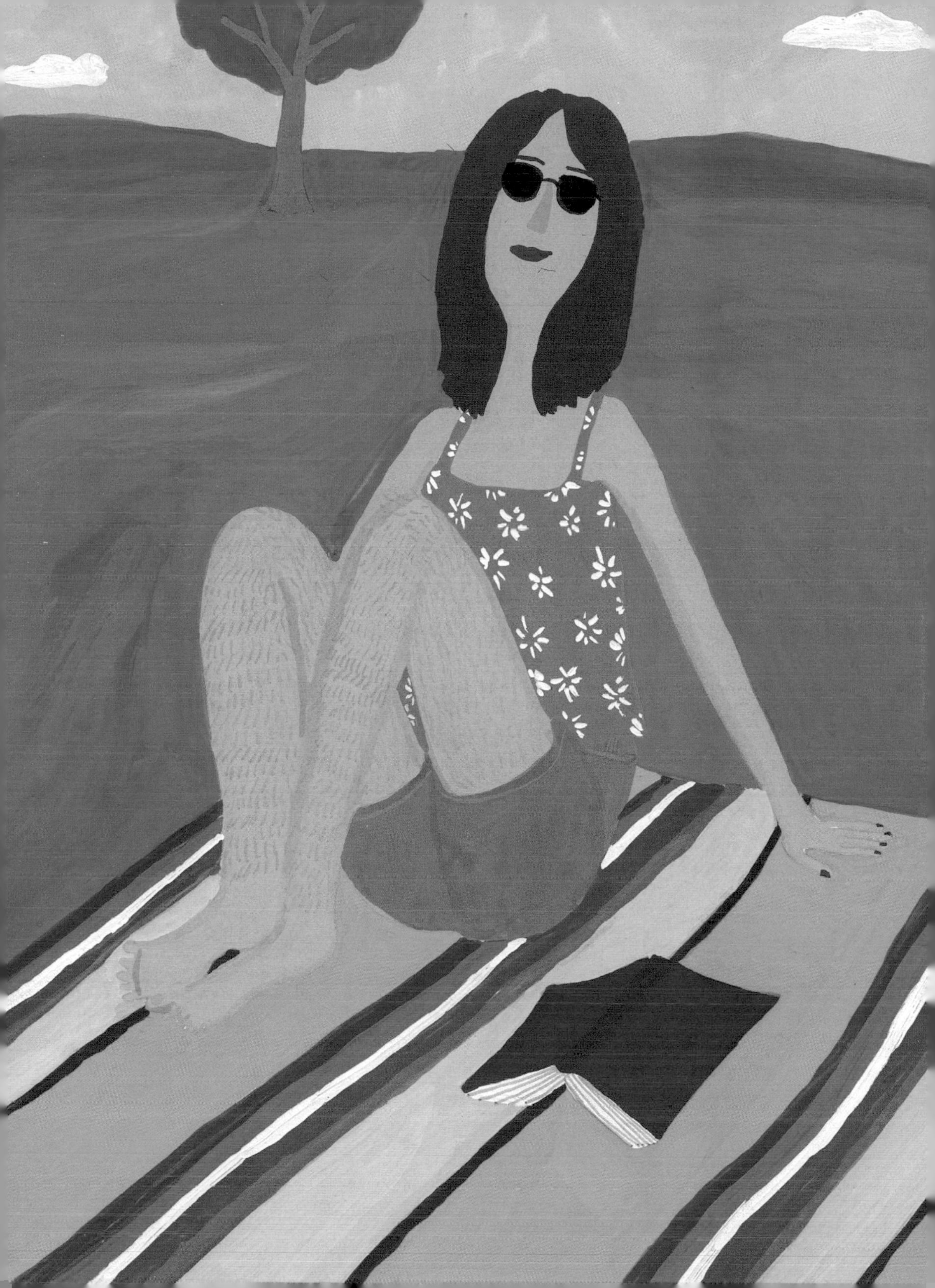

DAY 365: *Make chicken and dumplings*

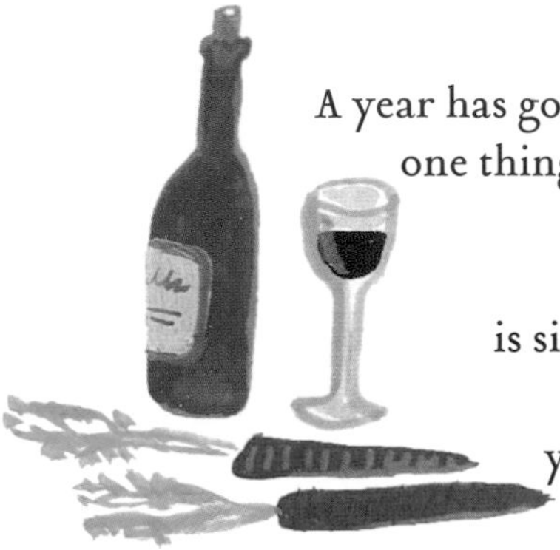

A year has gone by and you may still be feeling a lot of pain. If I could do one thing from the grave, it would be to help ease your sense of loss.

What we carry of other people, even when they're alive, is simply our perception of them, an idea. That means I'm here as long as you remember me. And since I'm here, I suggest you get busy living, seeking out happiness, moving forward.

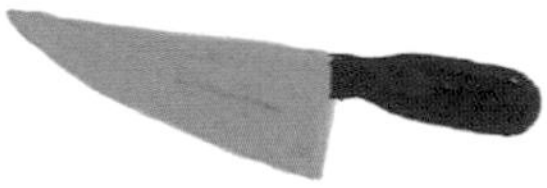

Let yourself feel how you feel. Then, realize that the sun is out, the dog needs to be walked, that huge pile of laundry could use some attention, and your neighbor might welcome some comfort food.

It's true, I'm not there in person, but chances are you know exactly what I would say: Make chicken and dumplings.

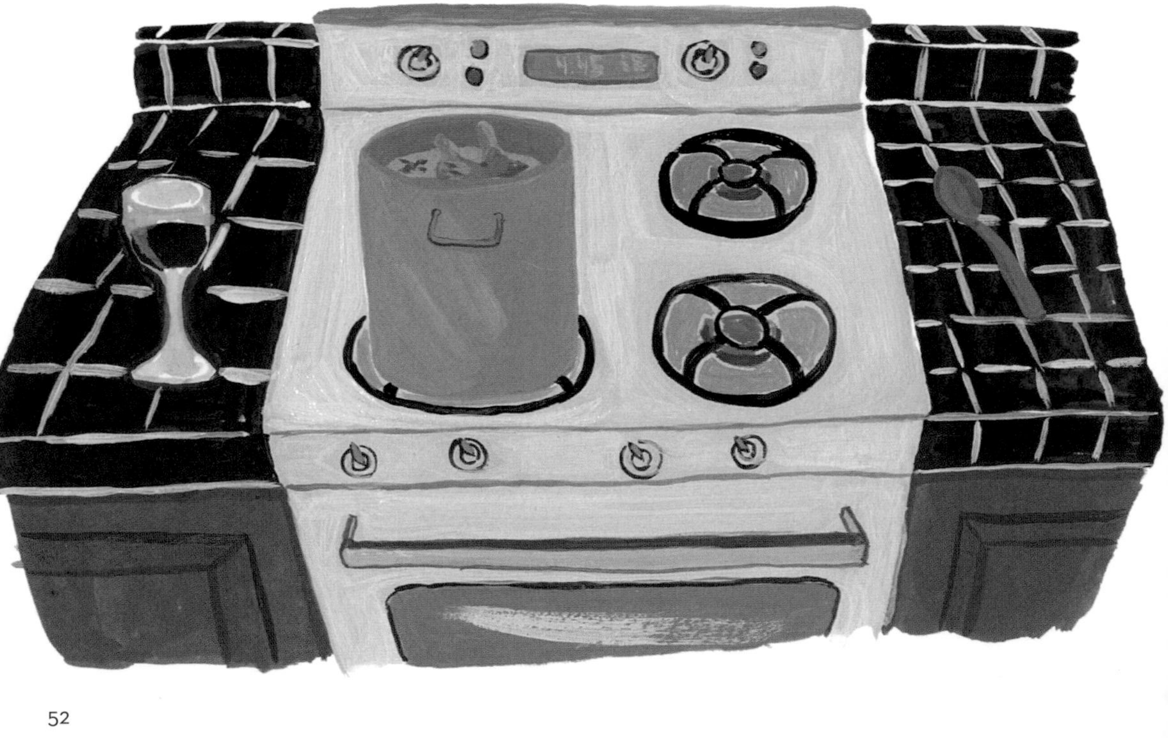

Whole chicken, rinsed
Celery, onion, carrots, and parsley
Salt and pepper, Italian and poultry seasoning
Flour and milk
White wine

Place the whole chicken into a pot, cover it with water, and add rough-cut chunks of celery, onion, carrots, and parsley. Add salt and pepper and the other seasonings. Cook over low to medium heat for a couple of hours, until the chicken comes easily off the bone.

Let it cool, strain the broth into a new pot, and use a fork to shred the chicken off the bone. Put the chicken in a separate bowl.

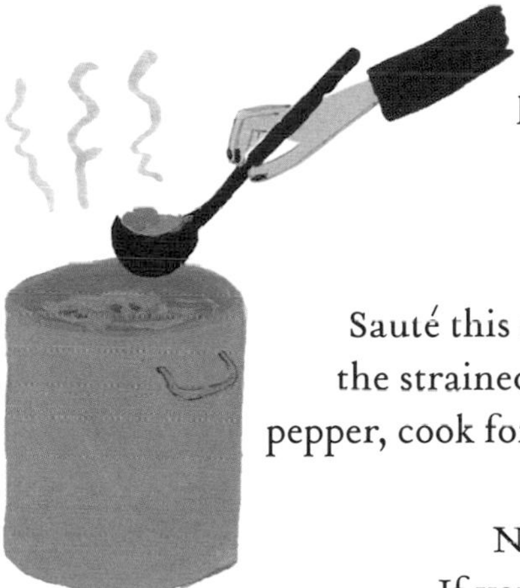

Dice a large onion and a few stalks of celery, leaves included. Sauté in butter until soft. Sprinkle a mix of Italian and poultry seasonings on top, and a bit of flour, and some white wine.

Sauté this mixture until it thickens a bit, then slowly pour in the strained chicken broth from the cooking pot. Add salt and pepper, cook for 15 or 20 minutes, then add in the cooked chicken.

Now for the dumplings: If you've never made these, they can be a bit tricky. Prepare by pouring yourself a large glass of wine.

1¼ cups flour
¼ cup cornmeal
1 tbsp. baking powder
1 tsp. salt
Parsley, diced
Italian seasoning
Ground pepper
~~~
2 tsp. butter, melted
1 cup milk

Mix the dry ingredients and parsley together. Mix the melted butter and milk, then add to the dry mix. Stir gently; don't overmix, so the dumplings stay tender. They will stick like glue to your intestines anyway. Spoon into the simmering soup and cook uncovered for 20 minutes.

By the way, the next day the leftovers turn into chicken pot pie. Cover the bottom of a pie pan with an unbaked crust, throw some diced potatoes and onions in, pour on the leftover chicken-dumpling stew, and set a crust on top. Bake at 350 degrees for 50 to 60 minutes or until the crust turns golden brown.

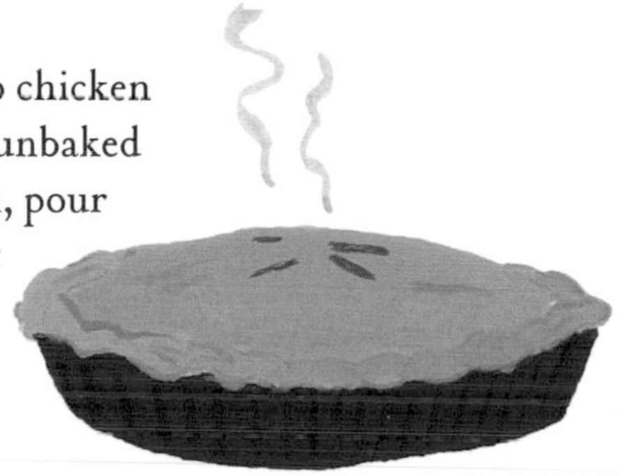
~~~

DAY 400: *Replace me*

> If you lose someone important to you, you should try to replace that person. Because if you live your life losing and not replacing, you'll end up at zero. I'm not saying you can replace your mother, and it won't necessarily be an even trade, but I'd like you to try.

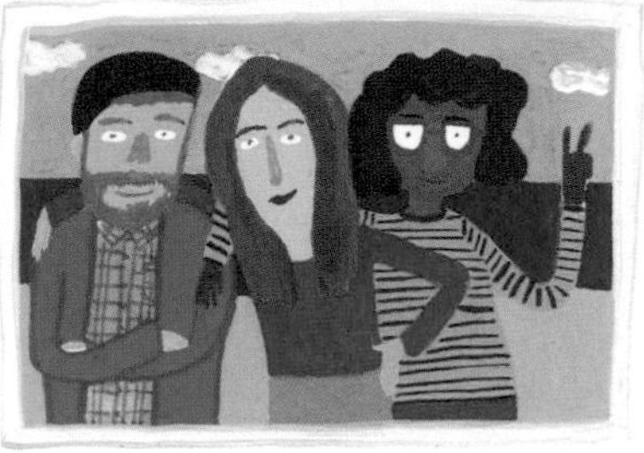

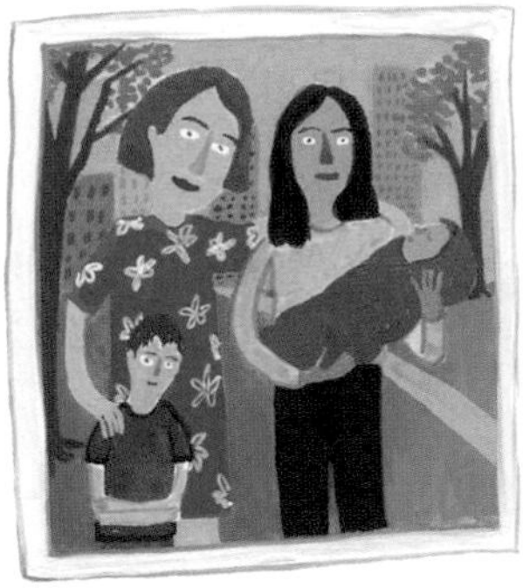

In your twenties and thirties you have dozens of friends. Suddenly you're forty and your circle narrows: People move, have families of their own, and lose touch amid busy, complicated lives.

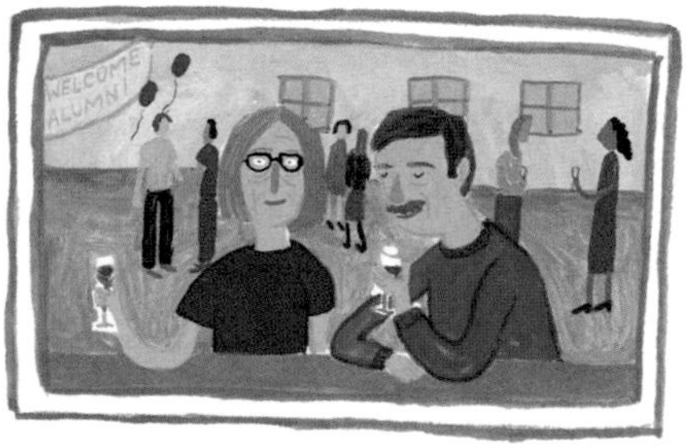
WELCOME ALUMNI!

In your fifties and sixties, more friends scatter: People divorce, loyalties shift, some die, some are born again or move to an ashram or just become obnoxious.

At seventy, eighty, people are dropping dead all around you. You have to replace those people just to maintain a supportive community, people who are with you and for you. Just make sure some of those new friends are younger than you are.

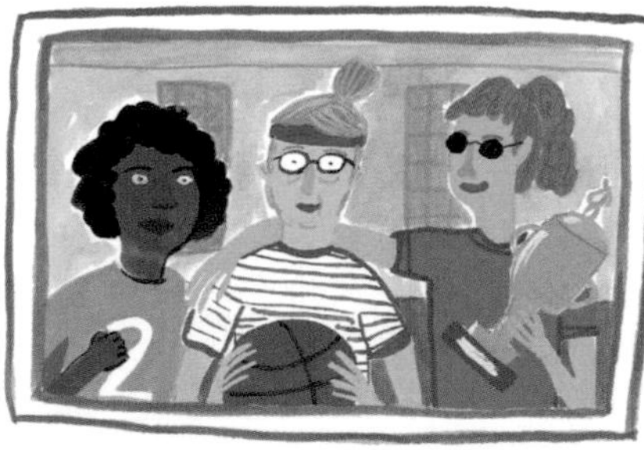
2

If this were an option, it would make things much easier, of course:

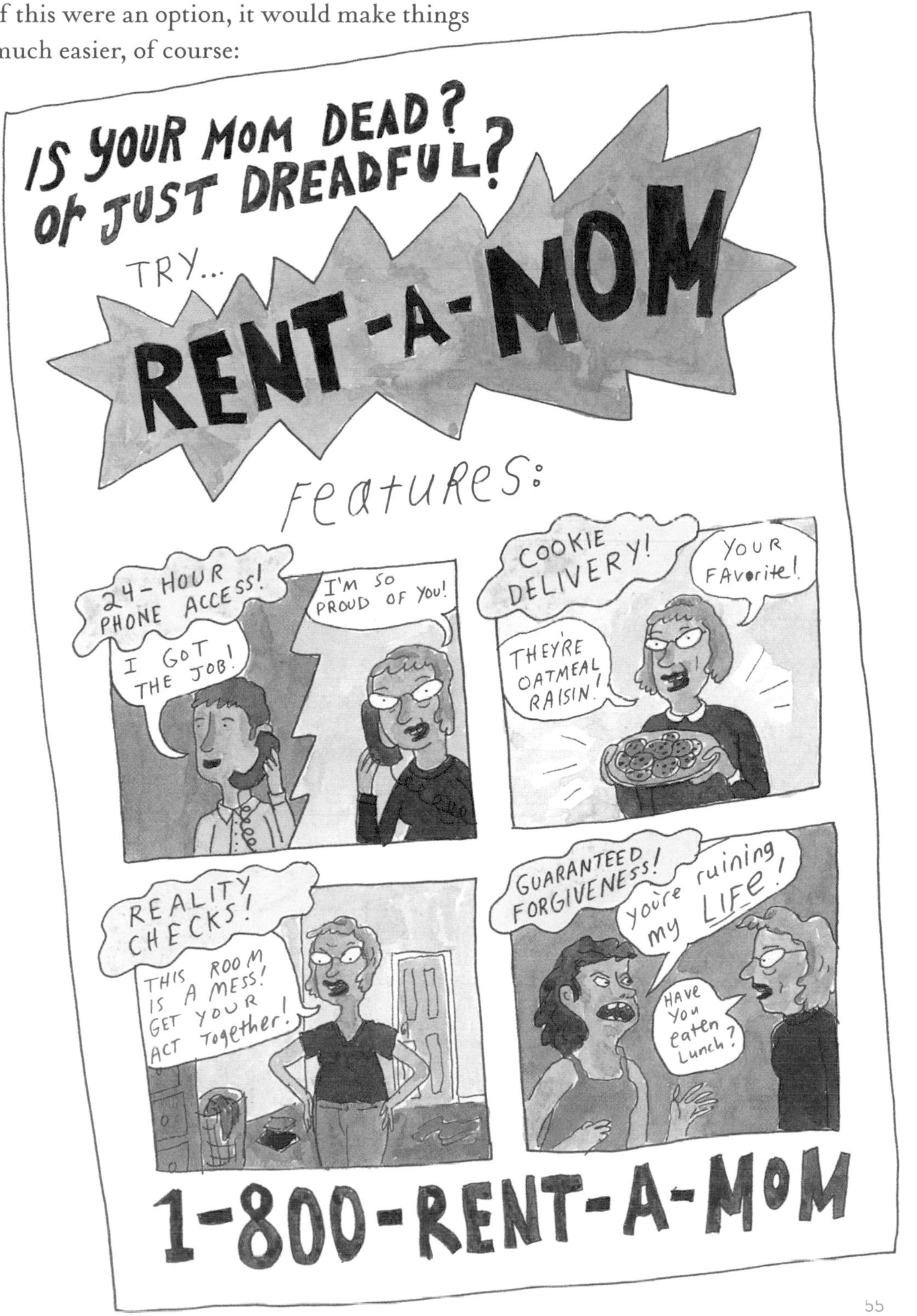

IS YOUR MOM DEAD?
or JUST DREADFUL?
TRY...
RENT-A-MOM
features:
24-HOUR PHONE ACCESS!
I GOT THE JOB!
I'M SO PROUD OF YOU!
COOKIE DELIVERY!
YOUR FAVorite!
THEY'RE OATMEAL RAISIN!
REALITY CHECKS!
THIS ROOM IS A MESS! GET YOUR ACT Together!
GUARANTEED FORGIVENESS!
you're ruining my LIFE!
HAVE you eaten Lunch?
1-800-RENT-A-MOM

DAY 450: *Look in the mirror and see yourself the way I saw you*

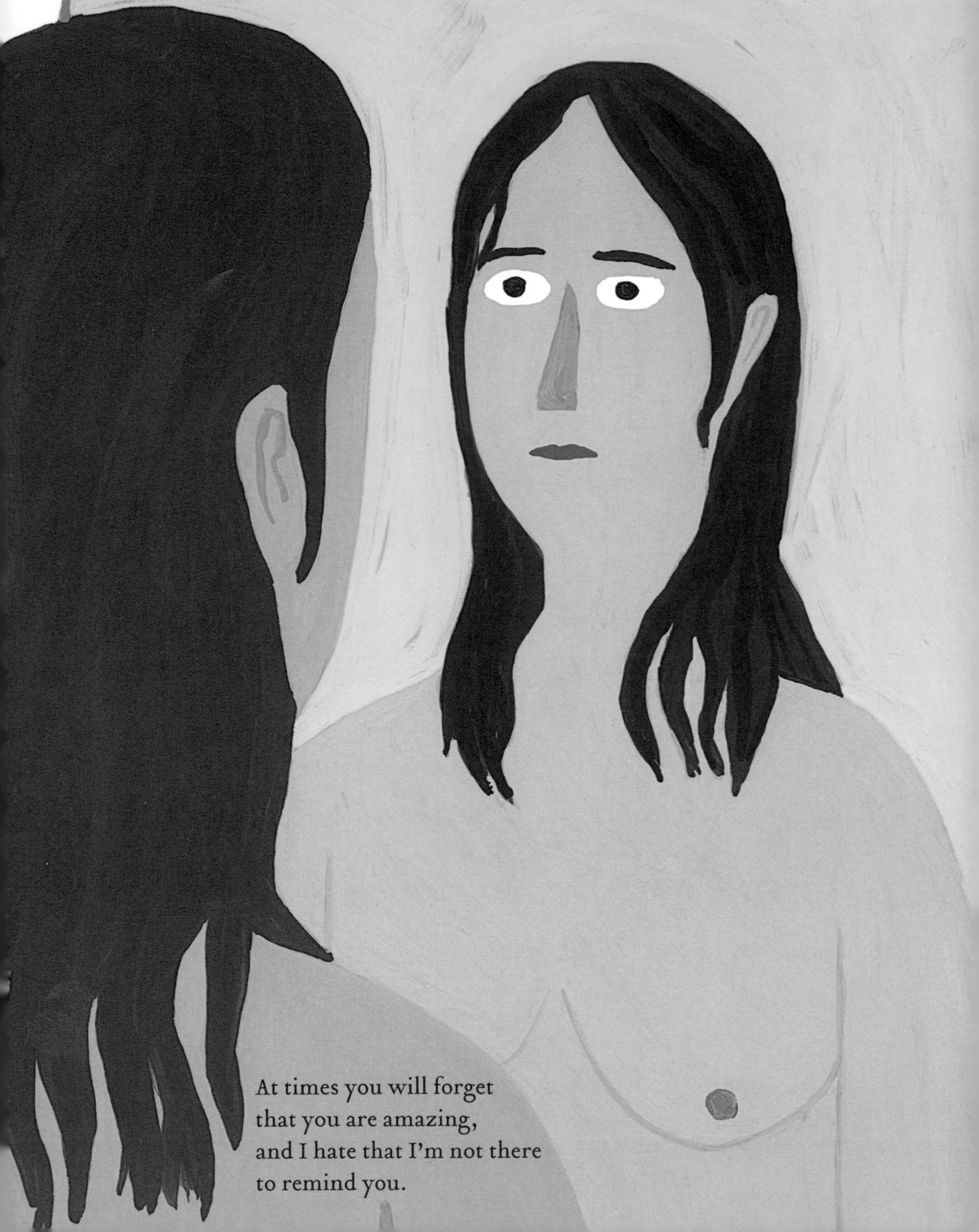

At times you will forget
that you are amazing,
and I hate that I'm not there
to remind you.

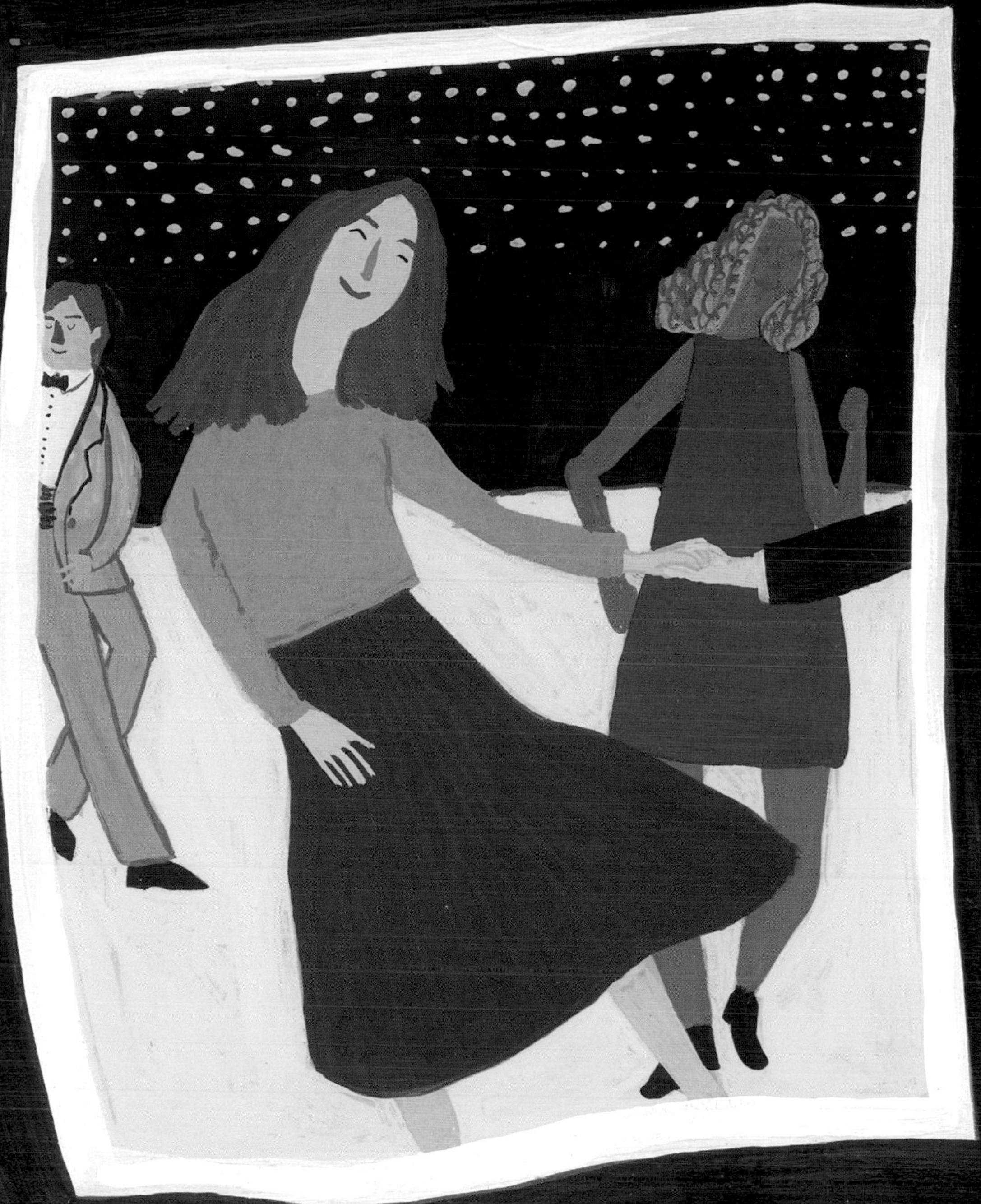

Because someday you will be old,
and you will look back at pictures
of yourself and you will see . . .
"I was beautiful."

DAY 500: *Take a bath*

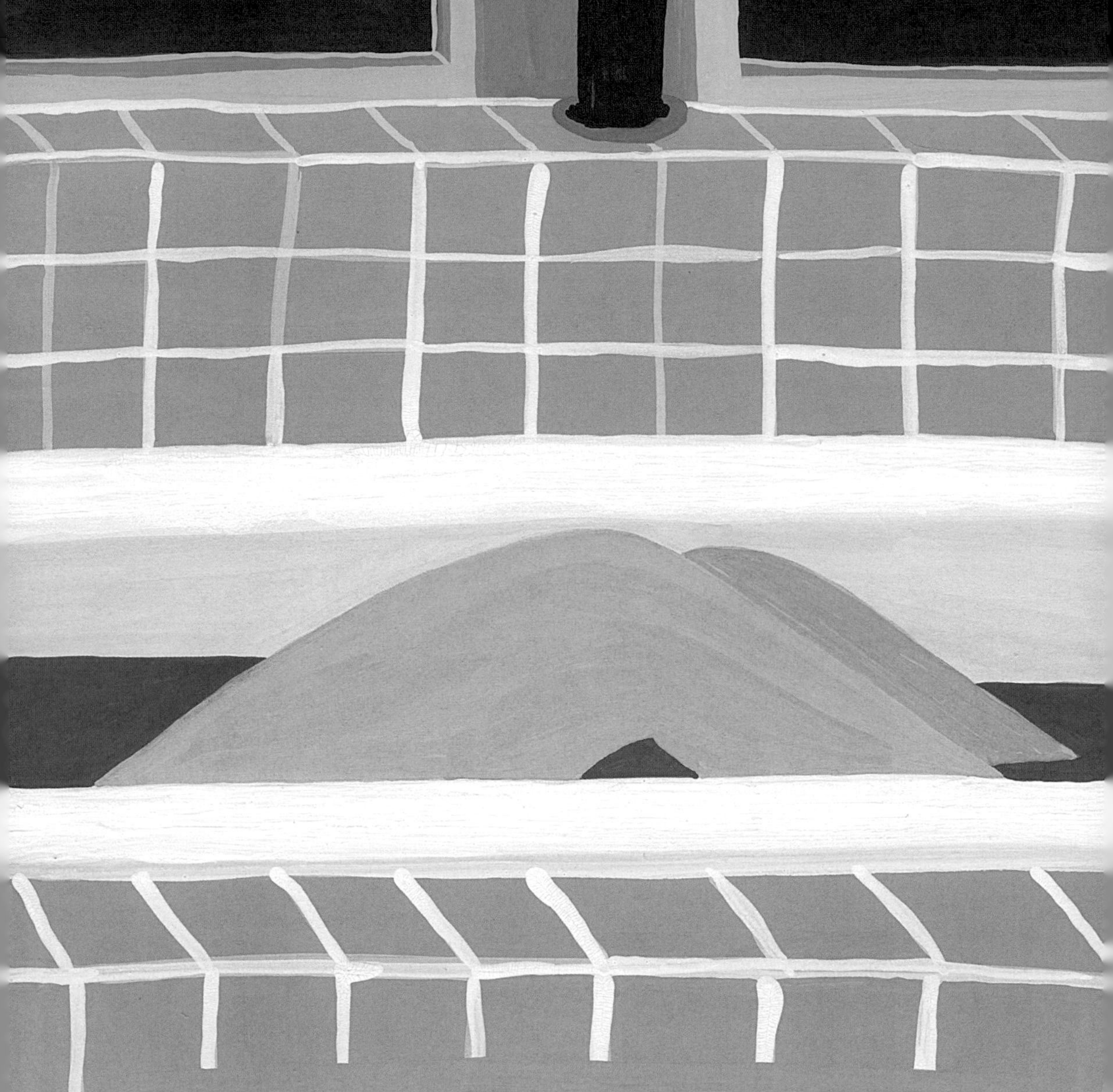

A bath is womb-like. It's warm, enfolding. Light a candle. Relax in the flickering light, the muted noises from outside. Stay in as long as you want to. I don't know if ghosts are real, but if they are, and I am one, I'll visit you. You'll know I'm there if the candle is flickering. Just make sure the wick is pretty long.

OTHER SIGNS I'M VISITING YOU FROM THE OTHER REALM

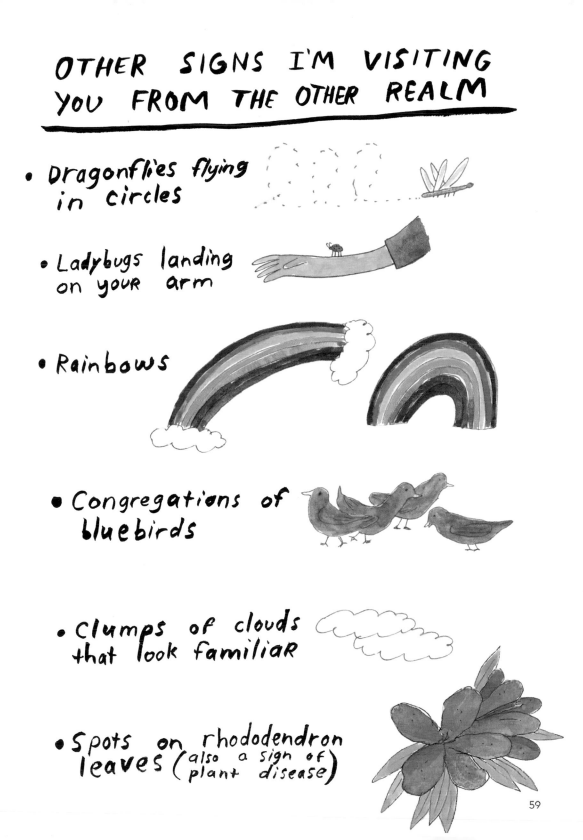

- Dragonflies flying in circles

- Ladybugs landing on your arm

- Rainbows

- Congregations of bluebirds

- Clumps of clouds that look familiar

- Spots on rhododendron leaves (also a sign of plant disease)

DAY 550: *Make a decision*

When there's a decision to be made—change careers, pursue a relationship, get out of one, move to a new neighborhood, start a business—the procedure is going to be exactly the same.

- Get a legal pad, ruler, pencil
- Draw a line down the middle of the pad
- Draw another line across the top 10 percent of the page
- Left is pro, right is con
- Beneath, list outcomes: best-case scenario, worst-case scenario
- If the best case is better than the worst case is worse, do it

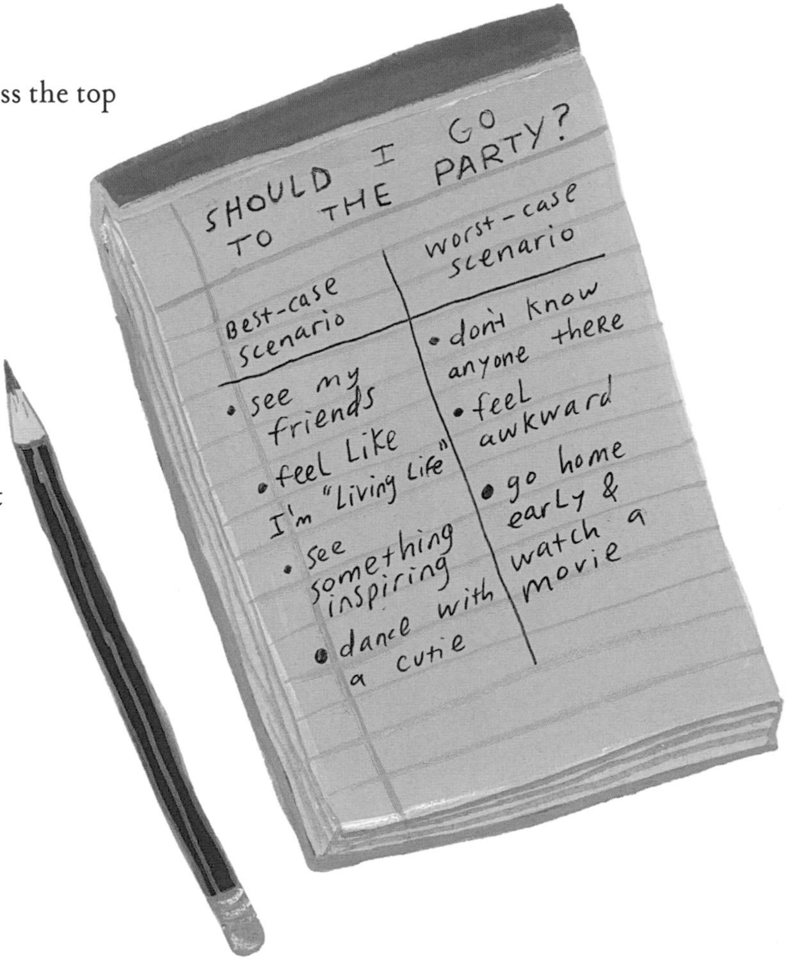

SHOULD I GO TO THE PARTY?
Best-case scenario
worst-case scenario
• see my friends
• feel Like I'm "Living Life"
• see something inspiring
• dance with a cutie
• don't know anyone there
• feel awkward
• go home earLy & watch a movie

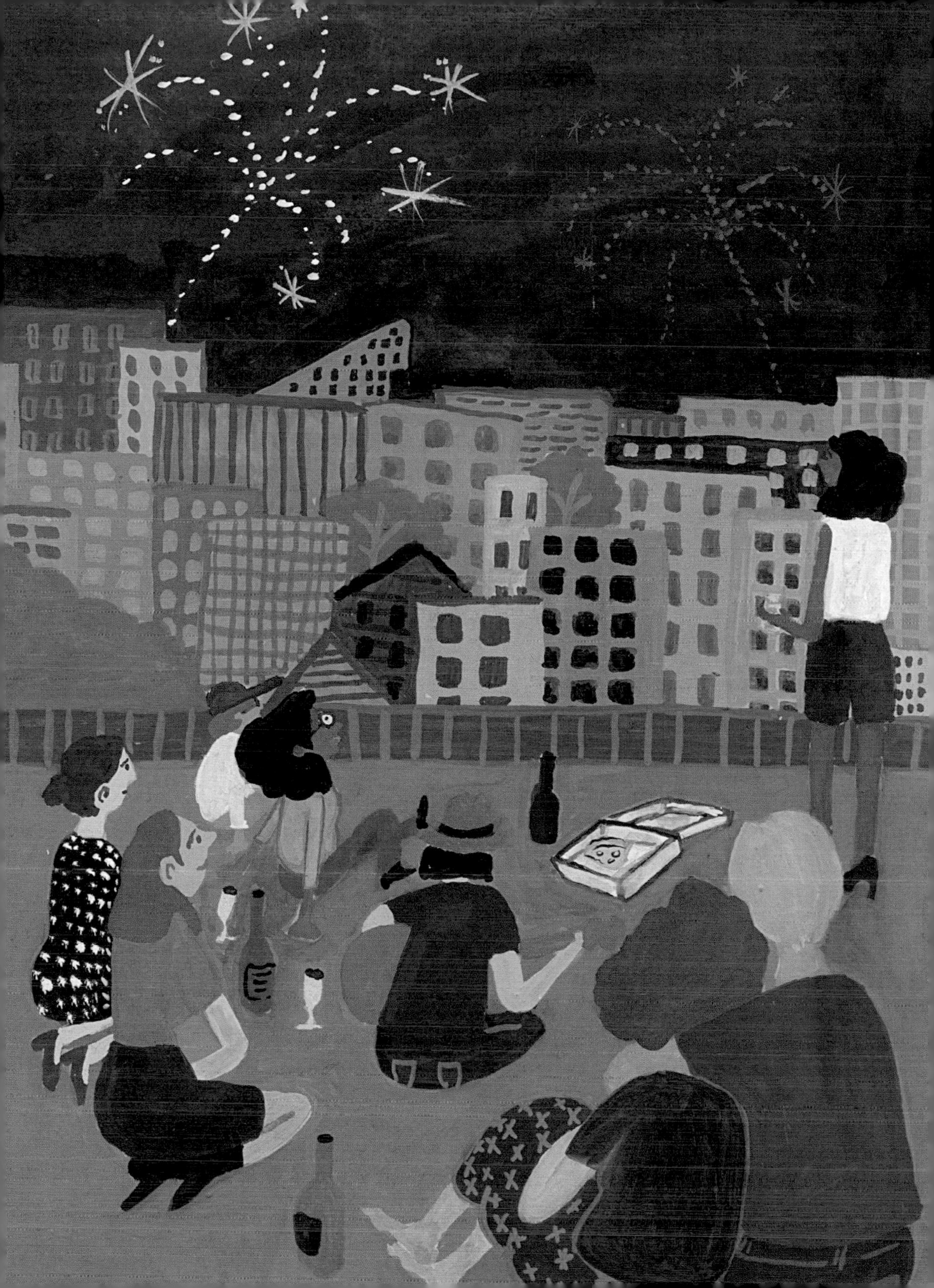

DAY 600: *Get some perspective*

If you're upset with someone, it's probably related to the fact that you love this person. Go to bed early and get a good night's sleep. The next morning, pretend that a meteor is going to hit the earth in five minutes, wiping out your neighborhood. Would you be worried about who's right and who's wrong, or would you just want to give a hug and never let go? Problem solved.

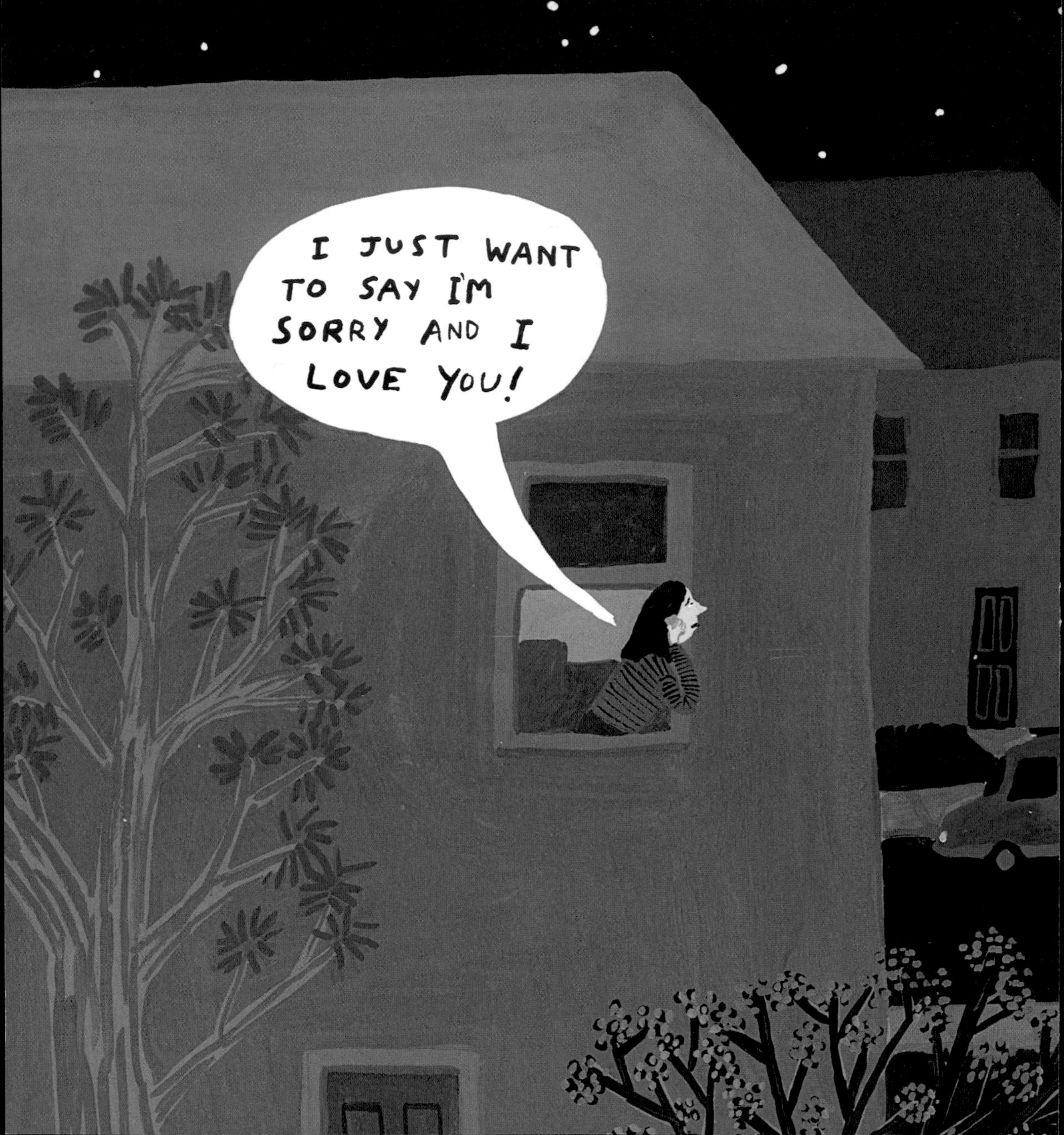
I JUST WANT TO SAY I'M SORRY AND I LOVE YOU!

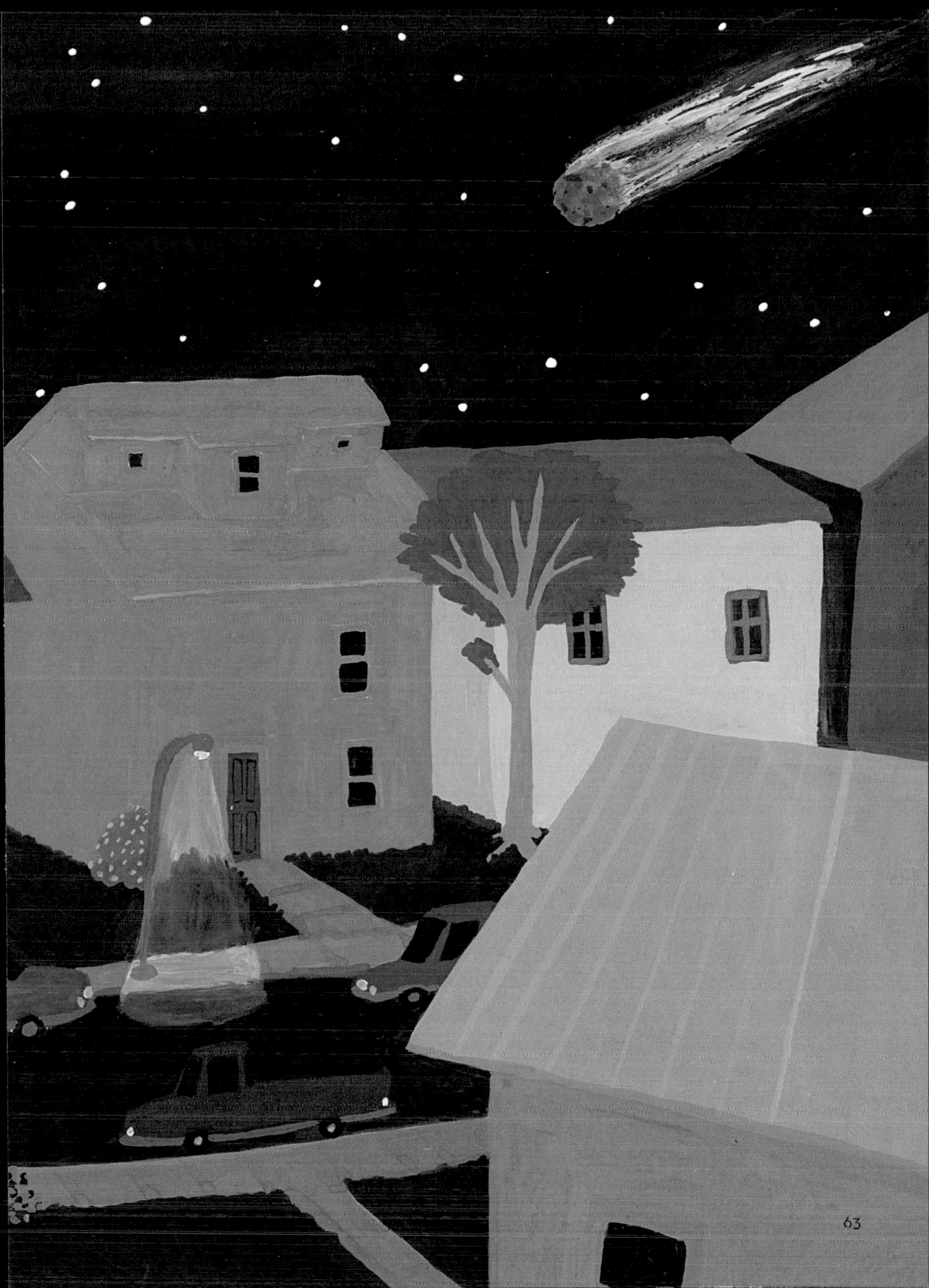

DAY 650: *Cure your heartbreak with curry*

Love can hurt. Curry can help.

Onions, butter, olive oil
Garlic, ginger
Potatoes, carrots, yams,
    apple, tomatoes
Broccoli, parsley
Curry powder (medium or hot)
Cumin, turmeric, cinnamon, brown
    sugar, fennel seed, cayenne, salt,
    pepper
Flour
Chicken or vegetable broth
Coconut milk

Dice a big pile of onions, then cook slowly over low heat in butter or oil with some fresh garlic and ginger. While they're cooking, peel and dice a handful of carrots, two or three yams, a couple of large red potatoes, a tart apple, a few ripe tomatoes, some broccoli and parsley.

You're unhappy with the amount of chopping involved? Deal with it. Sharpen your knife and be thankful you're not digging ditches for a living, or a heart surgeon, fixing people's hearts just so they can get hurt all over again.

Consider this curry-making time an emotional safety zone. Relax and enjoy the process of trimming, dicing, and excising rotten spots just as you would excise the blight of love gone wrong from your broken heart.

Next, prepare a small bowl of dry ingredients: curry powder, cumin, turmeric, a bit of cinnamon, a bit of brown sugar, some fennel seed if you're feeling crazy, cayenne, salt, and pepper. Sprinkle this mix on top of the caramelized onions and tumble over low heat.

Add a bit of flour, too, for thickening. Let this mixture cook for a couple of minutes, then add a few cups of vegetable or chicken broth. Next, add the vegetables, the toughest ones first, reminding yourself that you are also tough and will survive this emotional meltdown.

Let this mixture simmer for a while, then add coconut milk, more curry powder, salt, and pepper. Adjust the liquid as needed; add more, cook longer, whatever. It really doesn't matter. Curry is incredibly forgiving, even if you are not.

You could blend this mixture, but I like it chunky. Add the broccoli and parsley near the end so they don't overcook.

Your attention to all this detail will help take your mind off your broken heart. Curry can always help you through heartbreak. It involves making something new out of the old disorder of your life. Even more so if you invite a friend to dinner, or bring over a curry care package.

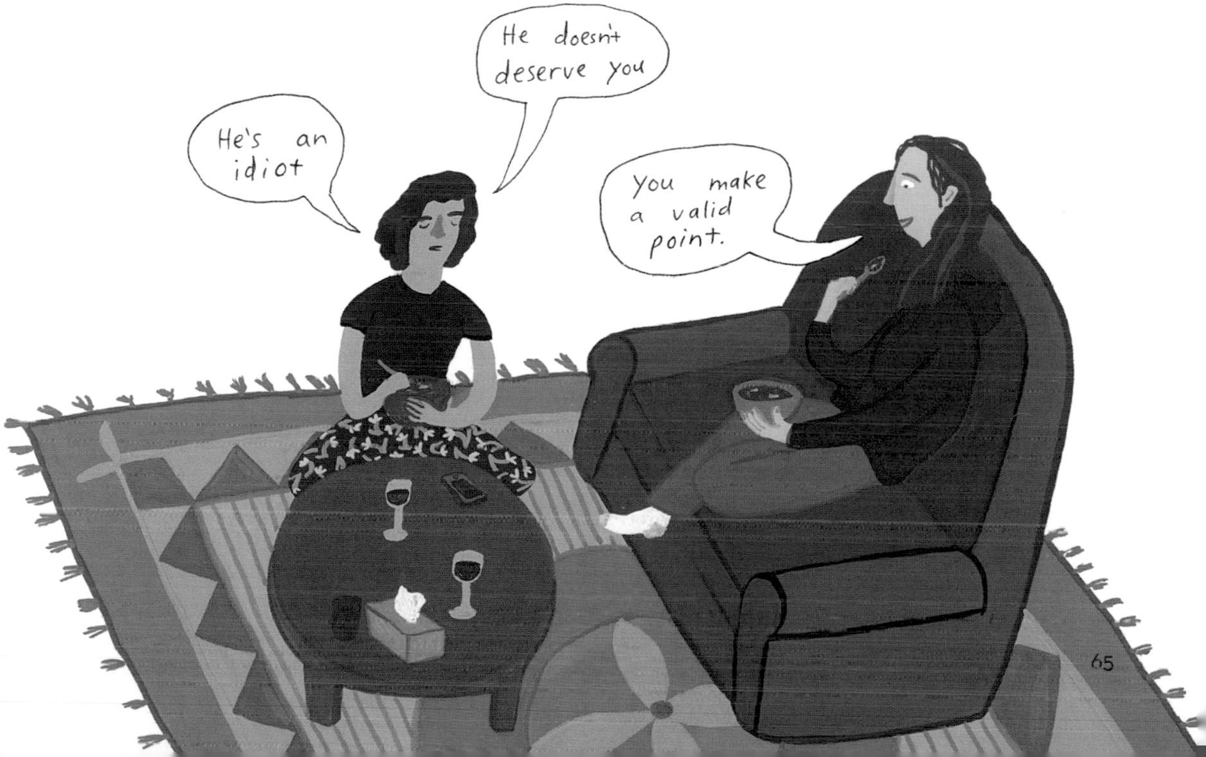
He's an idiot
He doesn't deserve you
You make a valid point.

DAY 700: *Raise the volume*

It's 3 a.m. and you can't call me because, well, I'm dead. If I wasn't, here's what I would say: "I'm sorry you can't sleep. Can I make you some tea? A nice bowl of curry?"

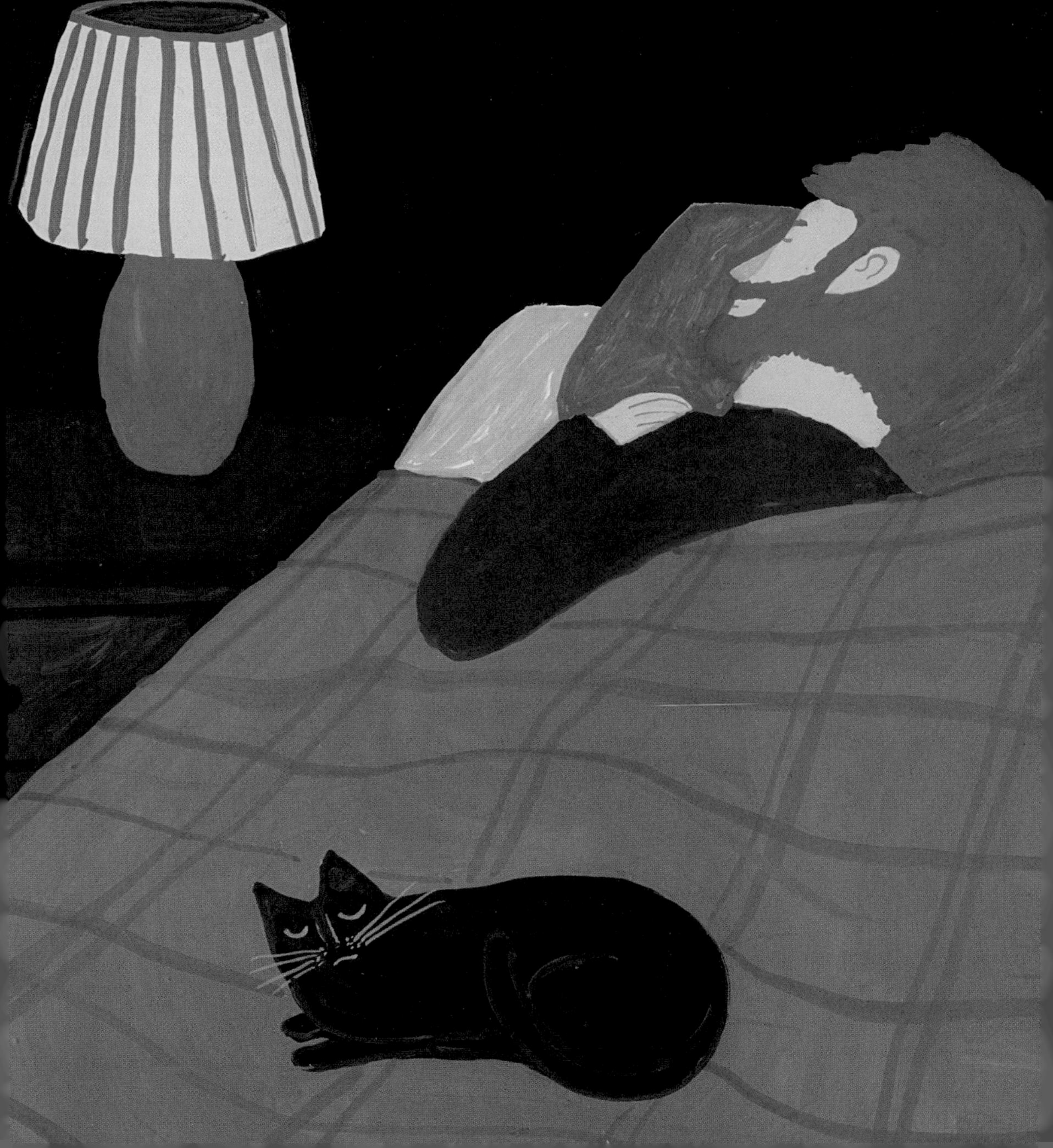

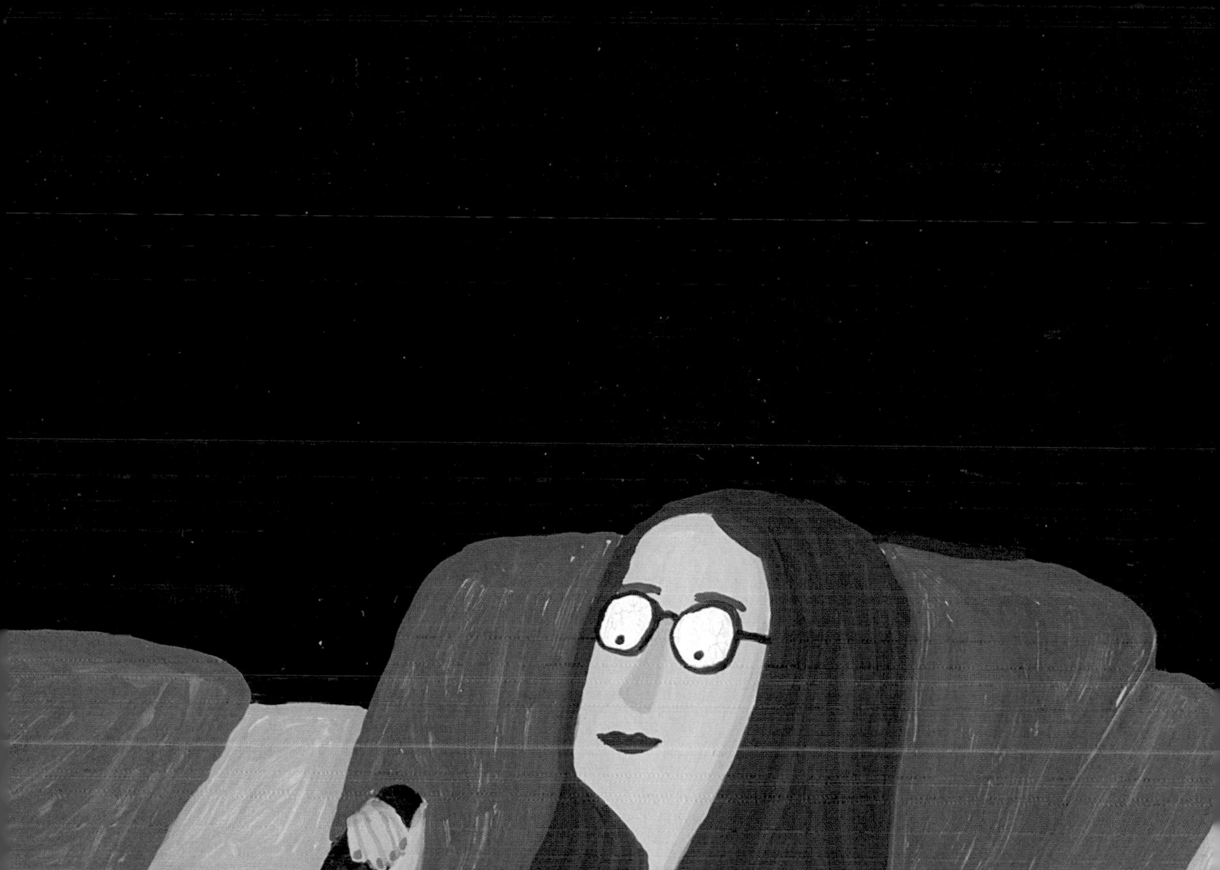

Your mind sometimes takes you places you don't want to go. Tune it out: Listen to a great song with the volume turned up to drown out that infernal internal screaming. If someone you care about is nearby, consider using headphones.

Better yet, read a great book. Let it transport you to another place and time, which—when you finally close your eyes—may help you appreciate where you are right now.

DAY 750: *Eat chocolate*

Are you with the right person?

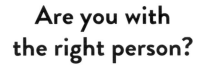

Someone who makes you laugh

Someone who cleans up if you're vomiting, then does the laundry

happy holidays!

Someone whose family welcomes you (it's true, you marry the family, too)

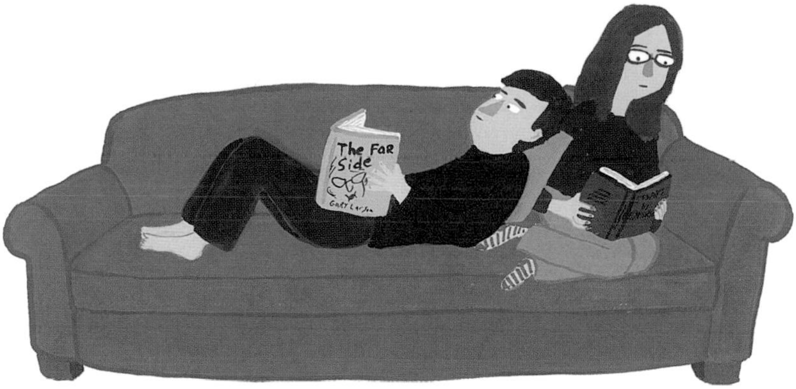
The Far Side
Gary Larson

Someone who is about as smart as you, definitely not too much dumber

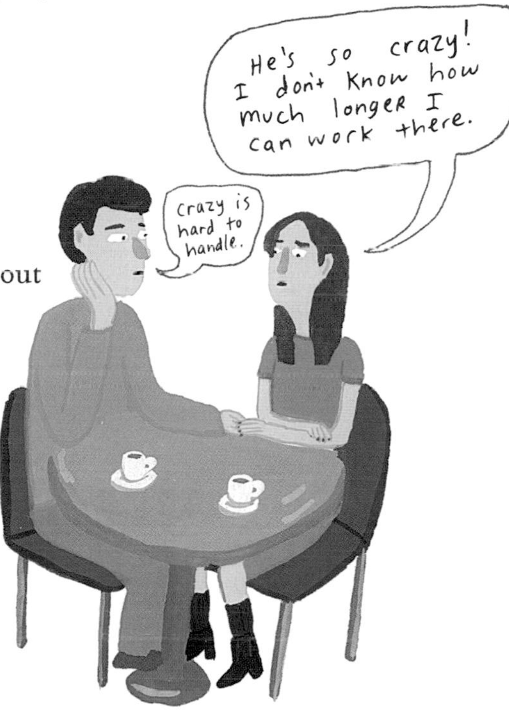
He's so crazy! I don't know how much longer I can work there.
crazy is hard to handle.

Someone who listens to your problems without trying to solve them

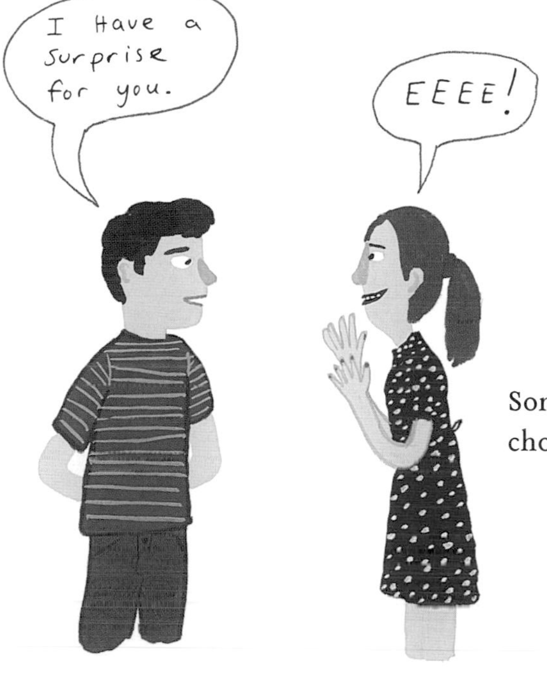
I Have a surprise for you.
EEEE!

Someone who brings home chocolate without being asked

DAY 850: *Talk to me*

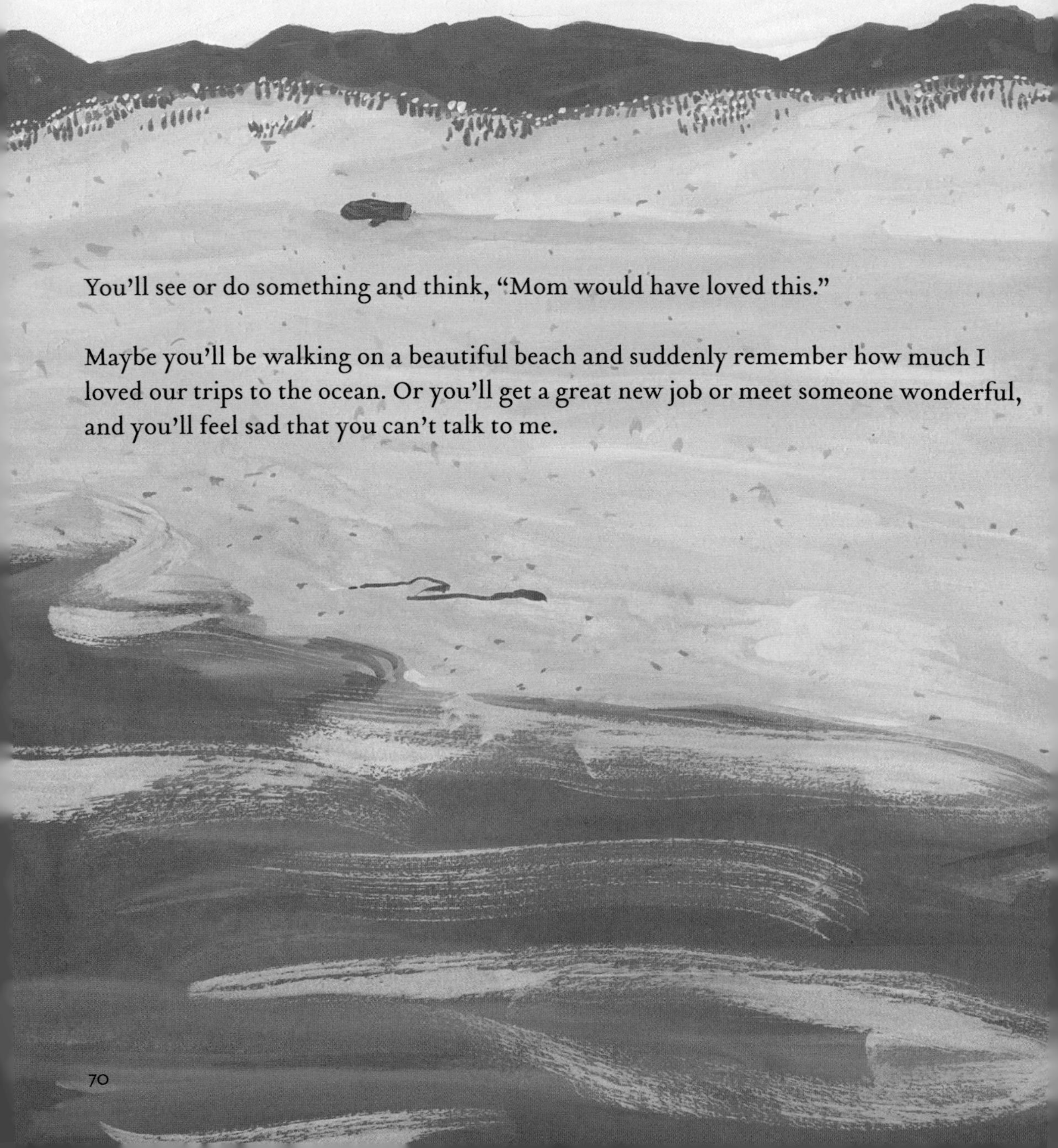

You'll see or do something and think, "Mom would have loved this."

Maybe you'll be walking on a beautiful beach and suddenly remember how much I loved our trips to the ocean. Or you'll get a great new job or meet someone wonderful, and you'll feel sad that you can't talk to me.

But you can.

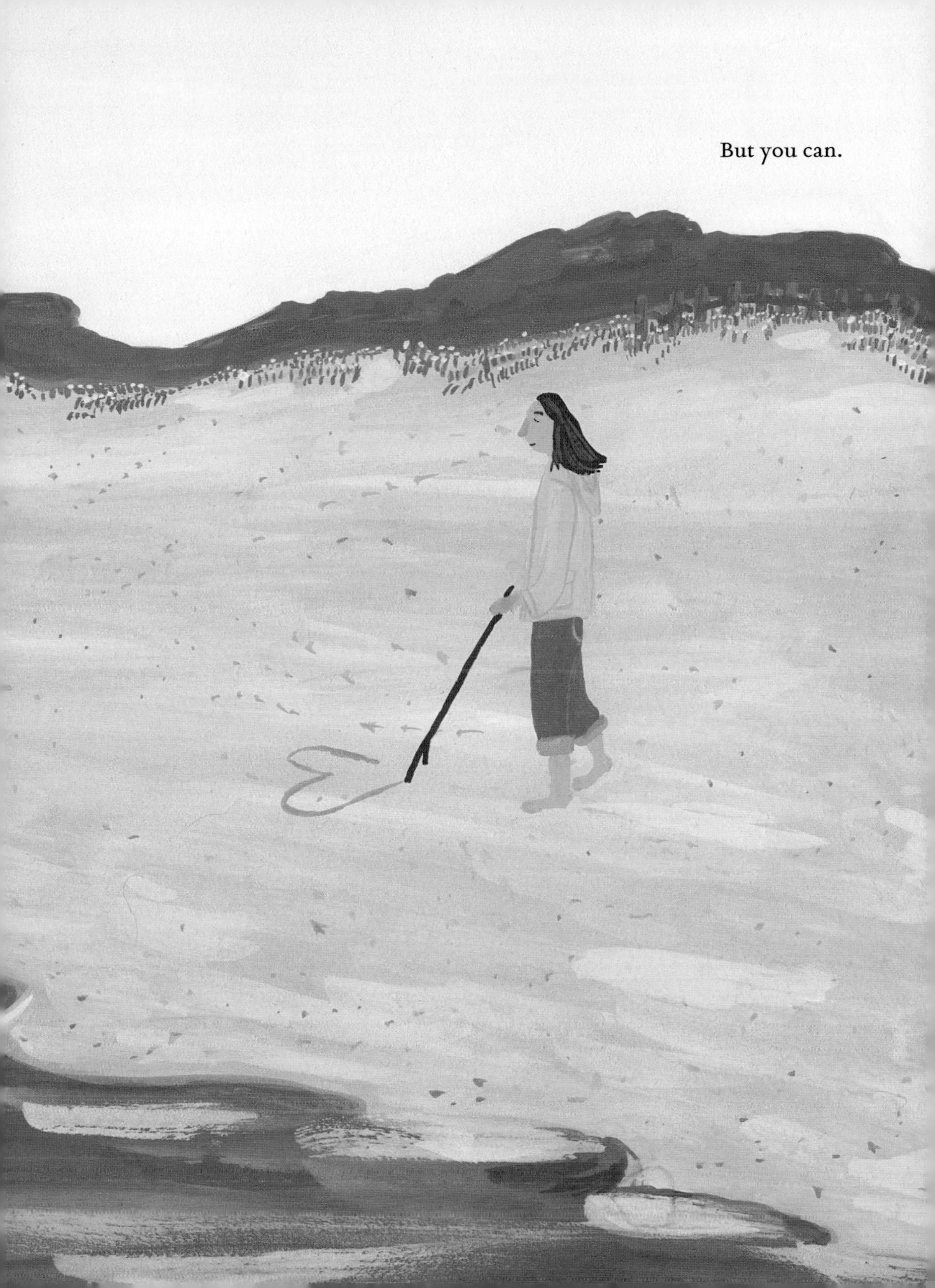

DAY 900: *Look up*

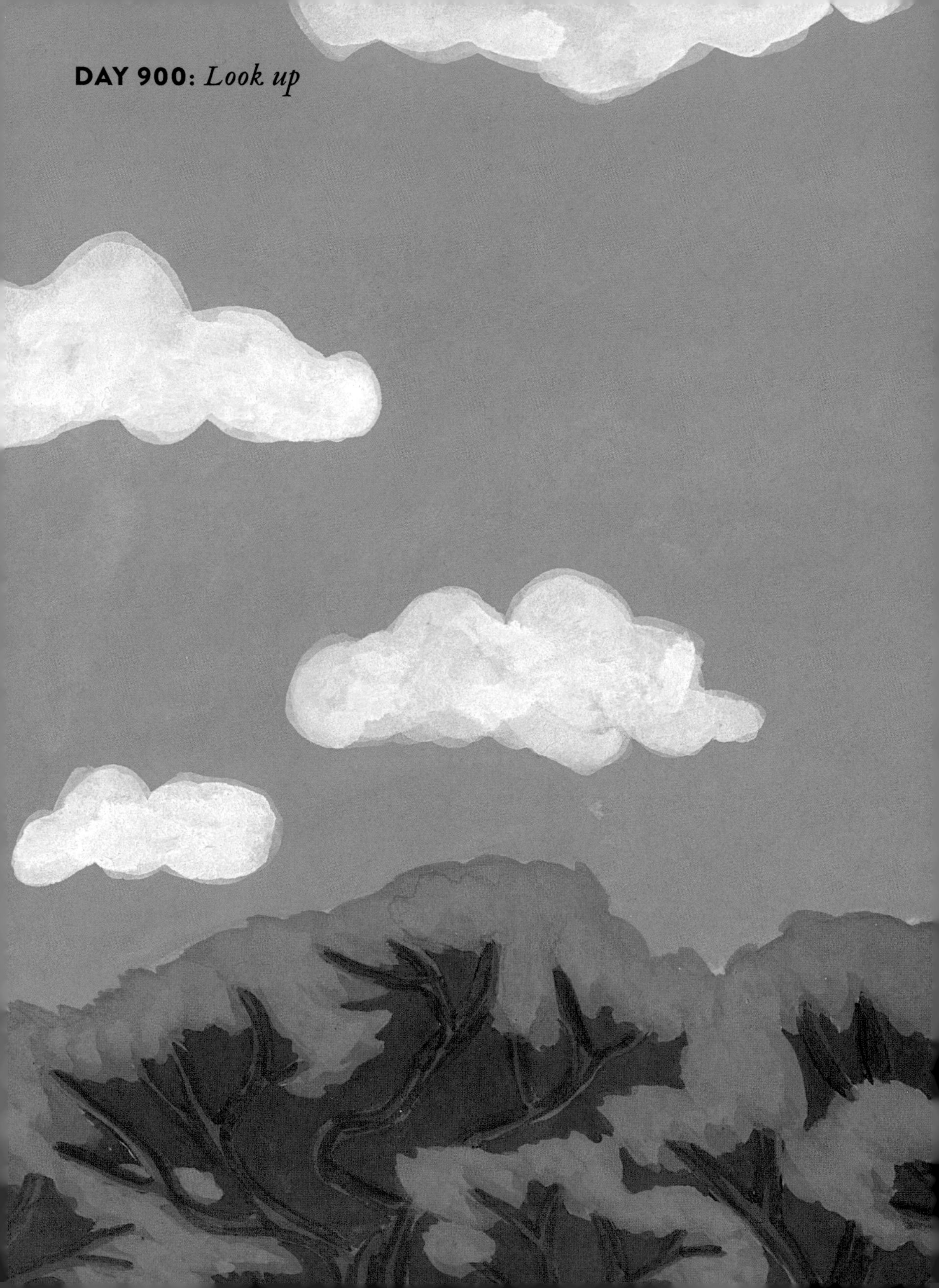

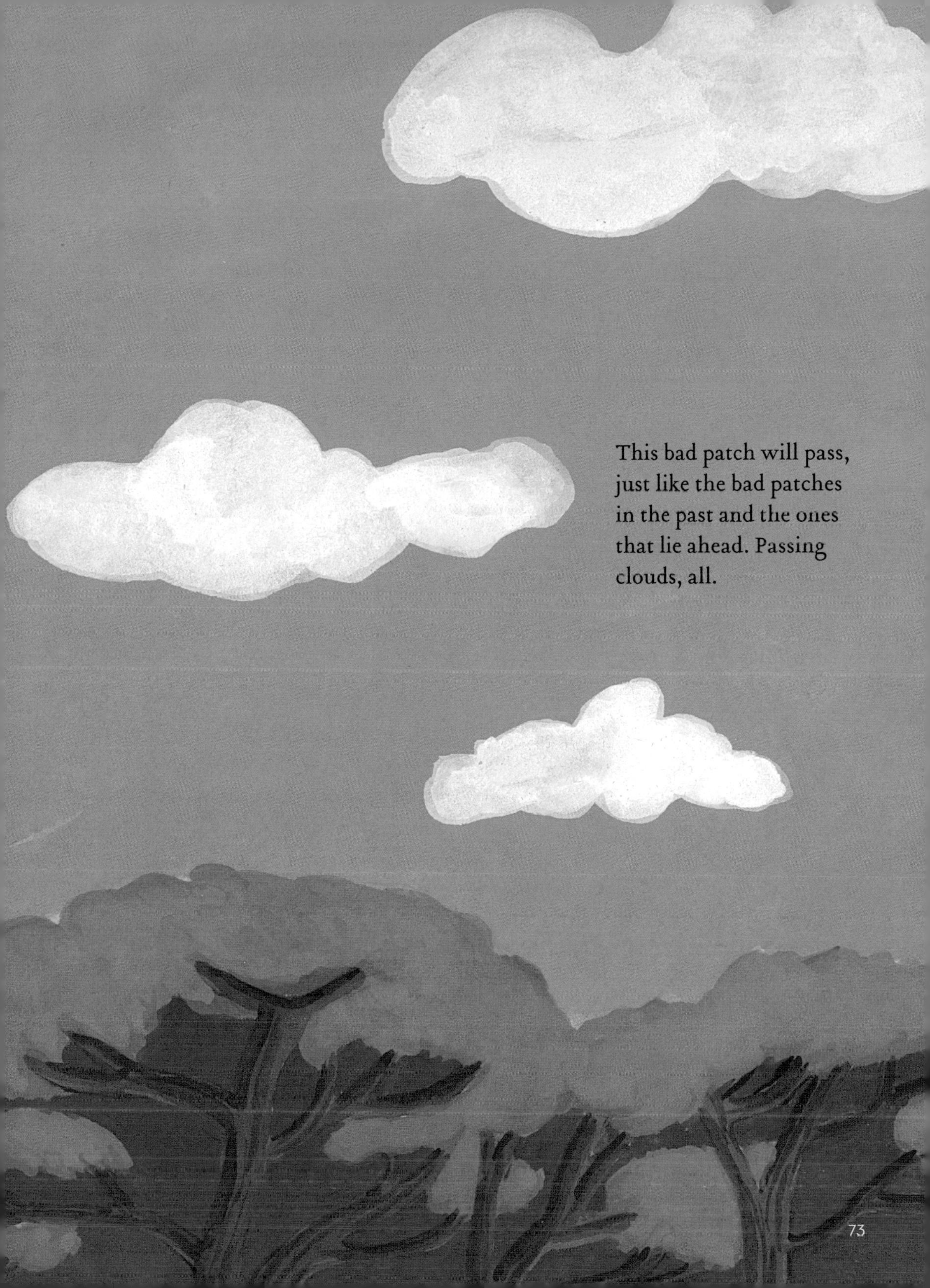

This bad patch will pass, just like the bad patches in the past and the ones that lie ahead. Passing clouds, all.

DAY 950: *Make chili*

People can be terribly inflexible. Chili is incredibly flexible.

Red onion, red bell pepper, celery, garlic
Olive oil
Chili powder, cumin, basil, fennel, rosemary,
    oregano, onion powder, cayenne, salt, pepper
Flour or flaxseed meal
Red wine
Diced tomatoes
Black beans, kidney beans
Vegetable or chicken broth
Diced carrots, yams, butternut squash
Tabasco sauce
Shredded cheese, sour cream, cilantro

This is a base recipe adaptable to big quantities. Before you get started, think of a few friends who would rather not cook tonight (they won't be hard to find) and invite them to dinner.

Dice and sauté a large red onion, red bell pepper, celery, and fresh garlic in olive oil for a few minutes, stirring occasionally.

Stir together the spices: chili powder, cumin, basil, fennel, rosemary, oregano, onion powder, cayenne, salt, and pepper.

Pour the spices over the onion mix, sauté for a minute or so, then sprinkle in two or three tablespoons of flour or flaxseed meal and cook for another minute. Add a cup of red wine and simmer the mixture until it thickens, then add diced tomatoes, black beans, kidney beans, and vegetable or chicken stock.

You can add more broth or additional diced vegetables at this point (I like carrots, yams, and butternut squash) and a splash of Tabasco.

Let this simmer for an hour or two. Test for spiciness and adjust. Serve with shredded cheese, sour cream, and fresh diced cilantro. This recipe can handle a lot of flavor and just gets better with age—and cornbread.

DAY 1,000: *Take a risk*

Q: We're in love and have talked about living together. How will we know if it's the right time?

A. When you'd rather be together night and day than apart.

Q: What if we live together and start to take each other for granted?

A. You will. Then you'll realize your mistake and refocus on your partner and strengthening your relationship.

Still, there may be times when you think the passion will never return, and when you feel invisible to your partner. Being in love is easy. Living together is harder. It's a learning experience, mostly about yourself.

At times you won't like how you behave or how your partner behaves. You won't always agree and the workload won't always be evenly distributed. At times you'll get angry and fight and have to work to reestablish communication. It sounds grim, but if you love your partner, it's worth the effort.

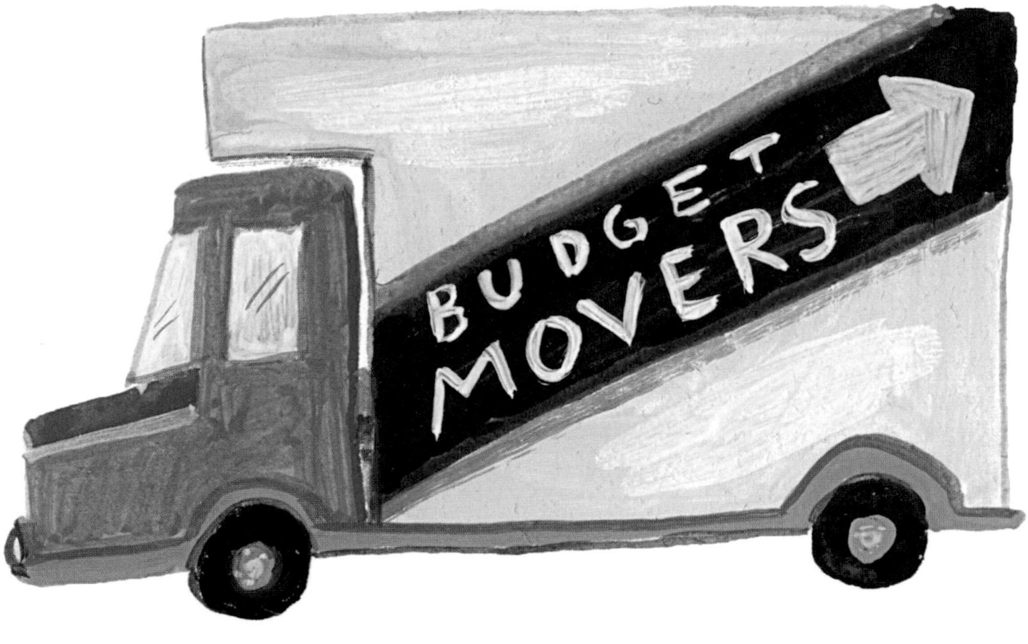
BUDGET
MOVERS

Q: What about marriage? Even if I find the person I want to spend my life with, I'm apprehensive about the institution and the strains it puts on a relationship. If nearly half of all marriages end in divorce, why risk it?

A. What is your reason for thinking about getting married? What do you think it will change? People get married for all kinds of reasons. Love, faith, sex, money, children.

Don't blame the institution: It's invisible. The problem is there's no instruction manual. People tend to be selfish and may not realize how much give and take is required. They may give up too easily. How much love and effort you put into marriage is a fair indicator of its success or failure. If you quit a few years in, you might miss out on wonderful time together when you're older and wiser.

All I can say is, it's worth it when you find someone who knows what you are going through and actually cares. Who knows your history and doesn't mind at all. Who knows what you are really like first thing in the morning and loves you anyway. Yes, it's risky, and yes, there are times when it's a lot of work. Take that chance.

Q: What if we work as hard as we can and still break up? What if I waste years on the wrong person? I'm scared I'll look back and cringe at how naive I was.

A: This person came into your life to teach you a lesson: You'll learn what you want or don't want in a partner. As for cringing, there's no need. Everyone is naive starting out.

It's what helps us say "I do."

DAY 1,500: *Have kids*

ARE YOU READY?

...TO BE CHAINED TO LITTLE HUMAN ROCKS FOR THE NEXT 20 YEARS?

...FOR THE POSSIBILITY THAT THEY WON'T HAVE TEN PERFECT LITTLE FINGERS AND TOES?

MO-OM!!!

...TO LOSE SLEEP YEAR AFTER YEAR?

DIAPERS

...TO PAY A FORTUNE FOR DIAPERS, FORMULA, CAR SEATS, SHOES AND SIPPY CUPS?

I HATE YOU!

...TO DEAL WITH TEEN RAGE?

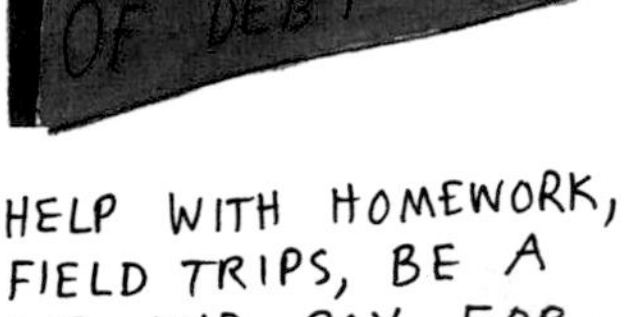

UNIVERSITY OF DEBT

...TO HELP WITH HOMEWORK, GO ON FIELD TRIPS, BE A CHAUFFEUR AND PAY FOR COLLEGE?

It's nice to think you'll give it this much thought. More likely, though, you will have sex with someone you love (or could grow to love), igniting a new life and rendering all your questions and worries moot.

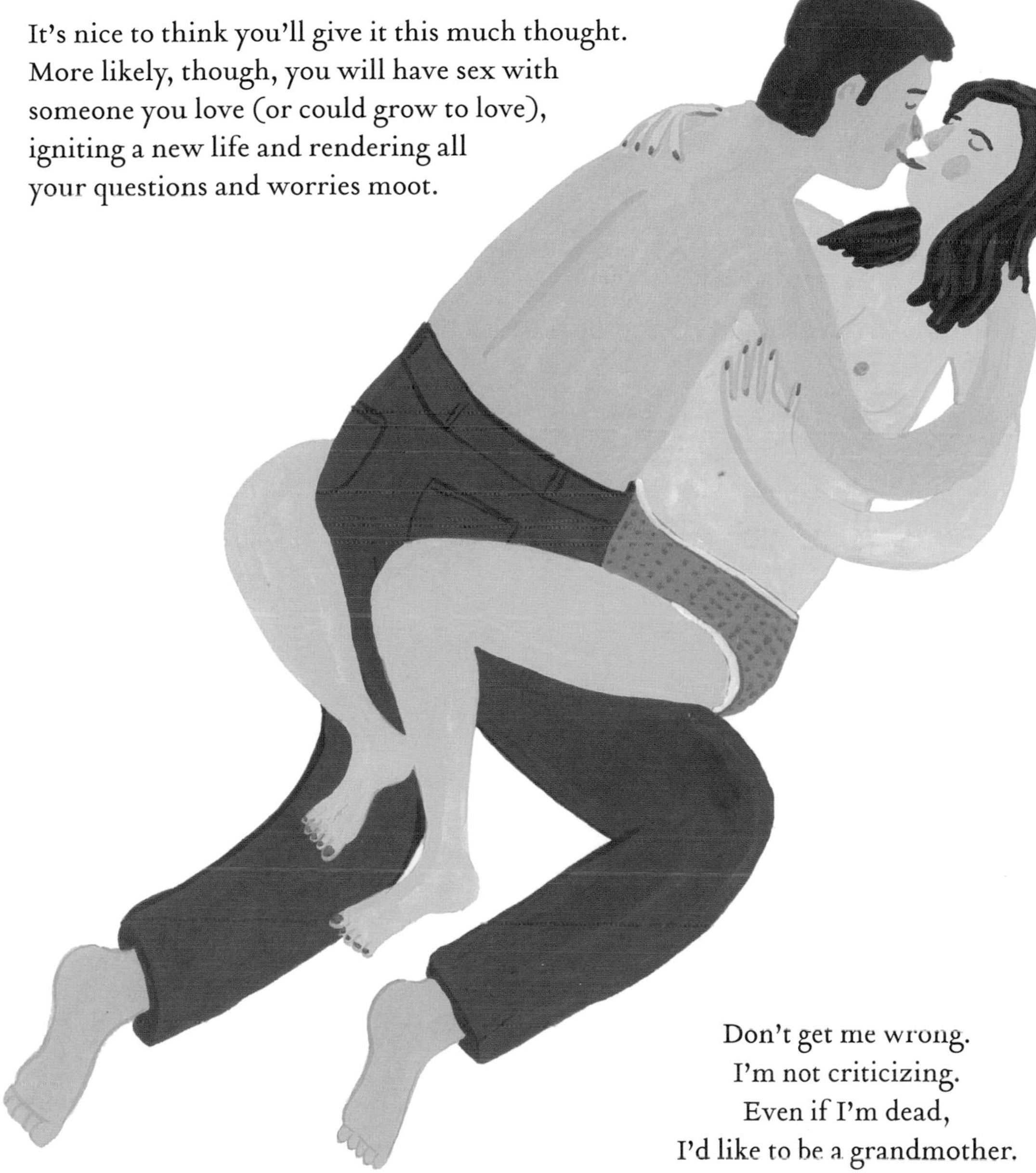

Don't get me wrong.
I'm not criticizing.
Even if I'm dead,
I'd like to be a grandmother.

DAY 1,775: *Do drugs*

Drugs can be a beautiful addition to a birthday. The pain you are likely to experience will be mind-bending, unless you are the one in one hundred women who say "I had the baby in ten minutes—I barely had time to finish my sandwich!"

This is a guilt-free zone: Ask for any drugs you are safely entitled to. When you first hold your baby, that pain will soon recede into memory because your future starts crying almost immediately.

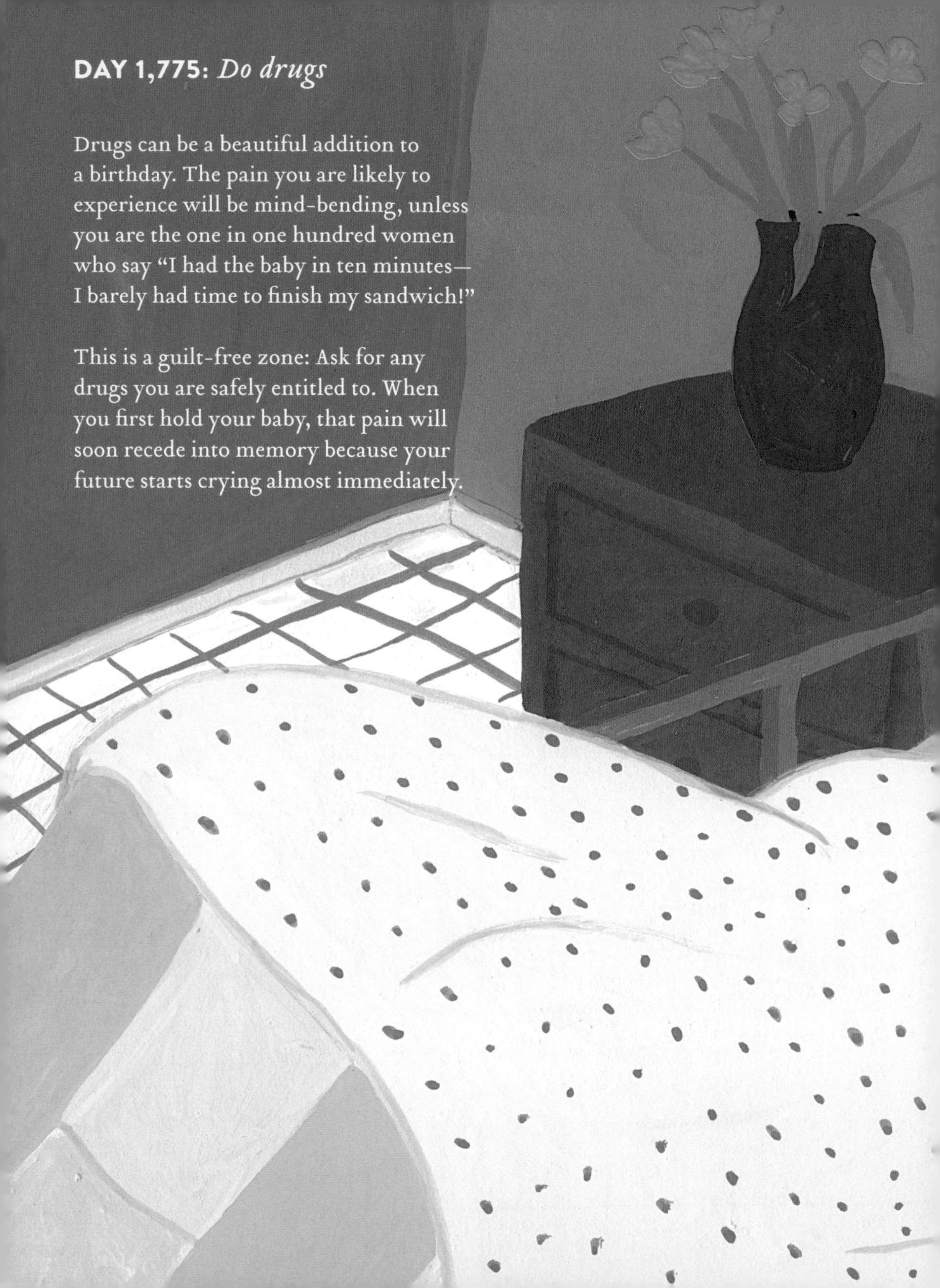

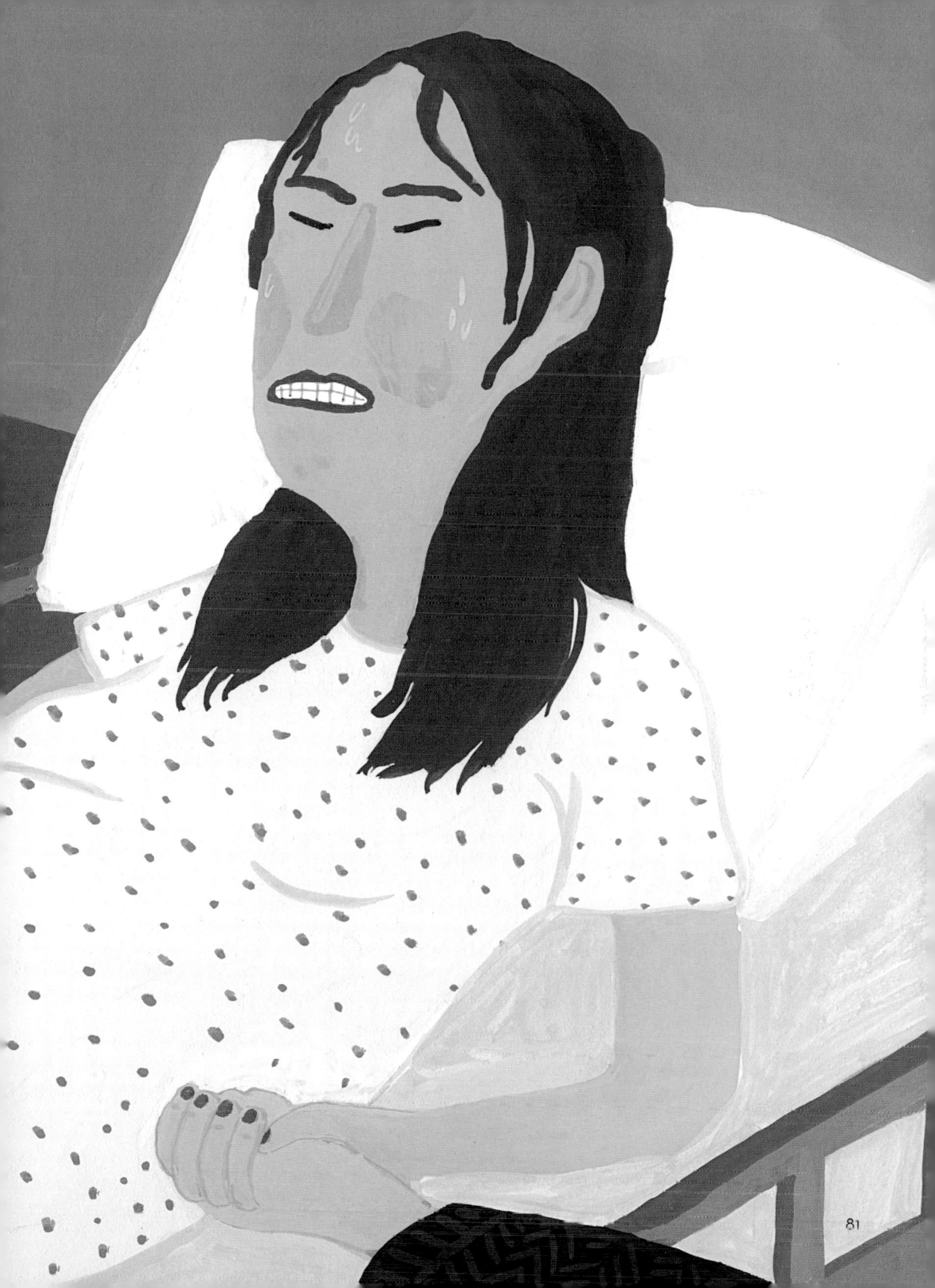

DAY 1,800: *Sing the lullaby I used to sing to you*

Daisy, Daisy, give me your answer true
I'm half crazy over the love of you
It won't be a stylish marriage
I can't afford a carriage
But you'll look sweet
Upon the seat
Of a bicycle built for two

Ruby, Ruby, give me your answer true
Will you let me pedal along with you
When you and I go cruisin'
You'll thank me for choosin'
You to come and have some fun
On a bicycle built for two

Billy, Billy, give me your answer true
I love riding, do you love it too
Slow or fast or faster
You lead, I'll follow after
The path flies by as you and I
Ride a bicycle built for two

A bicycle built for two

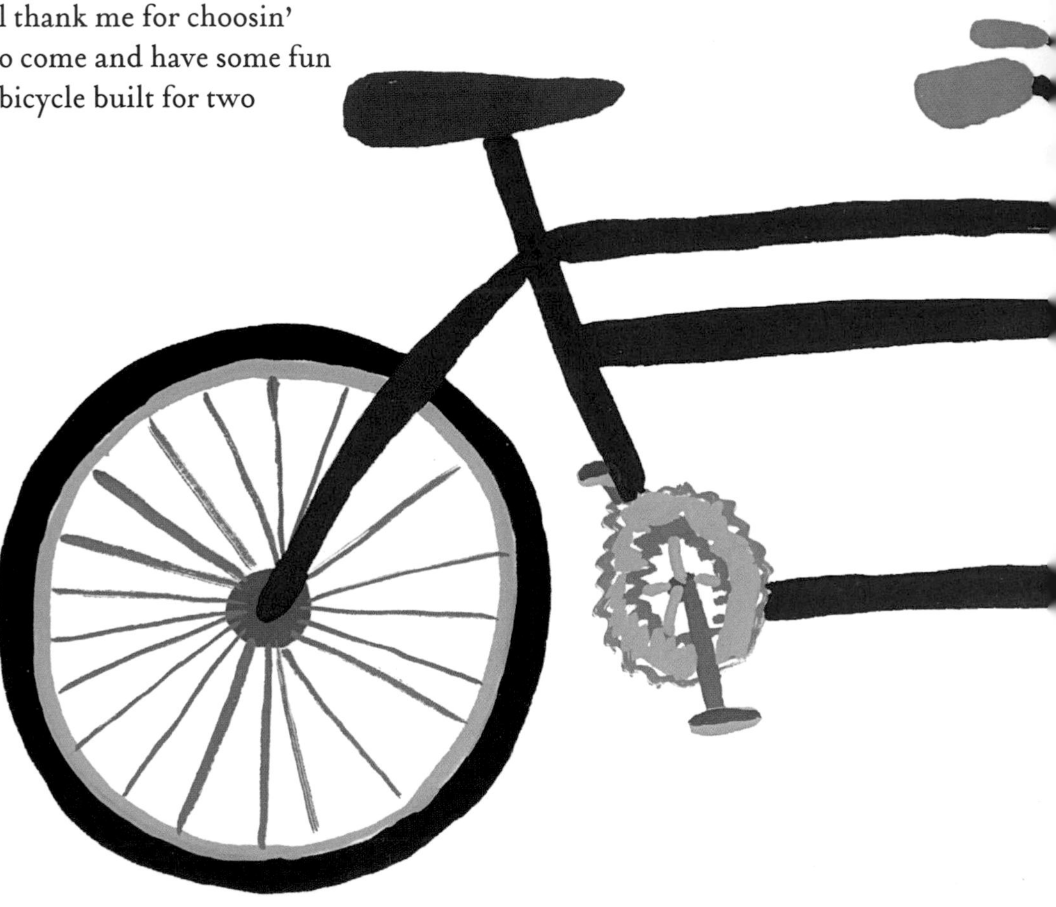

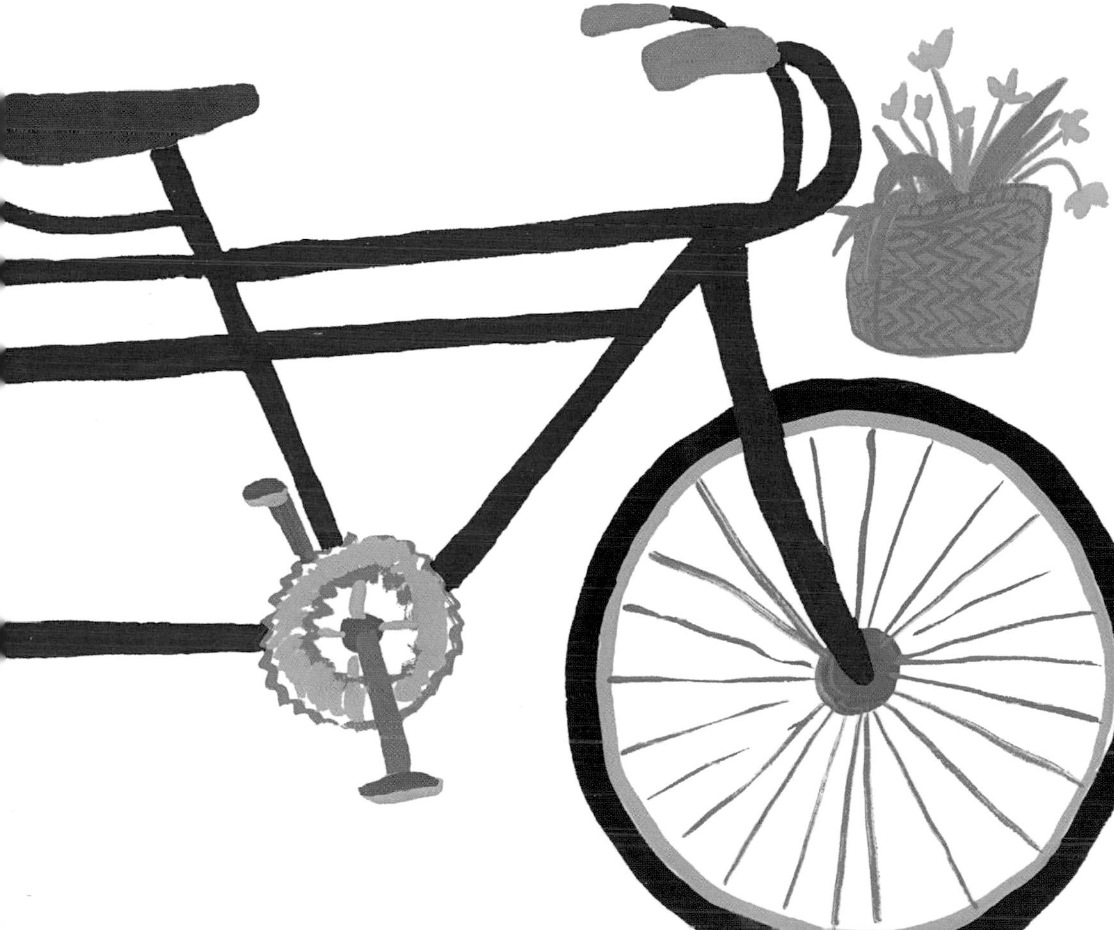

DAY 1,900: *Make amends*

If you have a fight with a sibling, friend, parent, try to mend it. Don't let little feuds turn into big ones. Let them know that despite what happened, you love and need them.

People need to know that you see them—that they are not invisible to you, taken for granted. Acknowledge what you did. Accept responsibility. Extend a sincere apology.

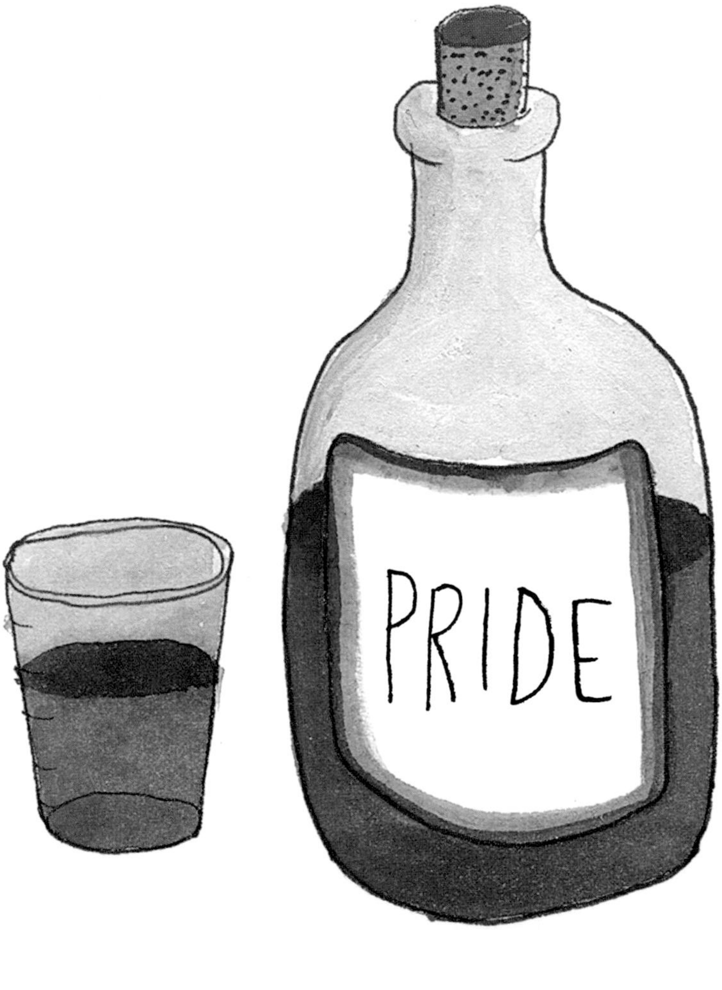
PRIDE

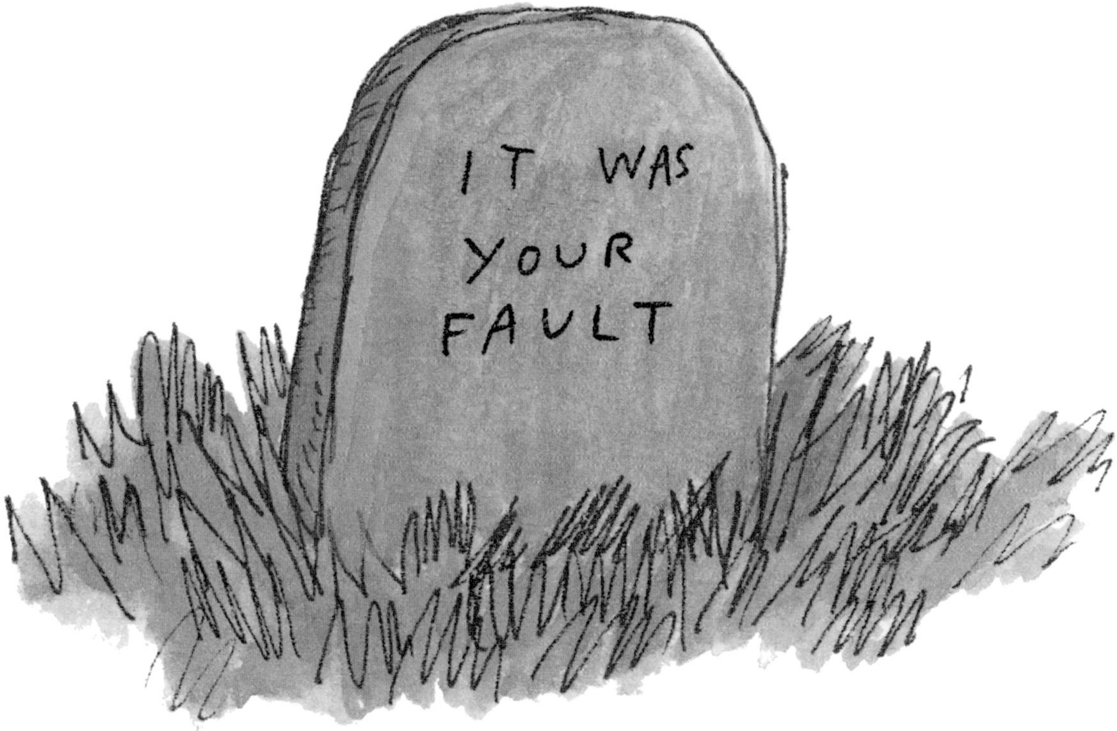
IT WAS
YOUR
FAULT

If you die angry, you've waited too long.

DAY 2,000: *Enjoy this dream*

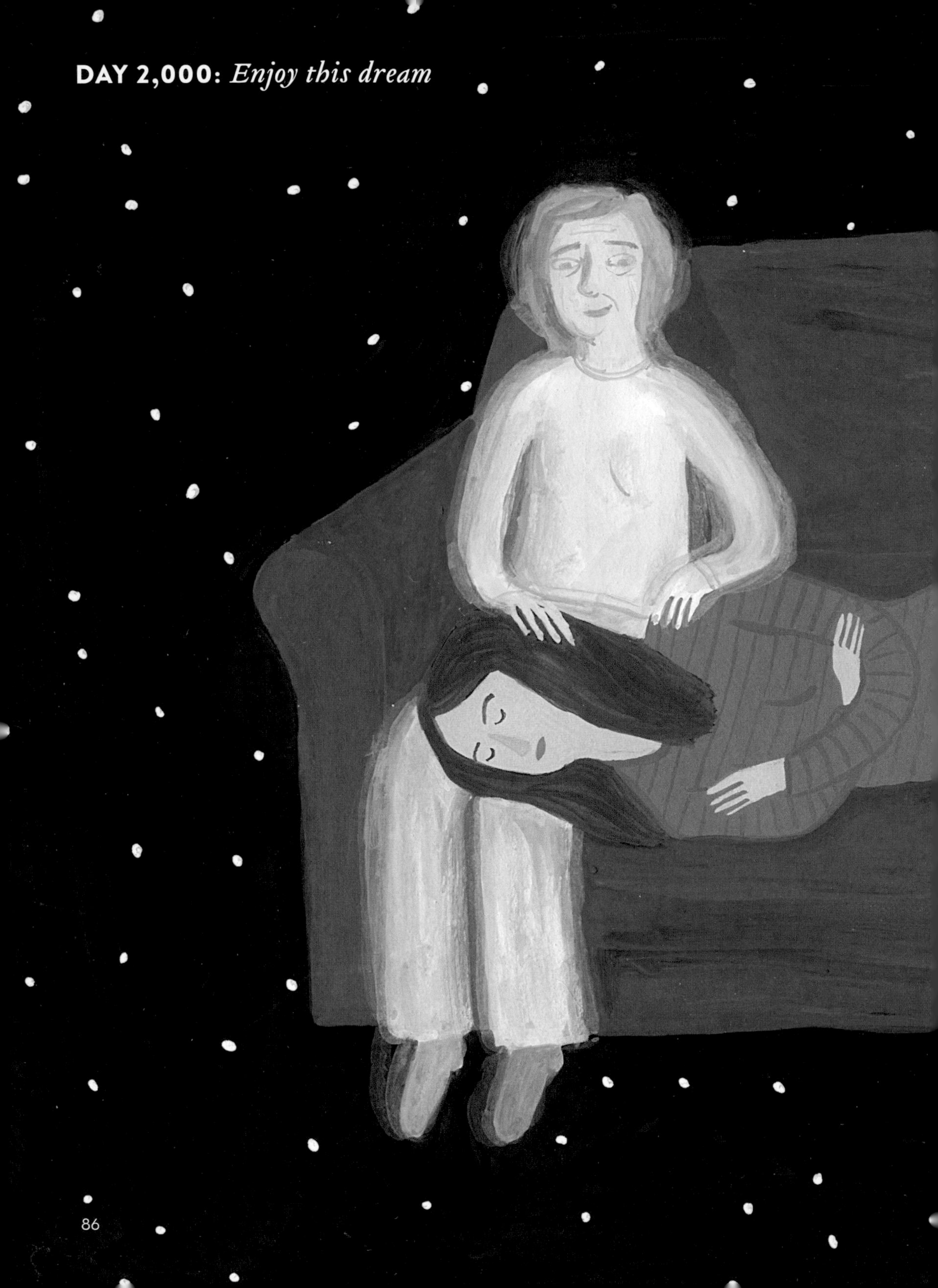

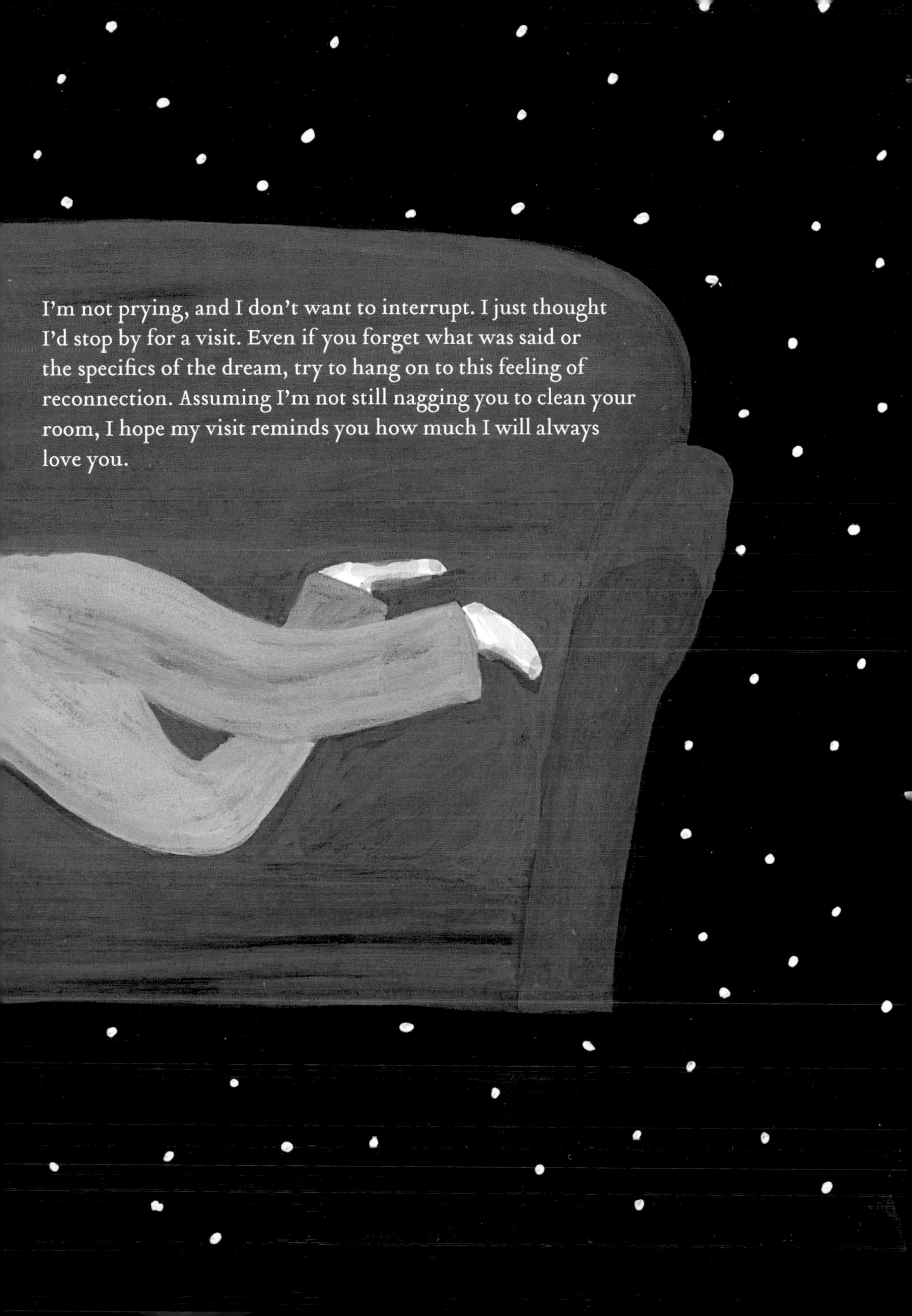

I'm not prying, and I don't want to interrupt. I just thought I'd stop by for a visit. Even if you forget what was said or the specifics of the dream, try to hang on to this feeling of reconnection. Assuming I'm not still nagging you to clean your room, I hope my visit reminds you how much I will always love you.

DAY 2,500: *Suffer*

You're going to get hurt. It's part of life. Just know that your sorrow and pain is not unique and not unmatched. There are lots of people who can outdo you on the suffering front. Find them. Take them cookies. You're in this together, even when it feels like you are the only one on earth dealing with this.

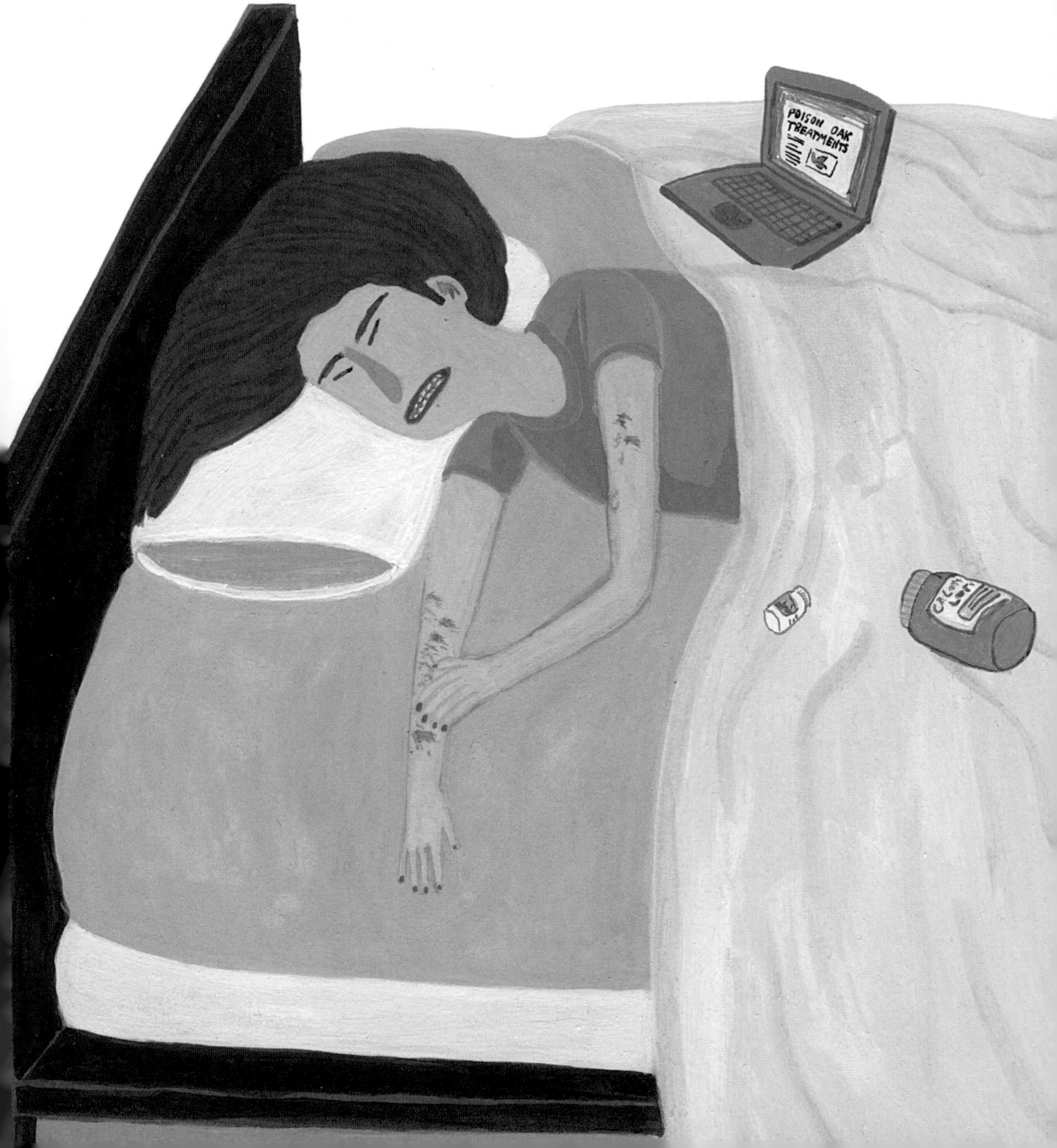
POISON OAK TREATMENTS

LET'S PLAY "WHAT'S WORSE?"

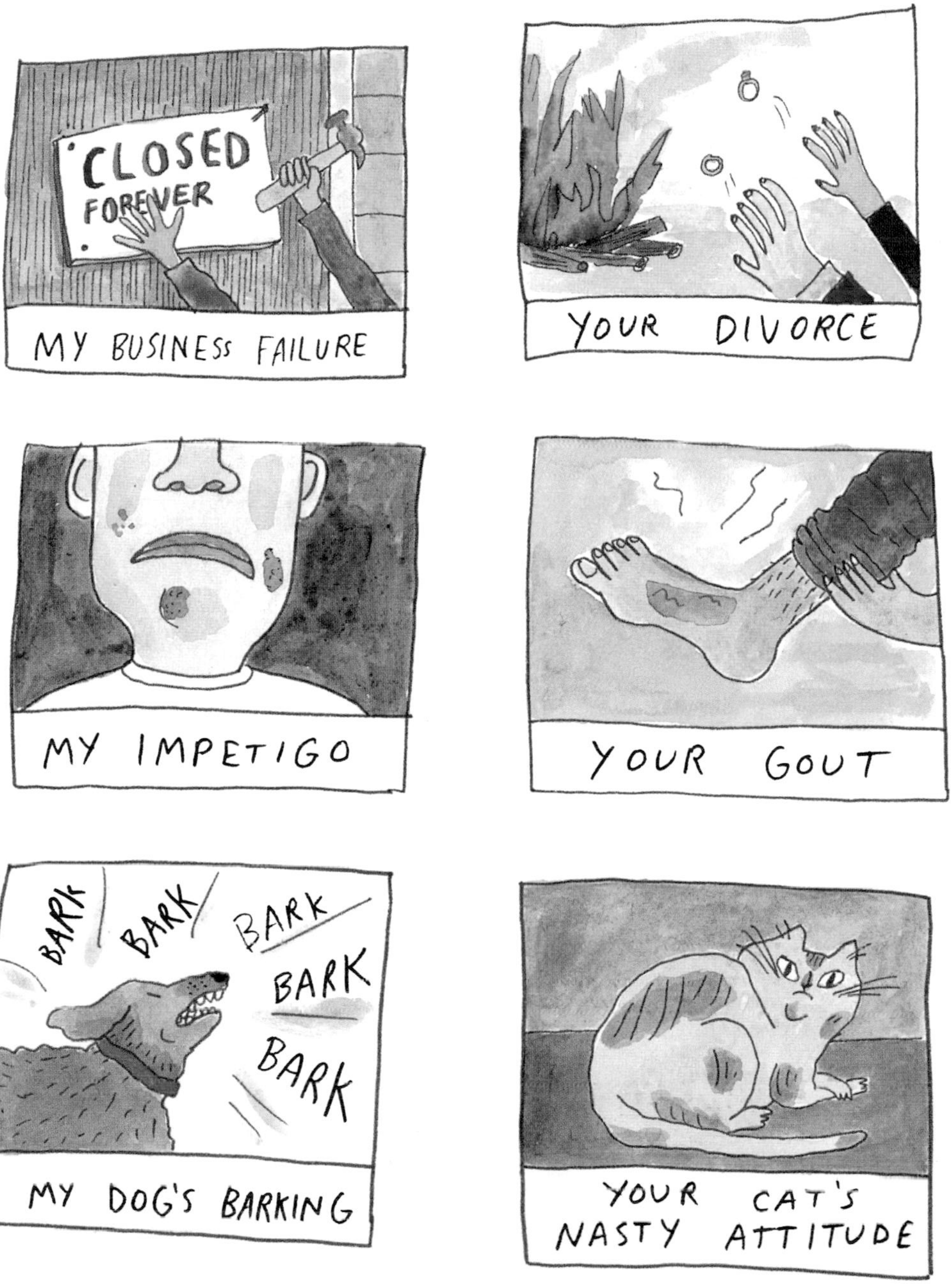
CLOSED FOREVER
MY BUSINESS FAILURE
YOUR DIVORCE
MY IMPETIGO
YOUR GOUT
BARK BARK BARK BARK BARK
MY DOG'S BARKING
YOUR CAT'S NASTY ATTITUDE

DAY 3,000: *Talk to your kids about death*

Cleaning and dressing the body, digging the hole, etching the stone. We used to be more connected to death. Now we are shielded from the reality of it, which adds to our unease.

Our culture, our families need to talk much more about death. In the same way you greet a new life you ought to honor a departing life.

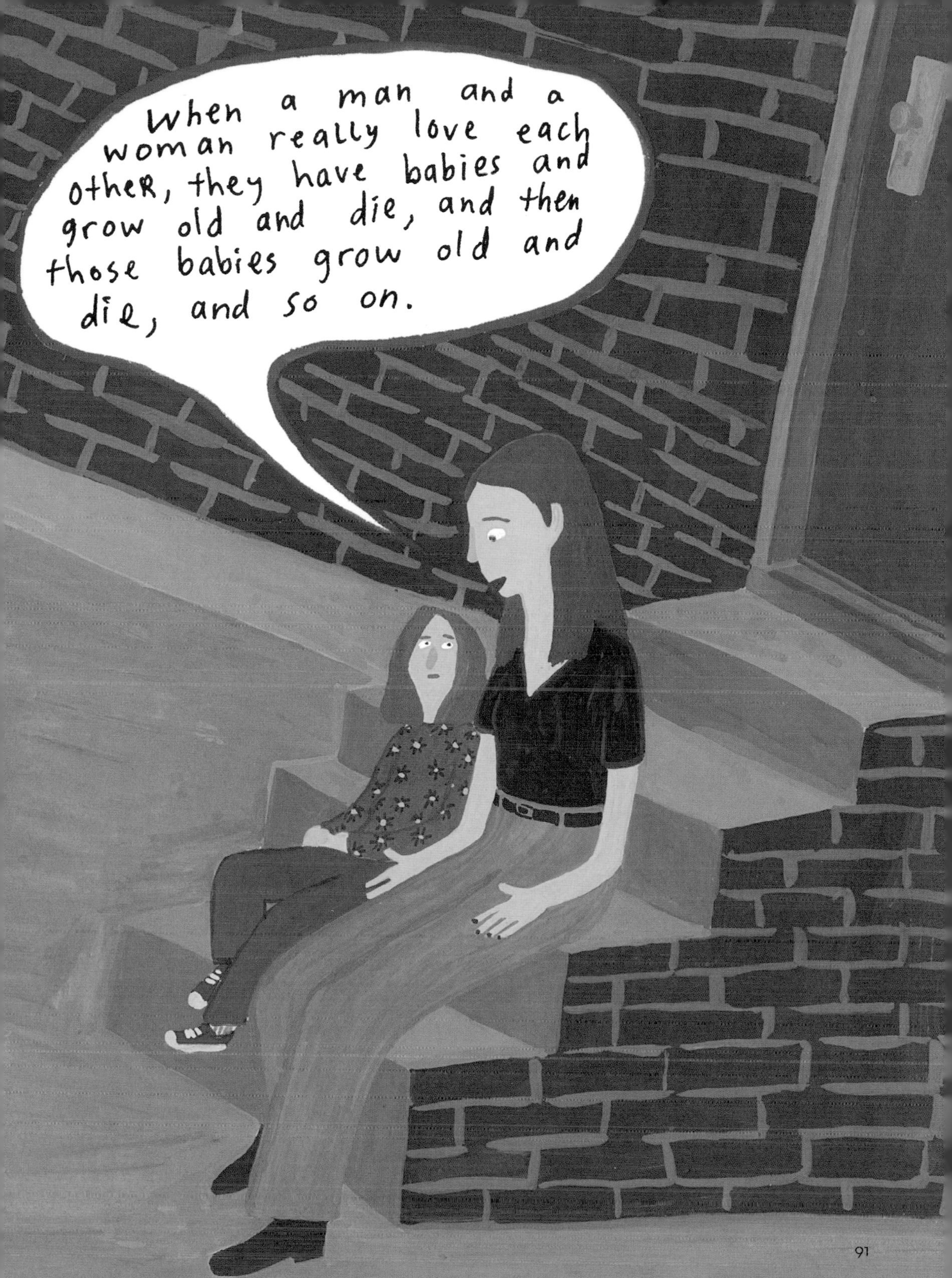
When a man and a woman really love each other, they have babies and grow old and die, and then those babies grow old and die, and so on.

DAY 3,500: *Make beauty*

The world will disappoint you. You'll be stunned by war, intolerance, hate, greed. You'll want a quick solution, but there isn't one.

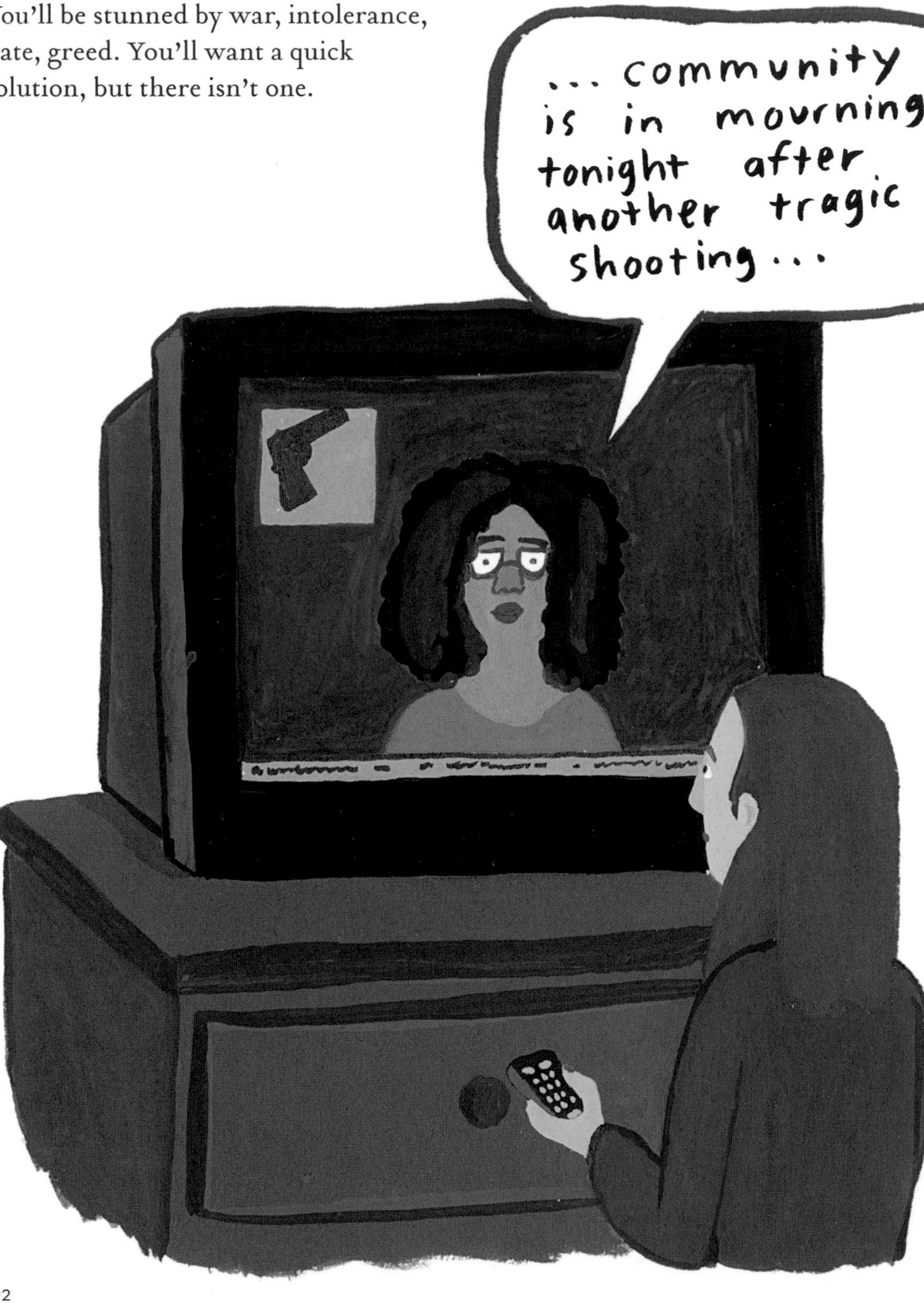
... community is in mourning tonight after another tragic shooting ...

Try to counter
those wrongs
by putting forth
something positive,
however small.

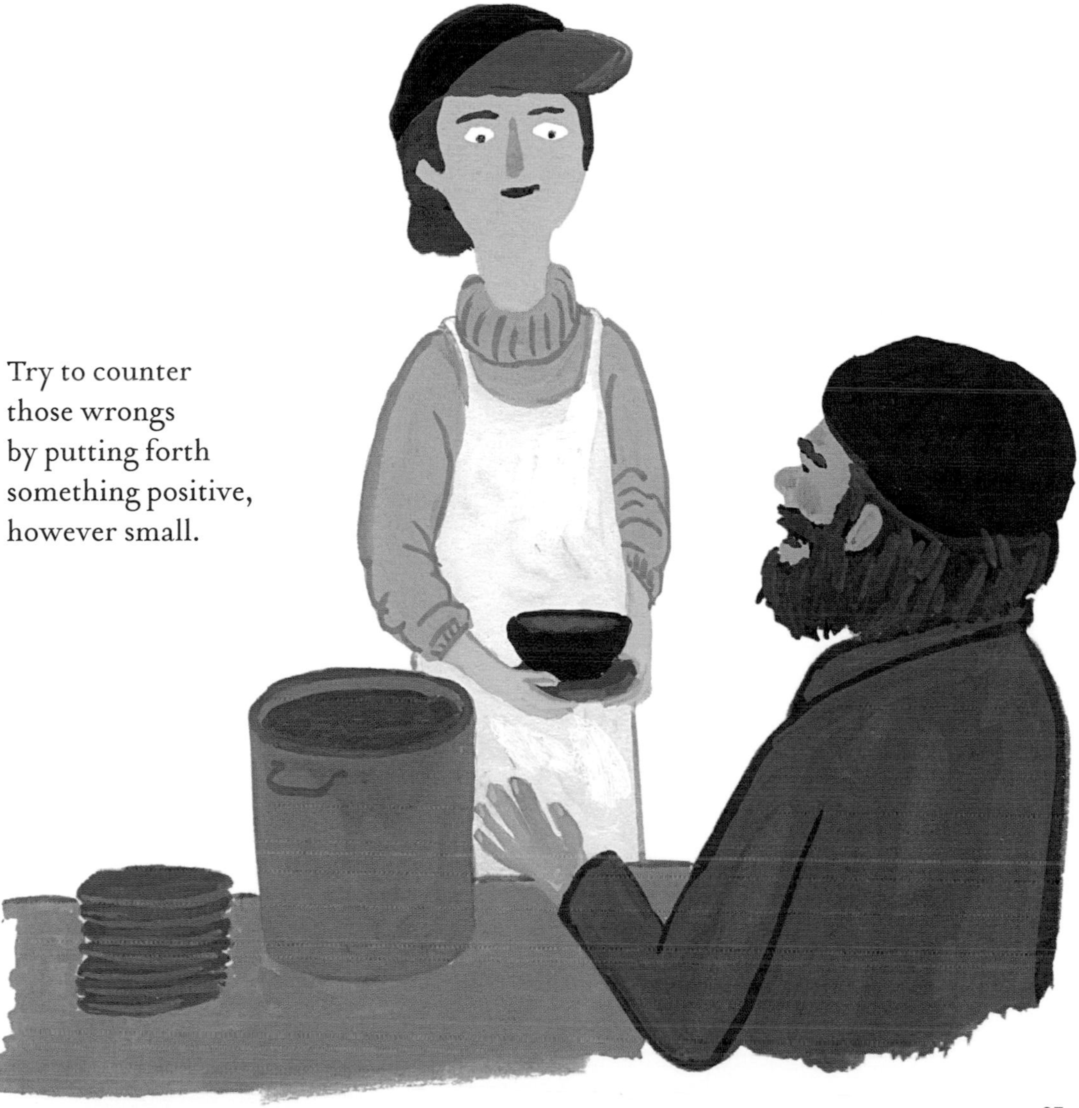

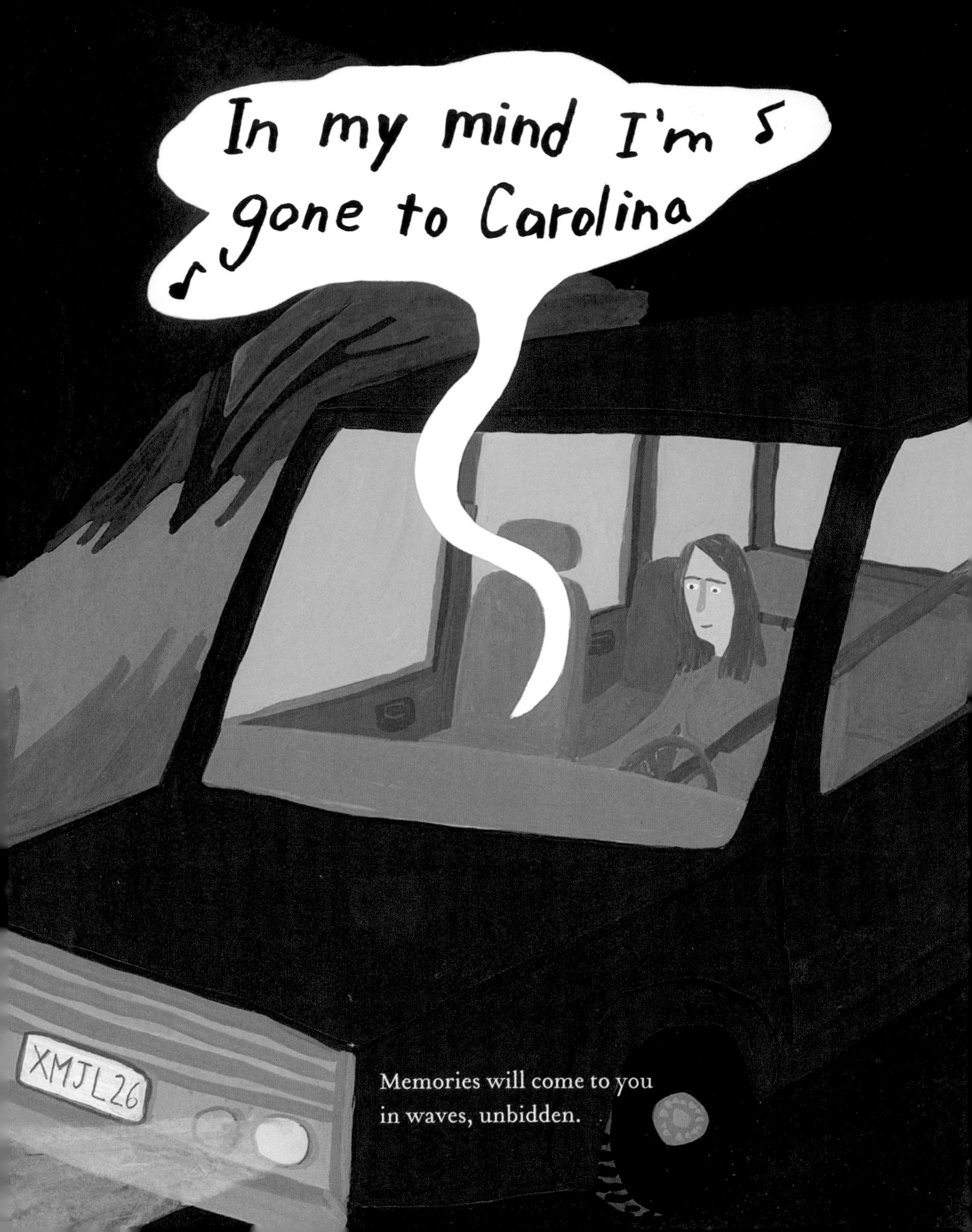
In my mind I'm gone to Carolina
XMJL26

Memories will come to you
in waves, unbidden.

Grief isn't the only byproduct of a death. And death isn't just subtraction. You're left with a treasure of memories that can be triggered by sights, sounds, smells—a record of how my life enriched yours.

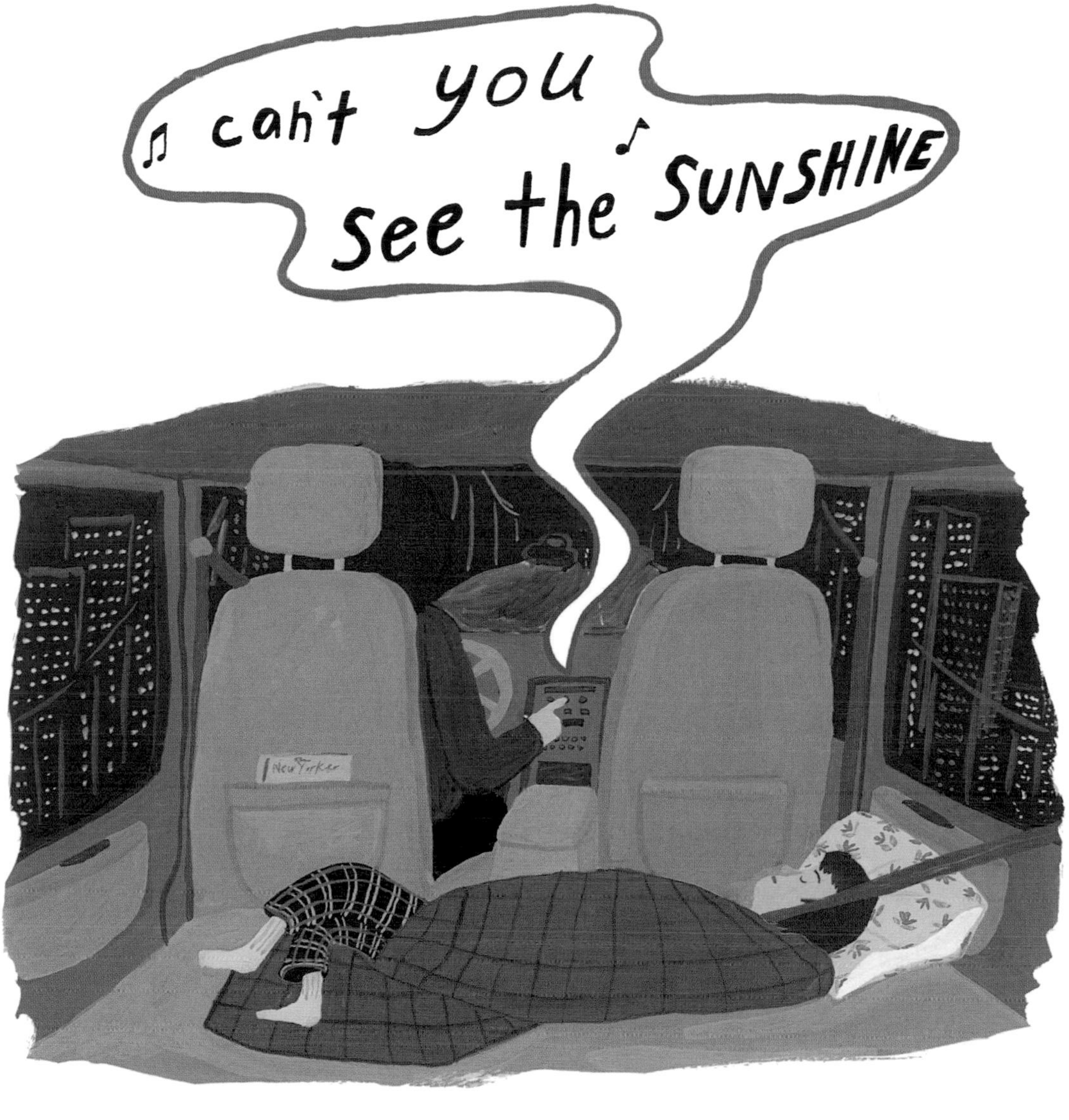
♫ can't you ♪
see the SUNSHINE
New Yorker

DAY 4,500: *Pinch yourself*

You're tempted to bail out of your relationship. The challenges outweigh the joys. You're thinking, "This is too much work. Wouldn't it be nicer if I had a little apartment where I could make popcorn at 2 a.m., drink a glass of wine, and avoid any and all emotional turmoil?"

Pinch yourself. Is that pain you feel, or just proof that you're alive?

Strip away sex and other expectations; at the heart of this is friendship. You signed on for a journey. You can't know how many times the train will stop, the detours, the duration of the trip, or even the destination.

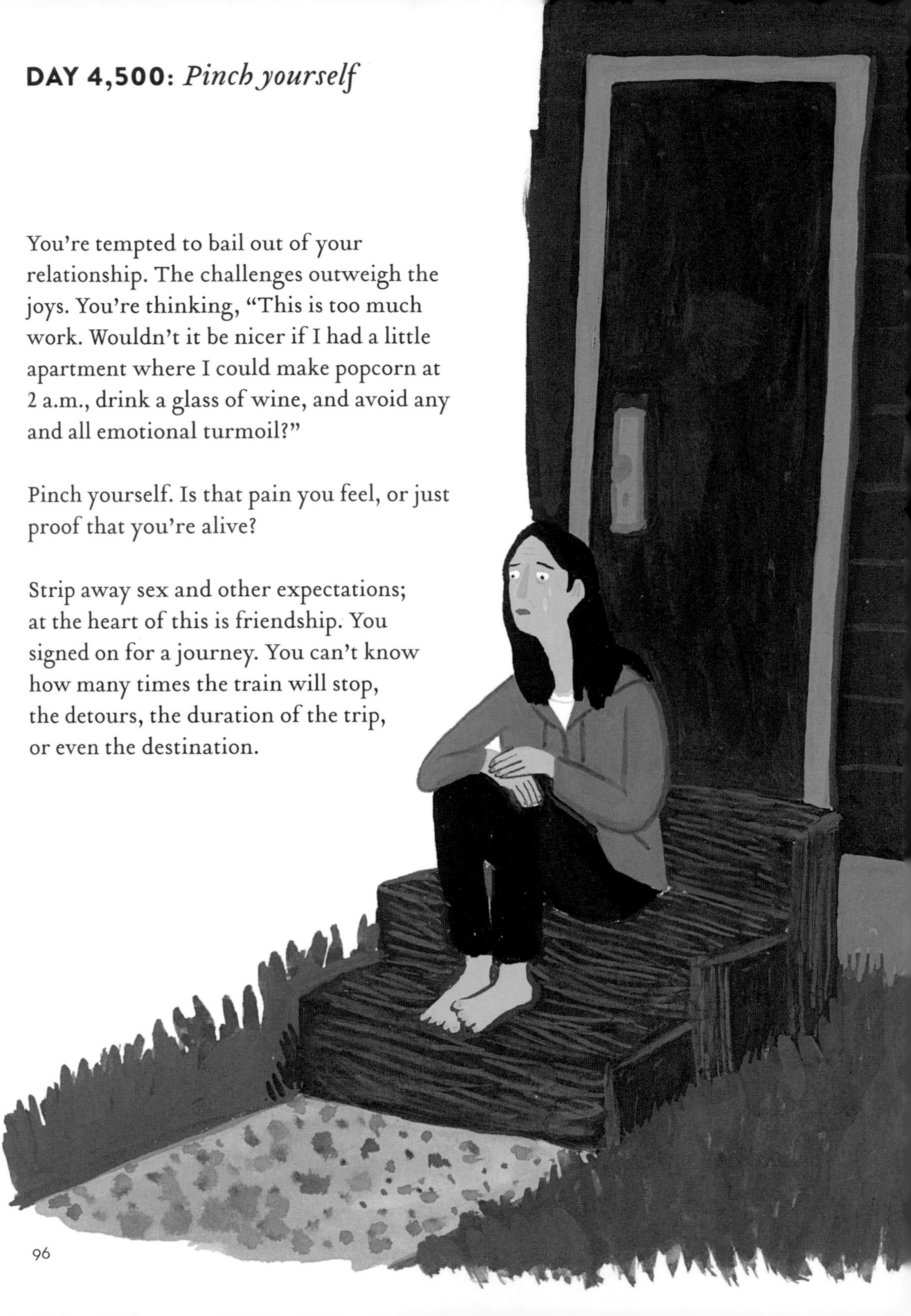

It's absolutely fine to leave when your partner:

- Doesn't respect you
- Can't beat an addiction or won't try
- Cheats on you (not twice; once is enough)
- Raises a hand to you (end of story)
- Is a serial killer (or even a non-serial killer)
- Kicks a puppy

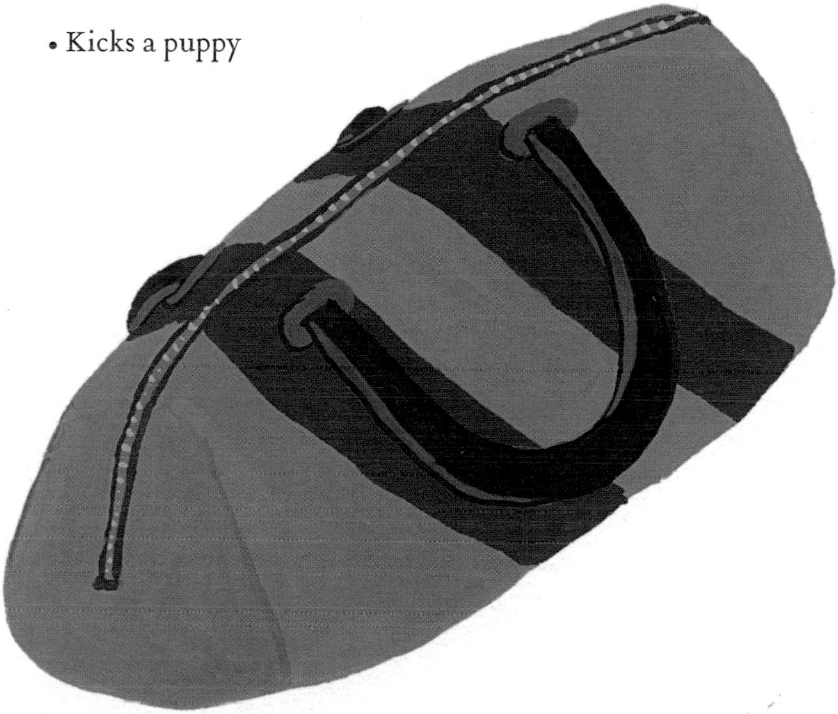

DAY 5,000:
Go to work

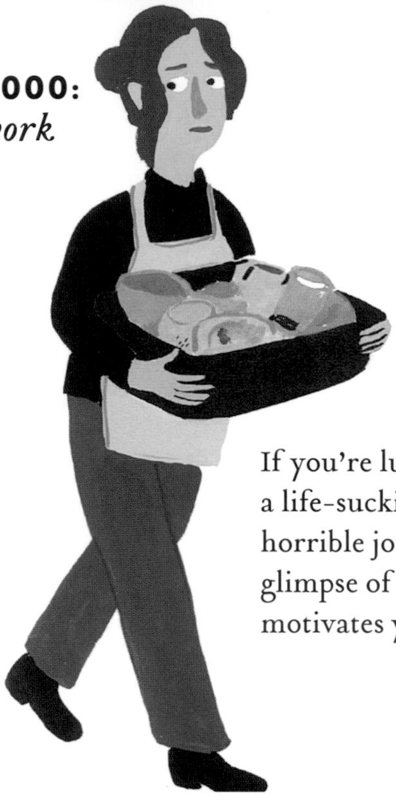

If you're lucky, you will get a life-sucking, stultifyingly horrible job early on. Having a glimpse of something dreadful motivates you to aim higher.

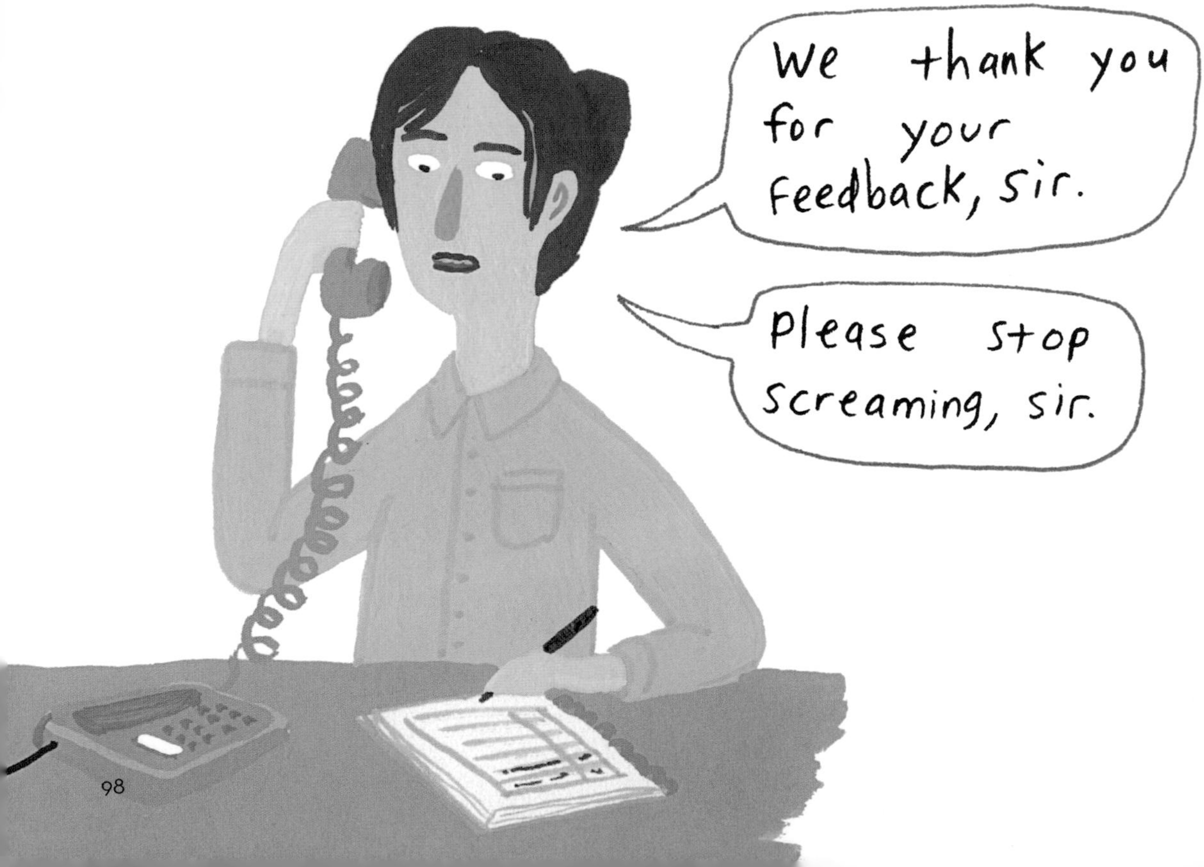
We thank you for your feedback, sir.
Please stop screaming, sir.

People sometimes think of work
as something that they have to do
so that their spare time can be
devoted to their real life.

But work isn't just a way to earn a paycheck. It's integral to your quality of life.
Seek out work you're excited about. Find a way to pursue your interests
and be well-compensated for it. It's no fun to be poor. Earn a bunch of money
and spread it around.

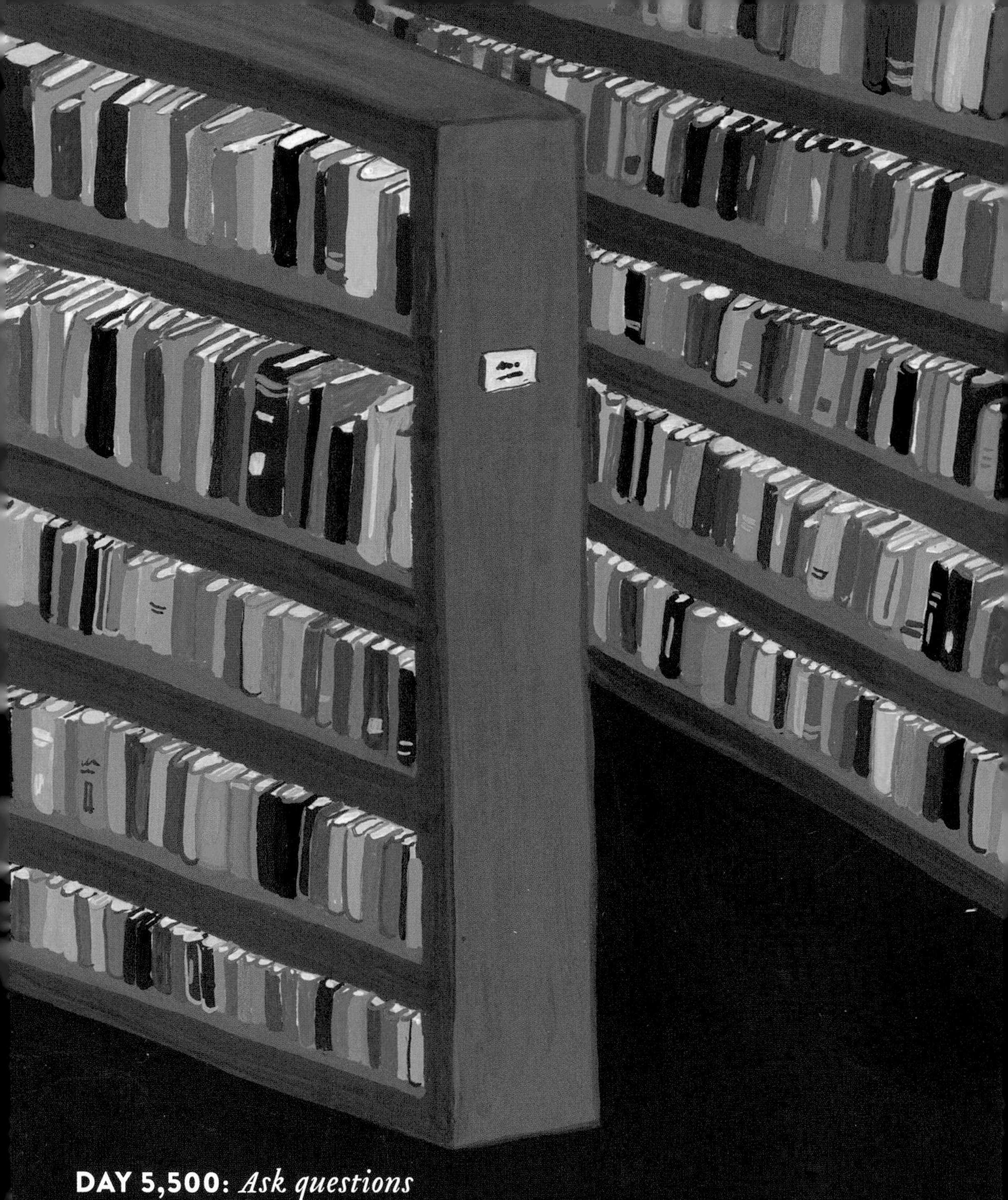

DAY 5,500: *Ask questions*

We're put here to look for answers. It's not that you're going to find them—it's that you're striving to find them.

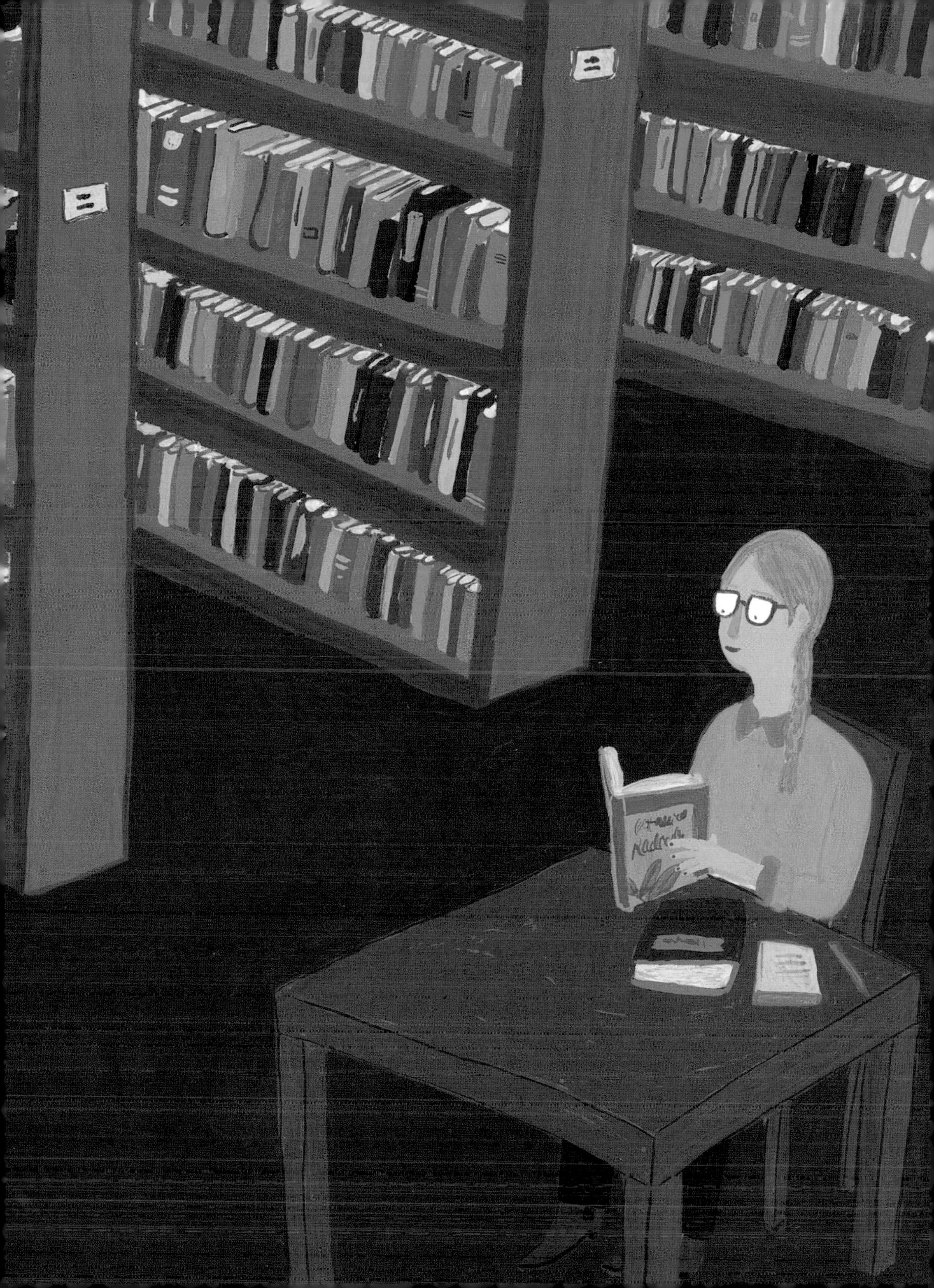

DAY 6,000: *Make a quiche*

In the face of calamity, quiche can restore order.

Onions, butter, garlic
Carrots, spinach, broccoli, zucchini, yam
Evaporated milk
Eggs, shredded cheese
Nutmeg, cinnamon, salt, pepper, cayenne
Unbaked pie crusts

Slice onions into thin pieces, sauté in butter or oil with diced garlic over low heat for 5 or 10 minutes.

While those are cooking, cut up the vegetables: shred a couple of carrots, dice a big pile of spinach, cut a head of broccoli into small pieces, shred a zucchini, and dice a semi-cooked yam.

Throw this all into a big bowl.

In a separate bowl, whisk a can of evaporated milk together with four or five eggs, then add a cup or more of shredded cheese. These measurements are approximate—keep in mind that life is a loose mix of odd circumstances that together can sometimes yield great results. Have faith that this will turn out well.

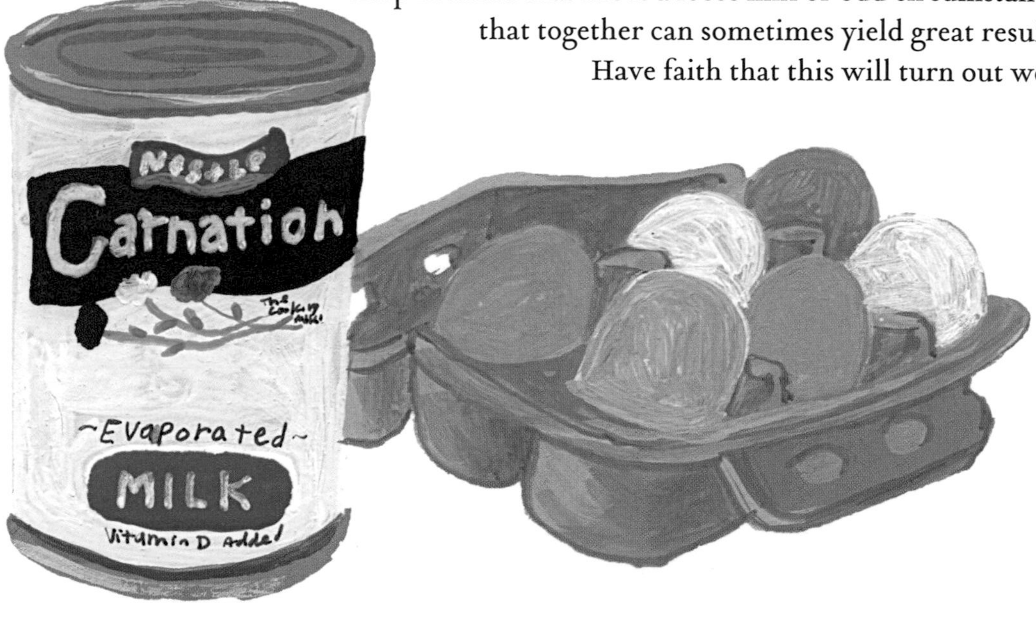
Carnation
~Evaporated~
MILK
Vitamin D Added

Add some seasonings to the milk-egg mix:
a bit of nutmeg, cinnamon, salt and pepper,
and cayenne are my favorites.

Dump this into the veggie bowl and stir together, then spoon
into unbaked pie crusts. This makes three or four quiches. Salt
and pepper the top, then cook at 350 degrees for about an hour—
until the middle has set and a toothpick stuck in the center
comes out clean.

You're using oven mitts, right? That pan is hot. Don't burn
yourself. If you do burn yourself, put your hand under cold
running water until the pain subsides.

Are you getting enough to eat?
Have some quiche.

DAY 7,000: *Prioritize*

You feel overloaded with work, life, whatever. Time for triage. Write down everything on your "plate," all the things you are responsible for or feel burdened by; include caring for yourself.

Imagine these are emergency-room patients waiting to be seen. Who should get help first, second, and third? And who shouldn't even be on the list, because their needs are far less urgent?

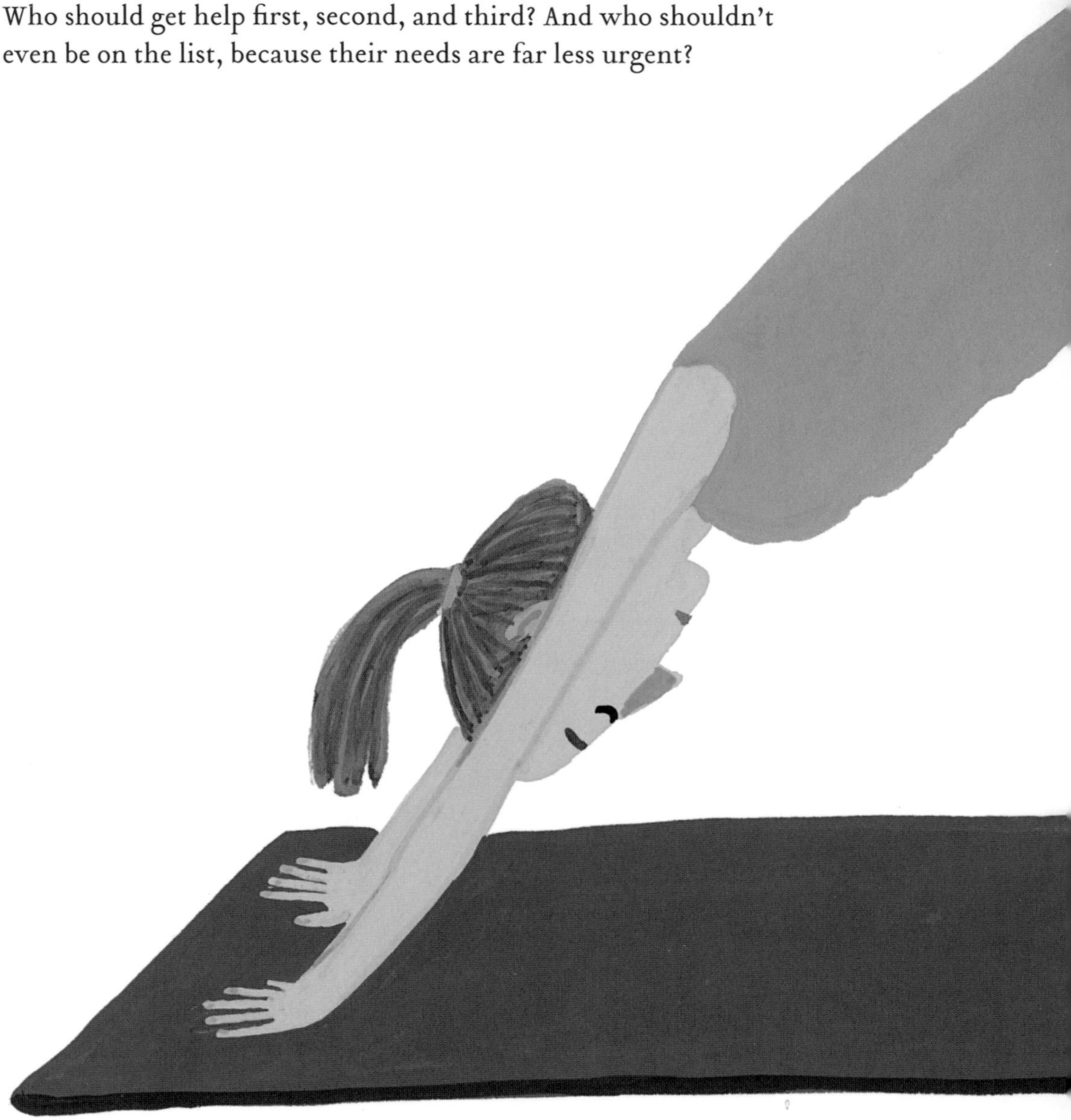

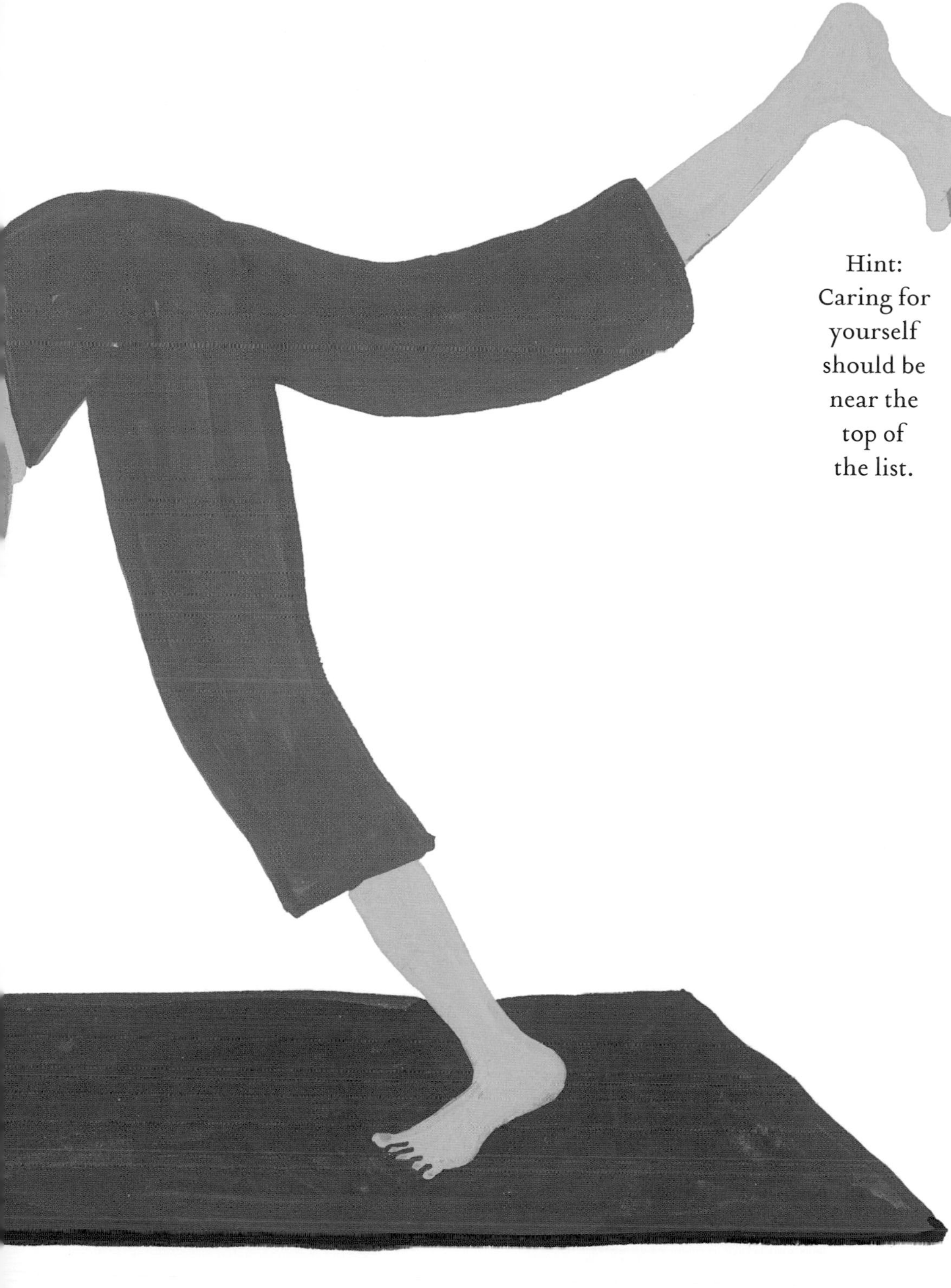

Hint:
Caring for
yourself
should be
near the
top of
the list.

DAY 8,000: *Redefine happiness*

I used to think happiness was something I would get to at some point, that one day everything would fall into place and stay there.

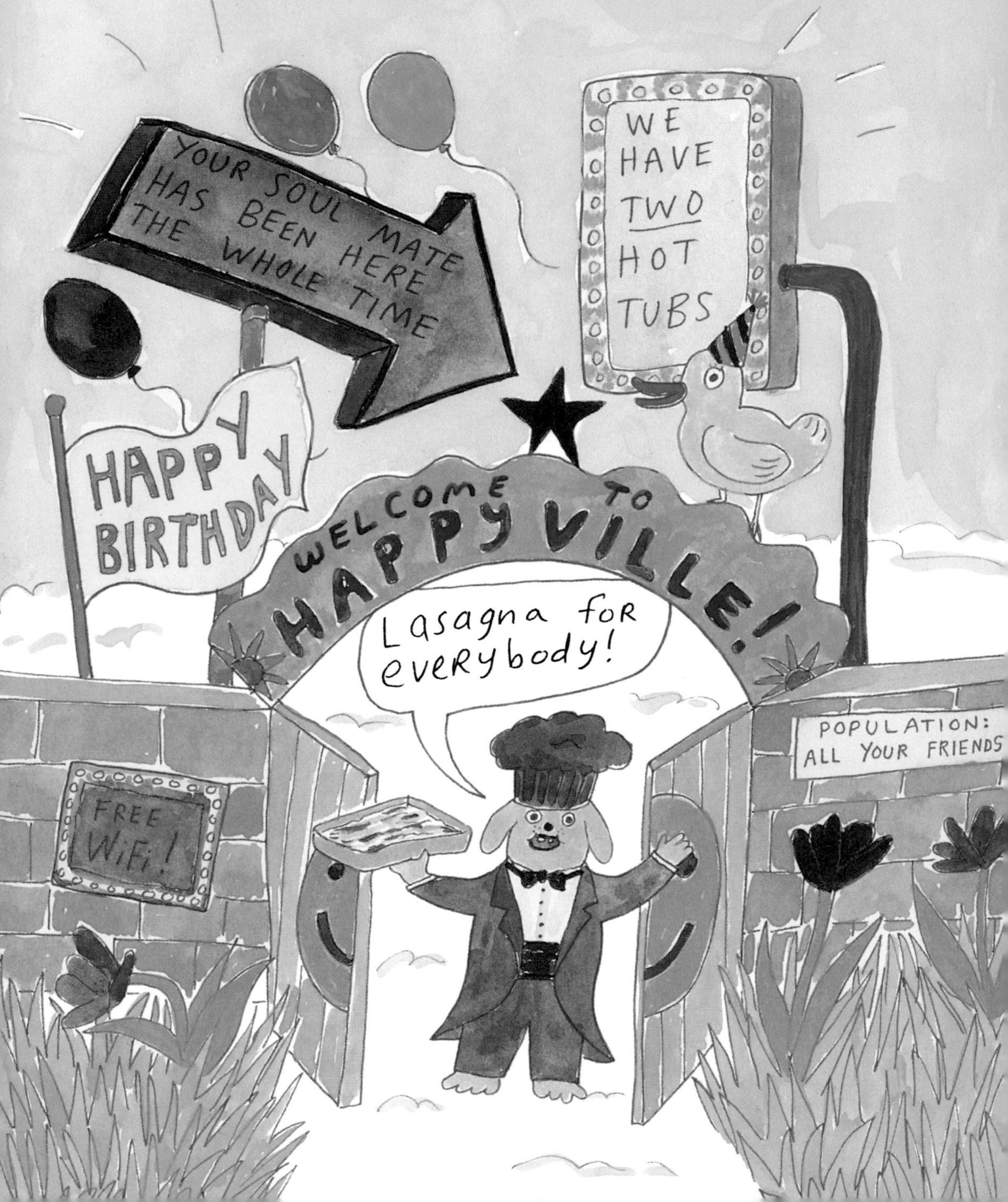
YOUR SOUL MATE HAS BEEN HERE THE WHOLE TIME
WE HAVE TWO HOT TUBS
HAPPY BIRTHDAY
WELCOME TO HAPPY VILLE!
Lasagna for everybody!
POPULATION: ALL YOUR FRIENDS
FREE WiFi!

It's not as if when you drop twenty pounds the world will be right
and will remain right as long as the twenty pounds stay off.
You can be fat and happy or thin and happy, and if you're lucky
you'll have many happy moments and days. Just don't expect
to have nonstop happy decades.

I see happiness
as contentment with what
you're doing right now.
That may be nothing at all, or
something ambitious,
or something in between.
It's a sense of not wanting
to be anywhere else.

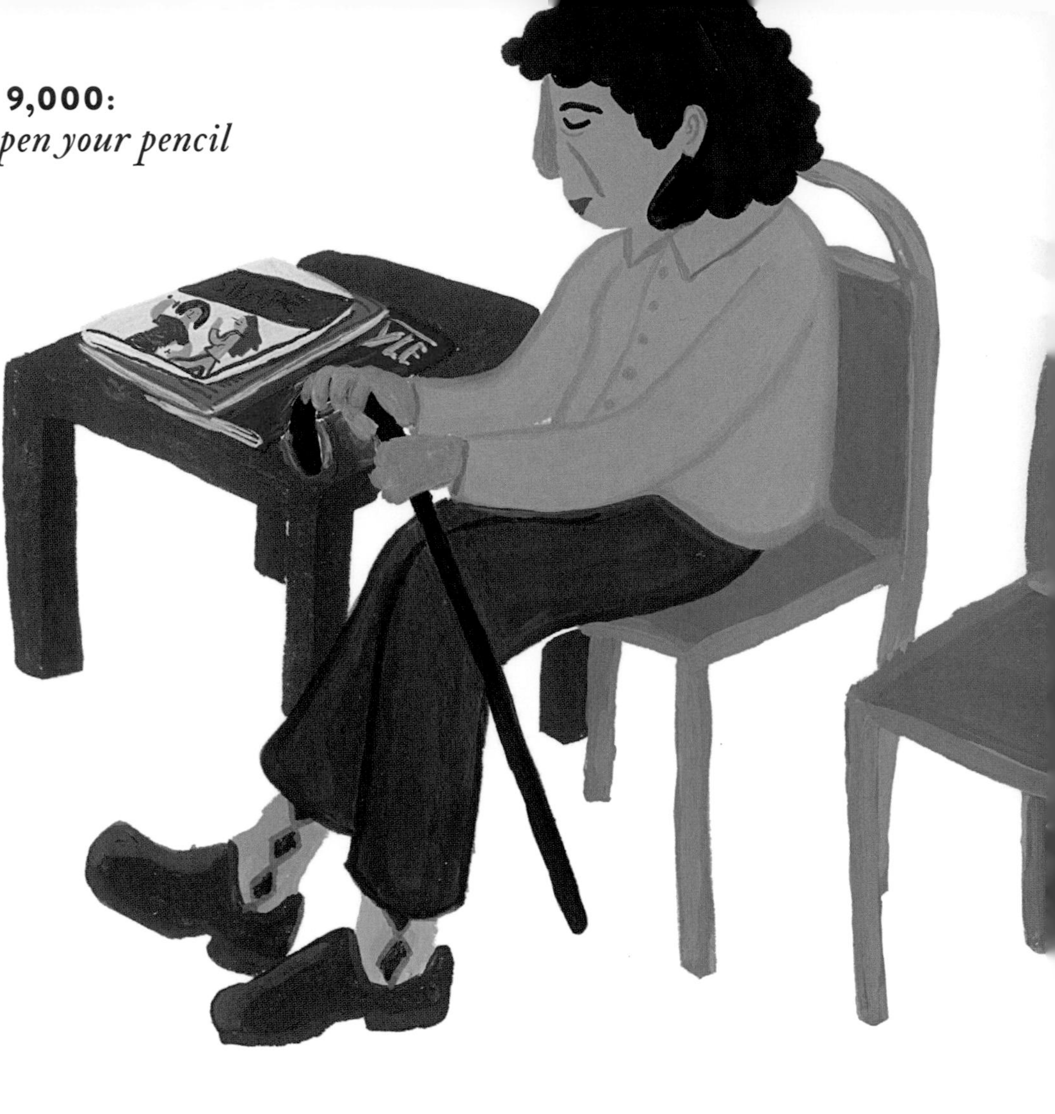

DAY 9,000:
Sharpen your pencil

You'll find yourself in times of transition, waiting for news: for an update, a prognosis, a signal of hope. Drink a cup of coffee and work on a crossword puzzle. The coffee will help you stay awake, and the crossword will keep your brain occupied. Do the Sunday *New York Times* puzzle only if you will be waiting for more than twenty-four hours and are unfazed by failure.

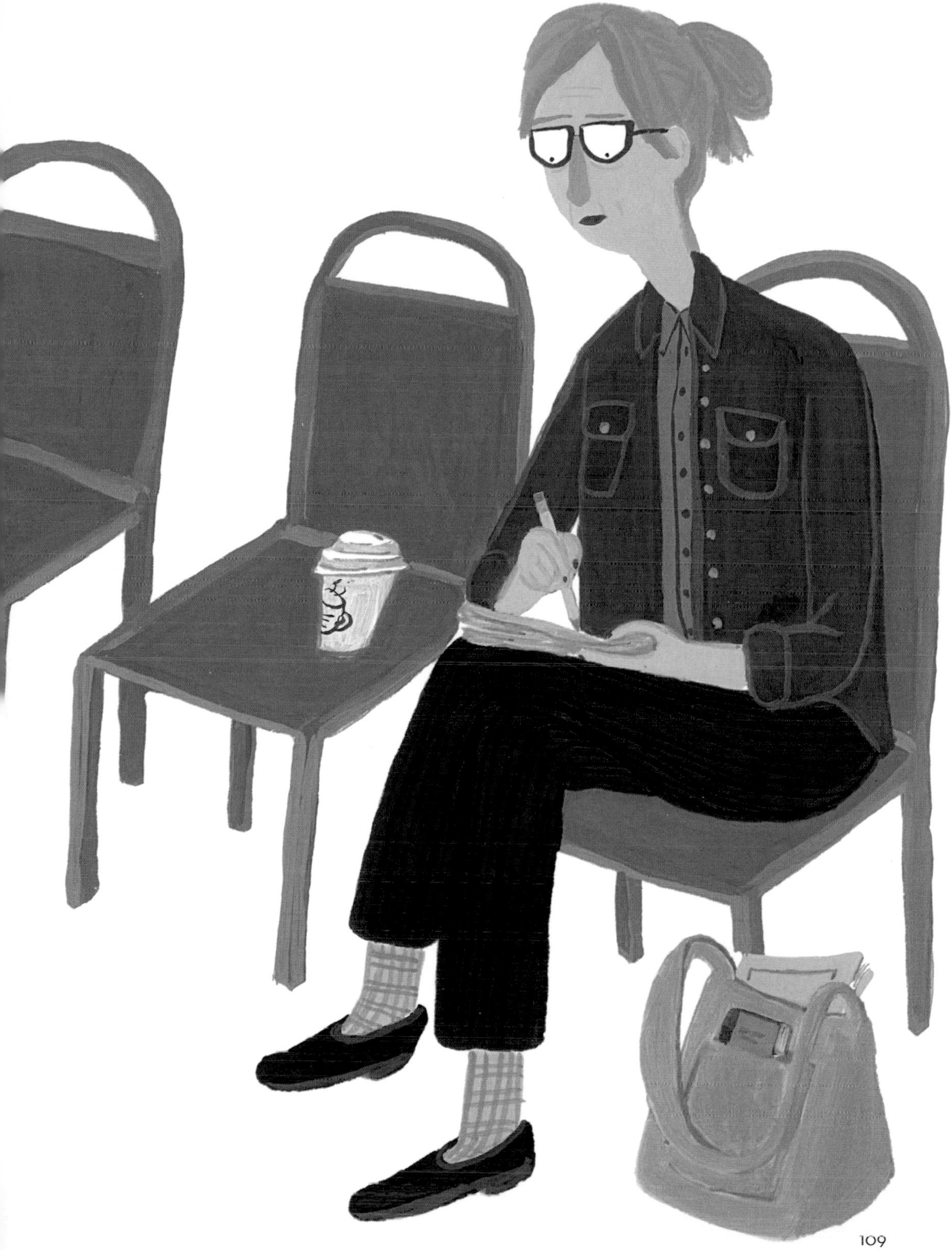

DAY 10,000: *Take a field trip*

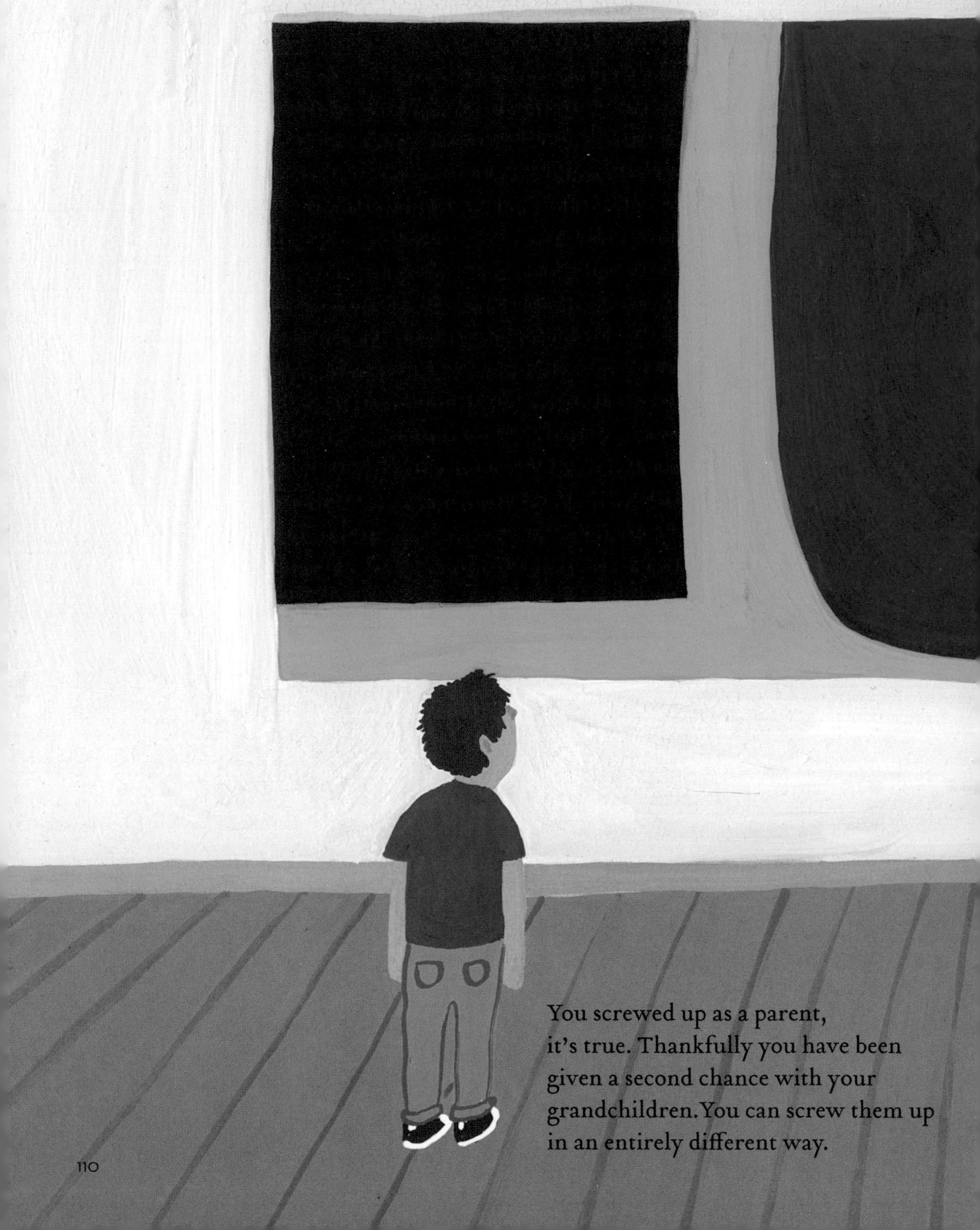

You screwed up as a parent, it's true. Thankfully you have been given a second chance with your grandchildren. You can screw them up in an entirely different way.

Or not.
Keep in mind that
they will be paying
close attention when
you least expect it.
Take time to play and
to see the world
through their eyes.

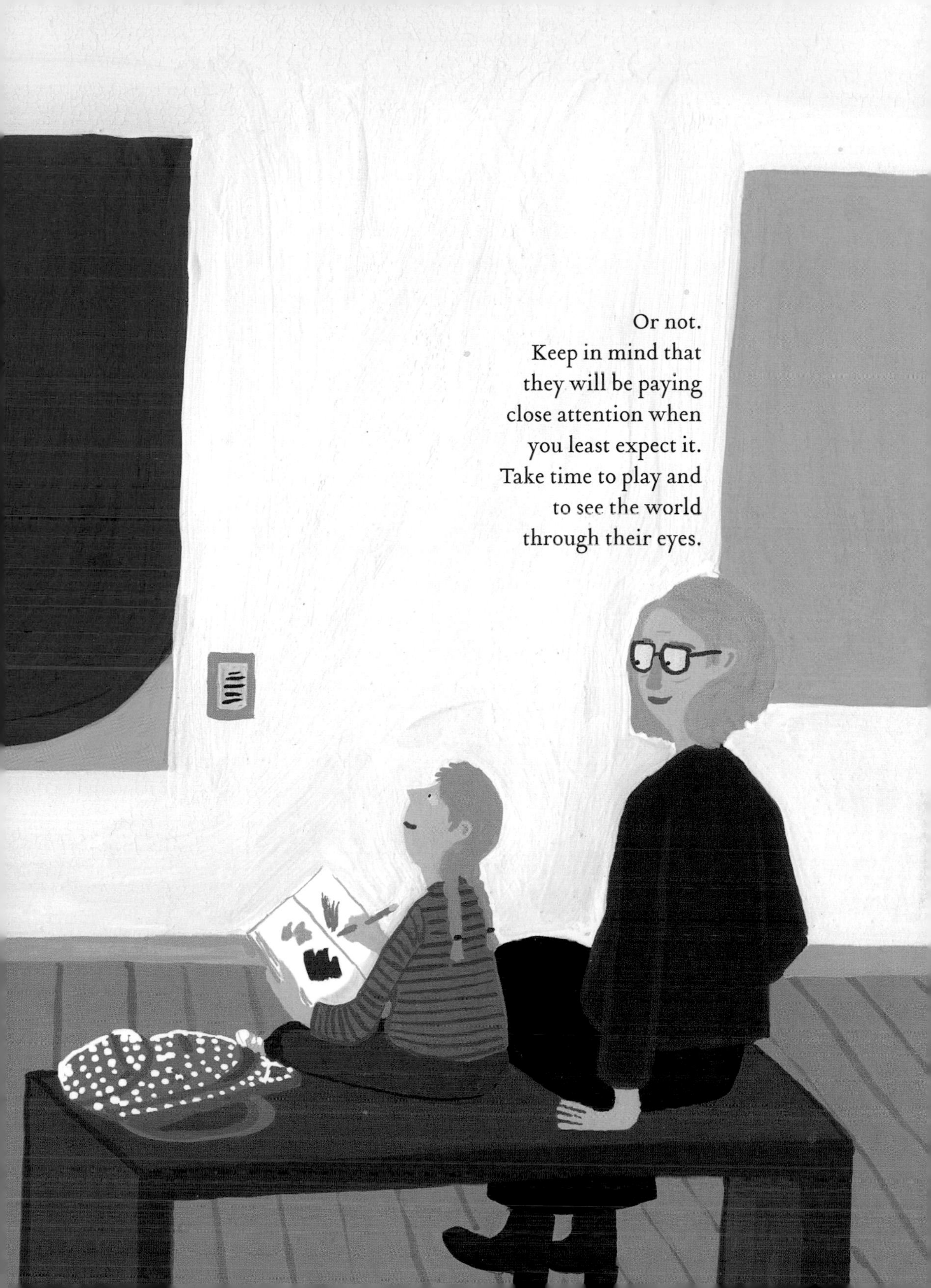

DAY 11,000: *Climb out of a rut*

Try to keep moving forward toward something—in both your work and personal life. Not backward to something you've done before, or standing still. Imagine that you aren't afraid of anyone or anything. Where would you go? What would you do?

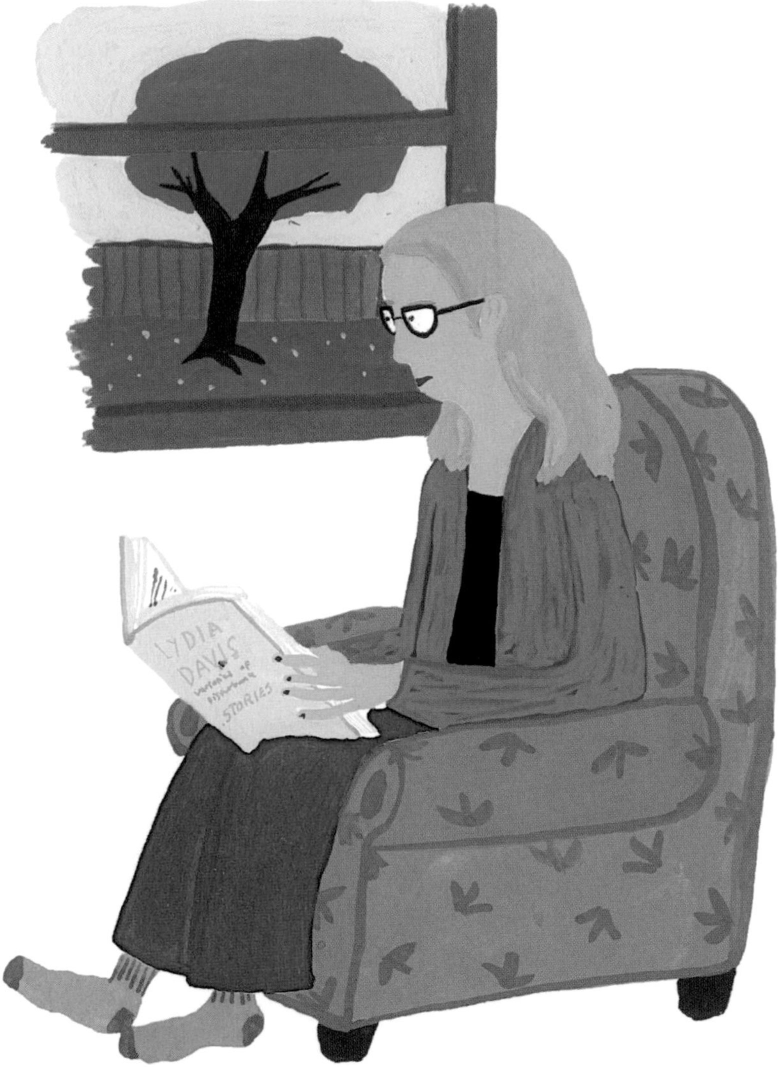
LYDIA
DAVIS
STORIES

Then get started.

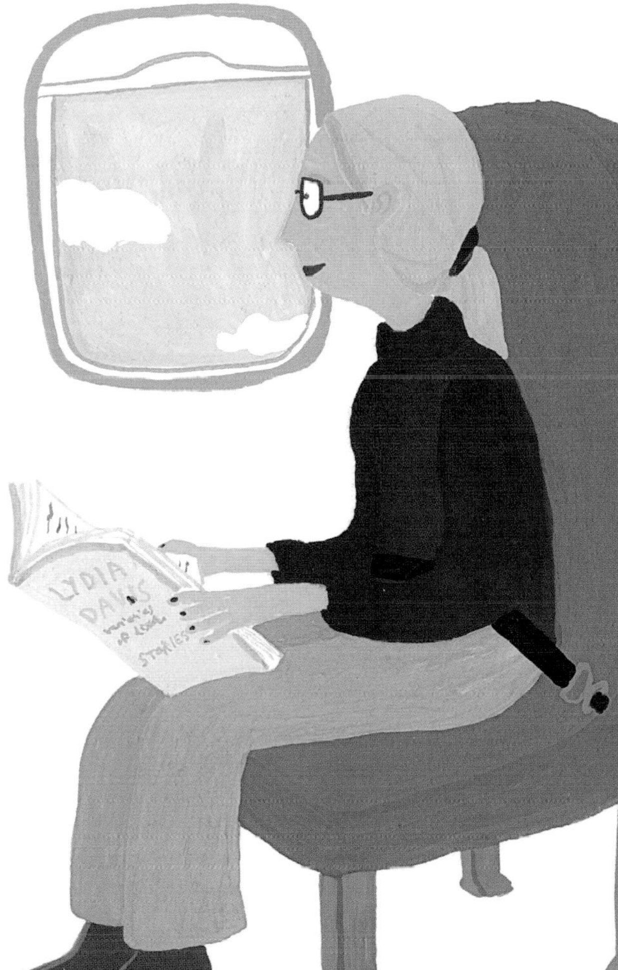
LYDIA DAVIS
STORIES

DAY 12,000:
Watch a funny movie

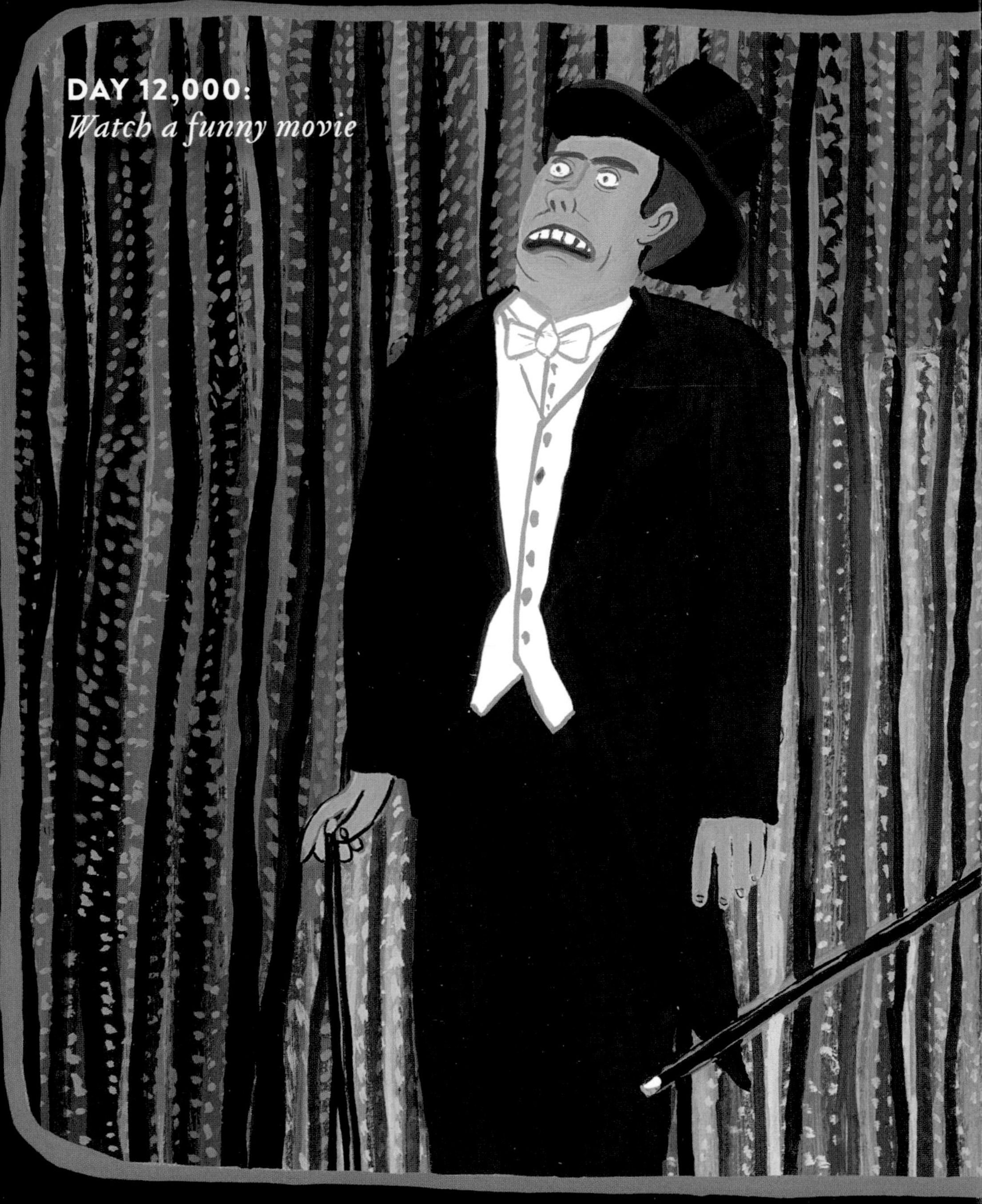

Because we are hardwired for survival, our brains are always looking for threats—and there are plenty to be found. You may have to rush a sick baby to the hospital. You might get an EKG that shows your heart misfiring, or hear the word "cancer" from someone in a white coat.

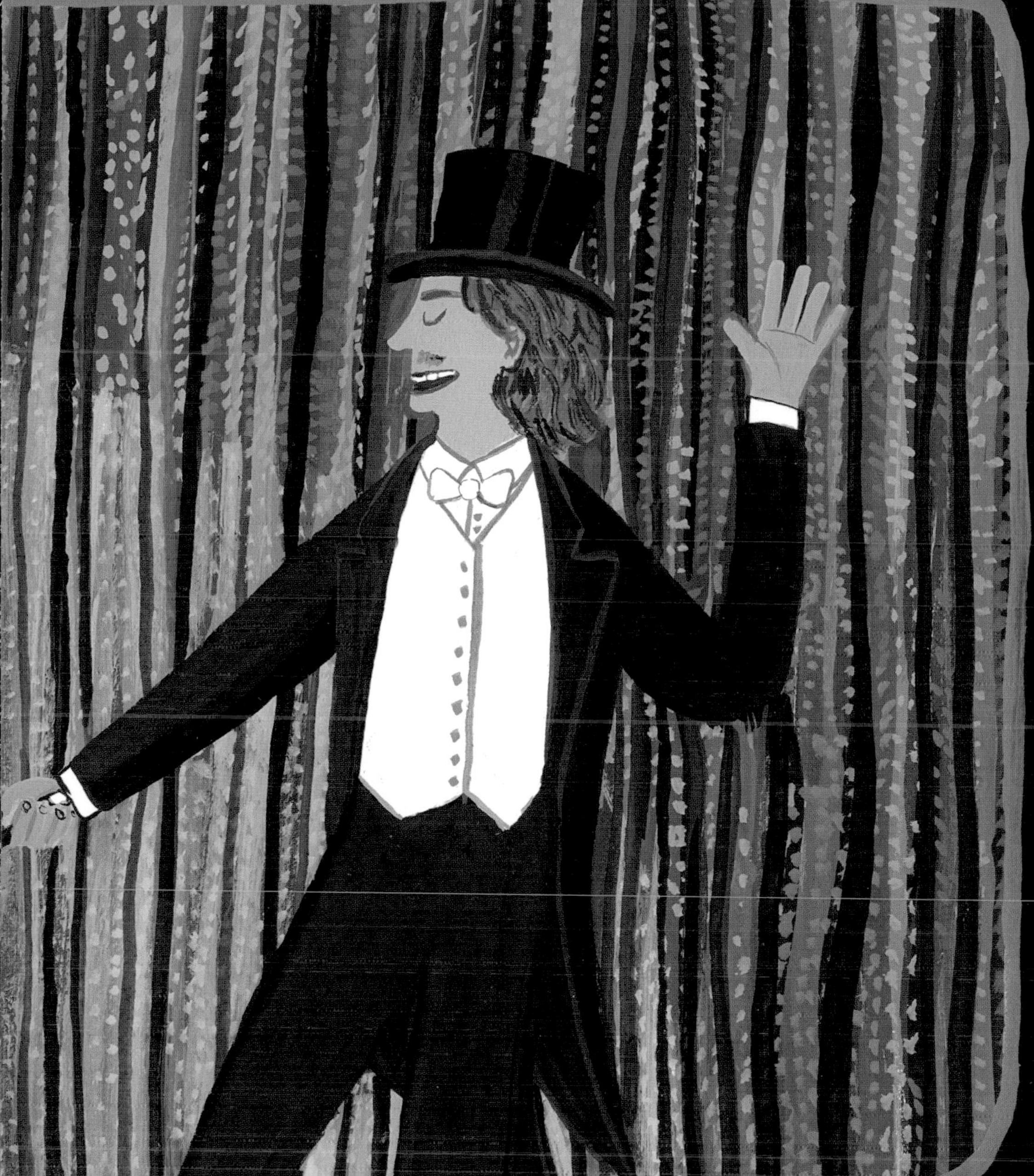

Fear is useful when it causes you to avoid an oncoming train or motivates you to make positive changes. Otherwise it's a life suck. When you're terrified, ask yourself: Is this helping? If not, laugh in fear's face.

DAY 13,000: *Step lively*

When you start saying and thinking that the world has gone to hell in a handbasket, you are officially old, whether you are thirty-four or ninety-five. Every generation probably thinks this, decrying the sad state of affairs, the dreadful mess politicians have made, the younger generation's sins, and so much more.

You are not the first to be in this position,
and you do not know everything,
and you are probably not in charge.
Absent a nuclear war or global pandemic,
you are in a more privileged position
than any generation in history.

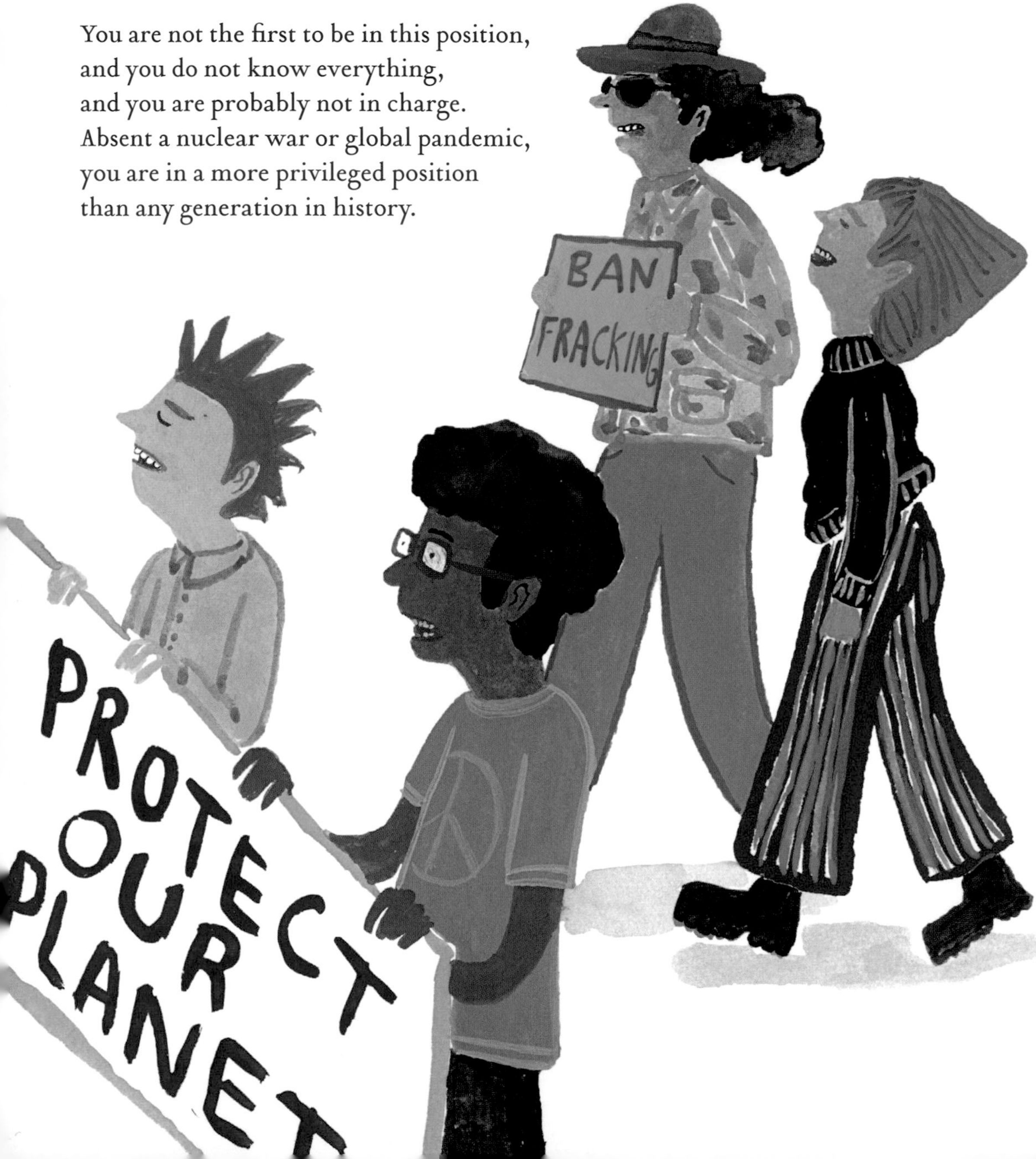
BAN FRACKING
PROTECT OUR PLANET

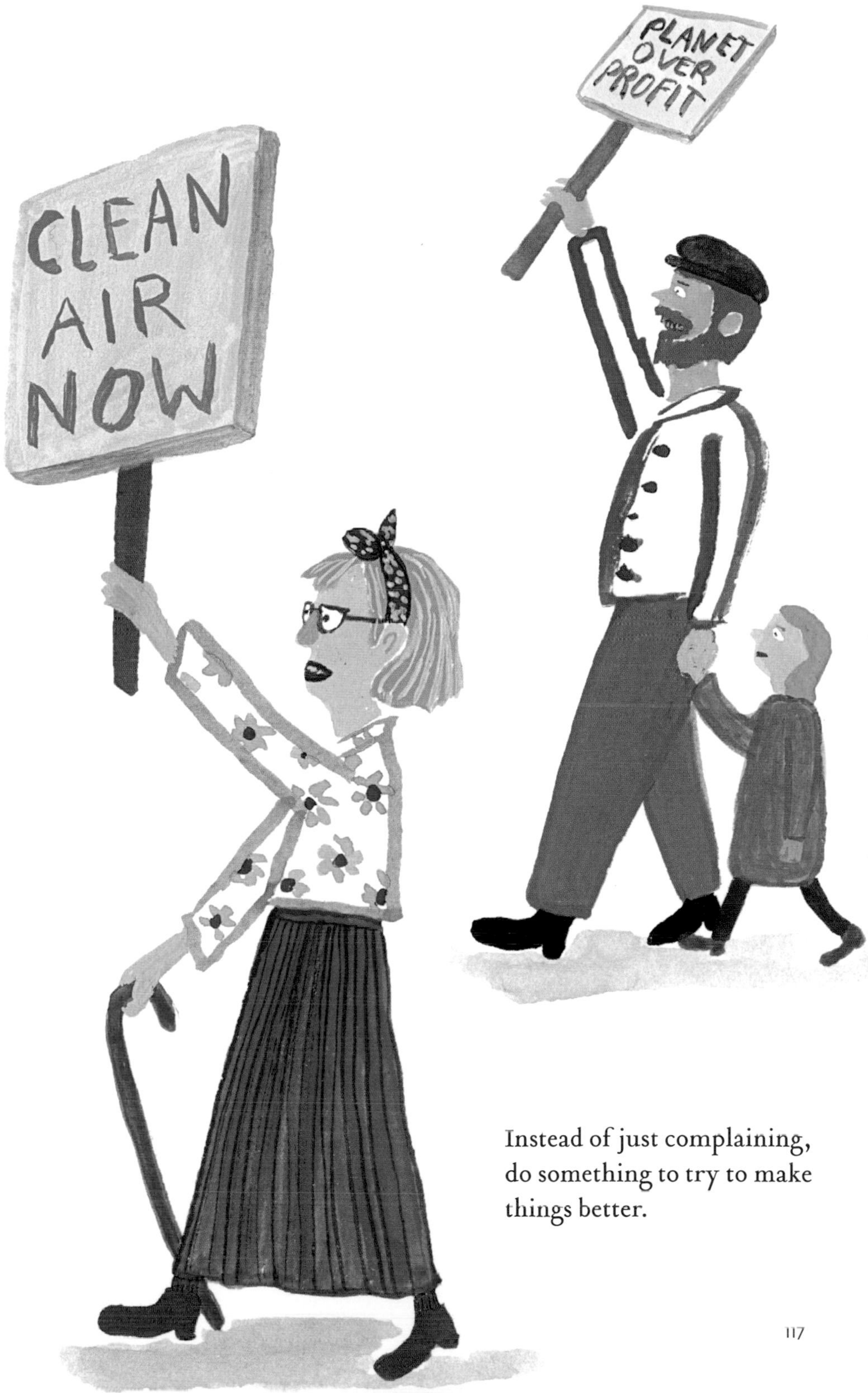
CLEAN
AIR
NOW
PLANET
OVER
PROFIT

Instead of just complaining, do something to try to make things better.

DAY 14,000: *Make a duck-it list*

People who have bucket lists are often the type of people who want to tell you all about themselves all the time. I don't want to hear it, any more than I want to hear about their trip to Peru.

Even if you did accomplish everything on the list, you set yourself up for failure. Let's say you finish the list but you're still not dead. Is it time to die? What do you do with all that time? Make another bucket list?

What about people who can't afford to have a good bucket list? Do they just make do with a mediocre one? "I'd like to go to Beaverton someday."

MADE IT!

NOW I JUST WAIT TO DIE!

Sitting and reading a good book, drinking tea, taking a walk with you. For me, those were life's best moments. Better even than seeing the Taj Mahal or sailing the fjords or skiing in Switzerland. Sitting around just talking about . . . stuff. That's what I really miss.

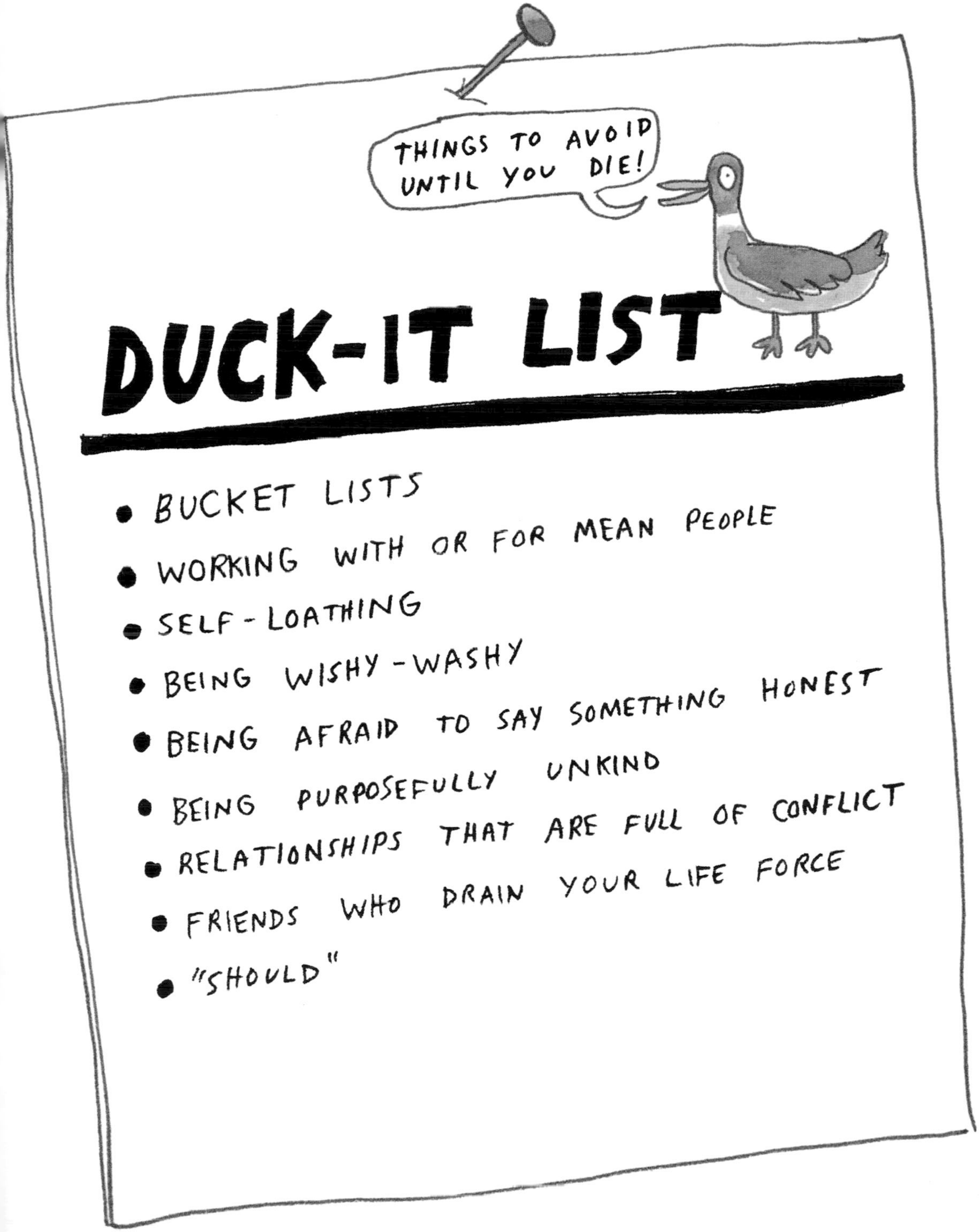
THINGS TO AVOID UNTIL YOU DIE!
DUCK-IT LIST
• BUCKET LISTS
• WORKING WITH OR FOR MEAN PEOPLE
• SELF-LOATHING
• BEING WISHY-WASHY
• BEING AFRAID TO SAY SOMETHING HONEST
• BEING PURPOSEFULLY UNKIND
• RELATIONSHIPS THAT ARE FULL OF CONFLICT
• FRIENDS WHO DRAIN YOUR LIFE FORCE
• "SHOULD"

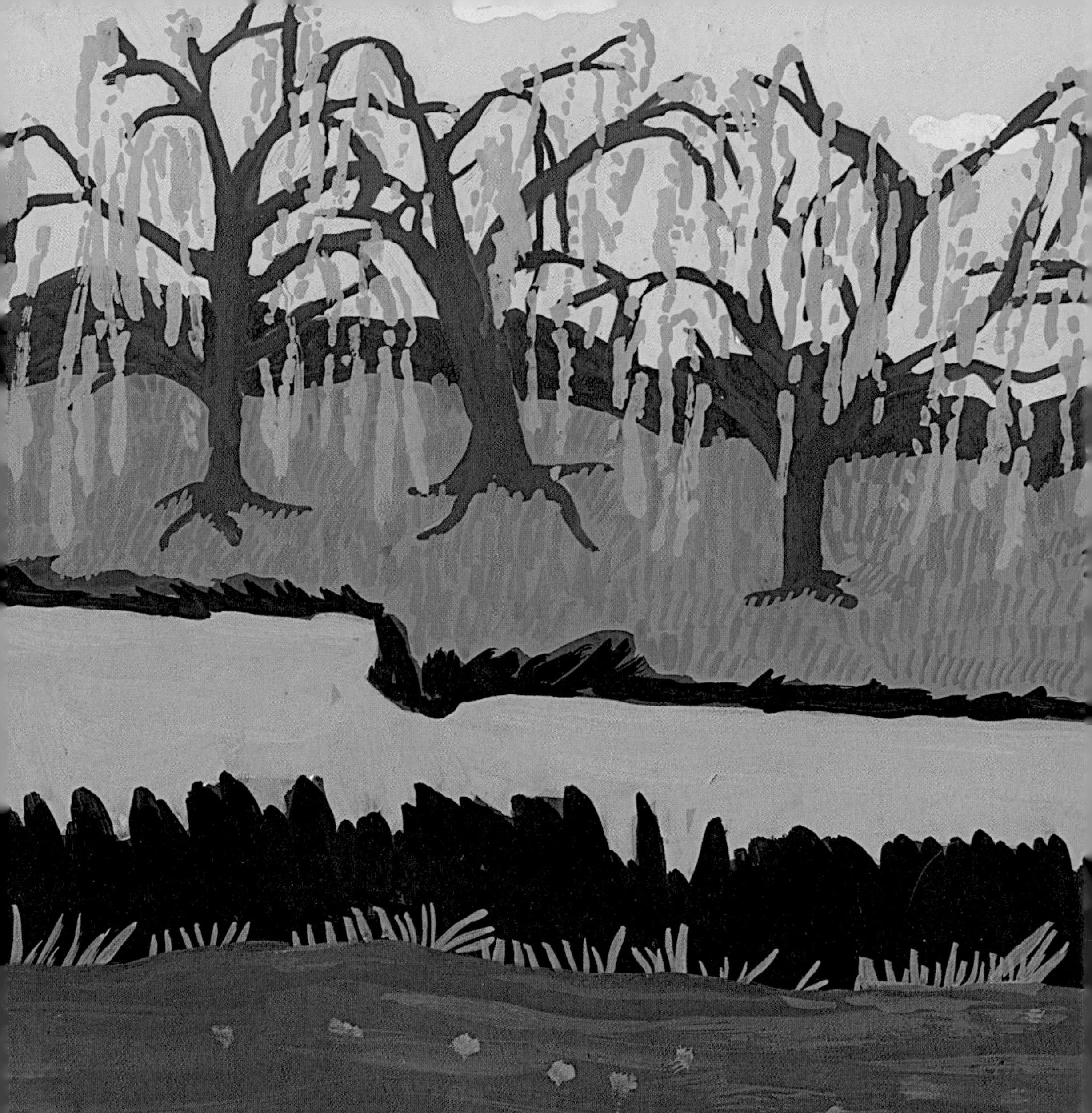

DAY 15,000: *Drop a crutch*

There will come a time when you understand that you don't need alcohol (despite earlier recipes) or drugs (despite childbirth advice). Don't worry, something will come along to replace it—endorphin rushes, whatever. Trust me, there will be other crutches.

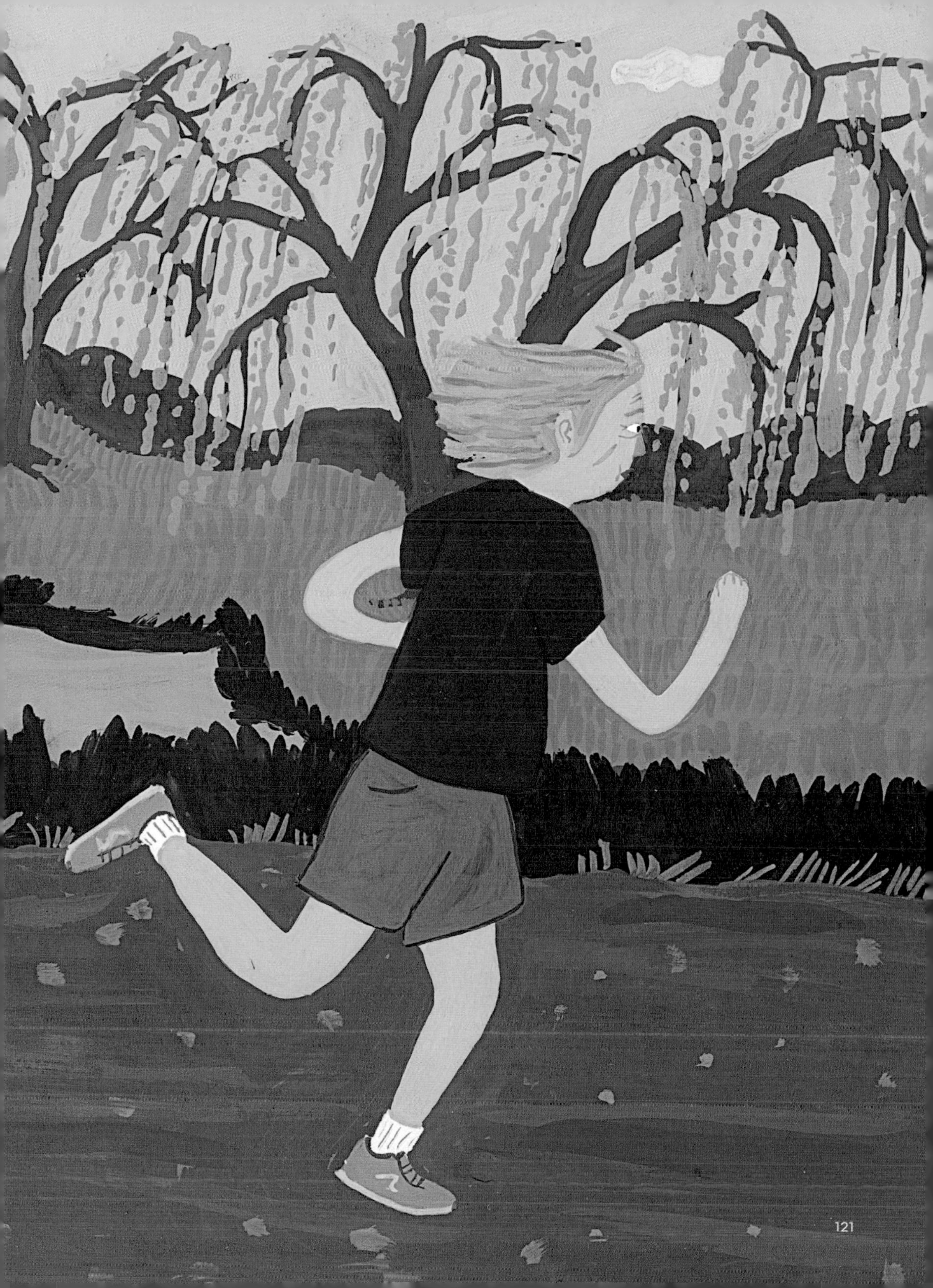

DAY 17,000: *Get a cane*

If you're lucky enough to get old, it's probably going to hurt.

You'll fall and break something. Doctors will have to cut things out of you, then they'll put fake stuff back in. At some point you may have trouble walking. And sitting. And eating. And hearing. And sleeping. You get the idea.

If legislation were passed that required everyone in their twenties to be confined to a wheelchair for six months, they might gain lifelong empathy for the elderly and disabled. But like you, most people have had to learn patience and acceptance in other ways over the course of their lifetimes.

Trust me, you have the tools you will need to cope with these new challenges.

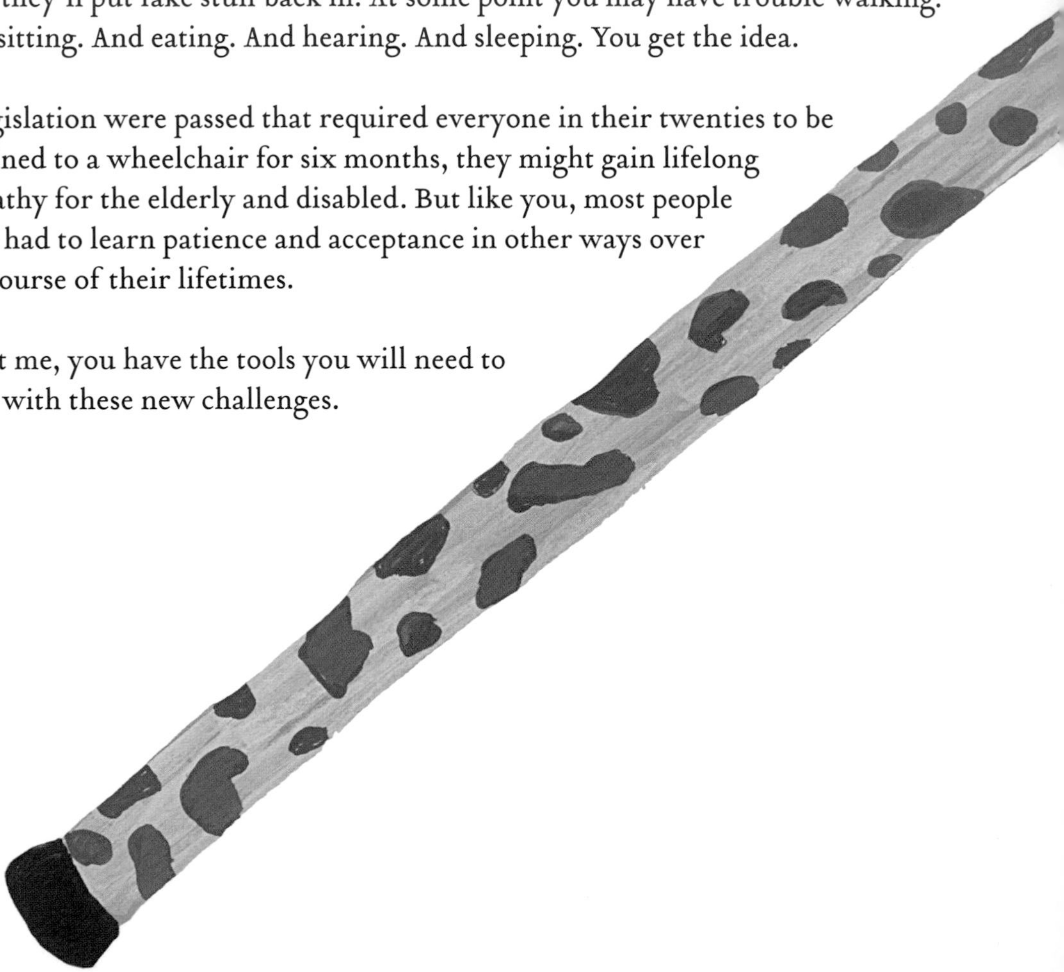

Except for the cane,
which you need to buy.
Make it a flashy one.

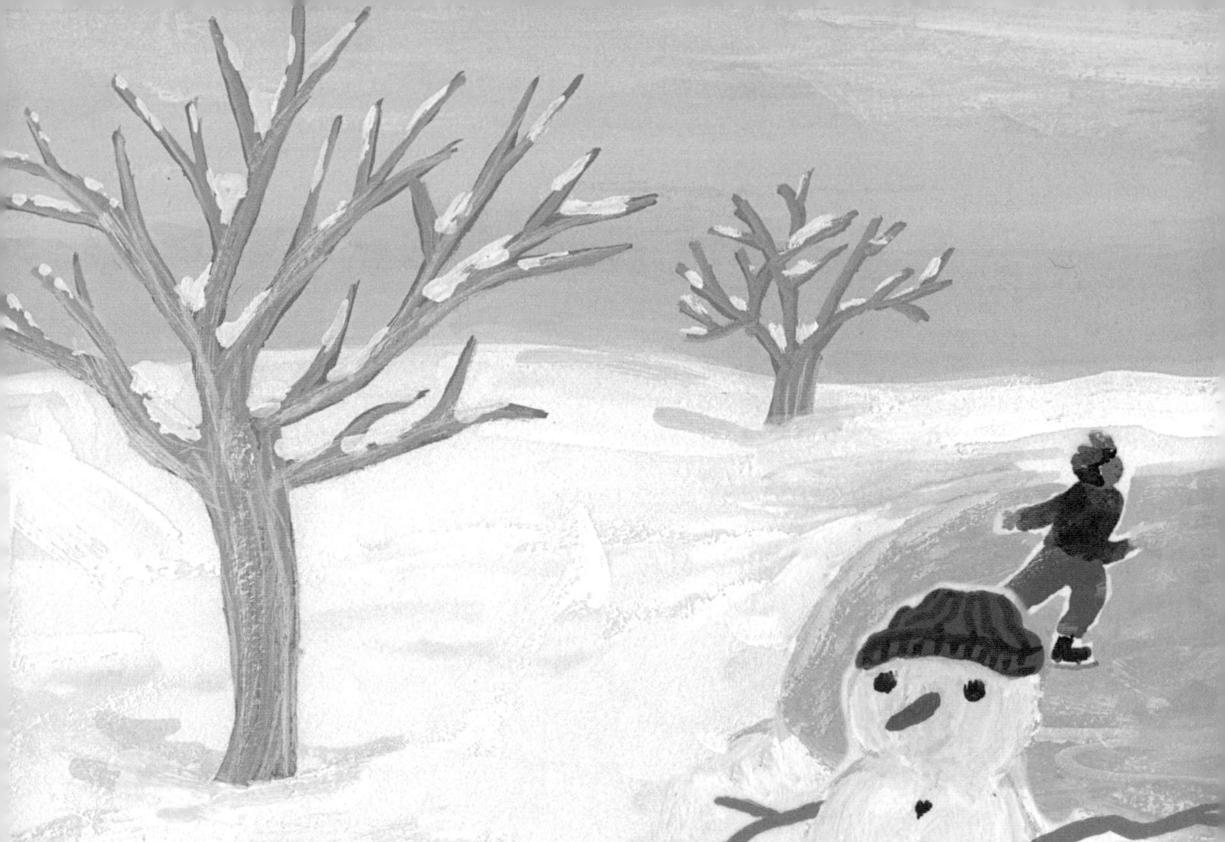

DAY 18,000: *Show compassion*

When part of your body falls apart—heart, bones, brain, whatever—you will suddenly realize you are not invincible. Until now, you probably thought you were exempt. These things are supposed to happen to other people, not you. Time to show yourself some serious compassion. Be kind to yourself. No matter your age, you deserve clean clothes and a hot meal and good company.

Don't go it alone: Accept help and friendship when it's offered. And if it isn't offered, ask for it. Allow extra time and be patient with yourself. Ask other people to be patient, too. They may need to be reminded.

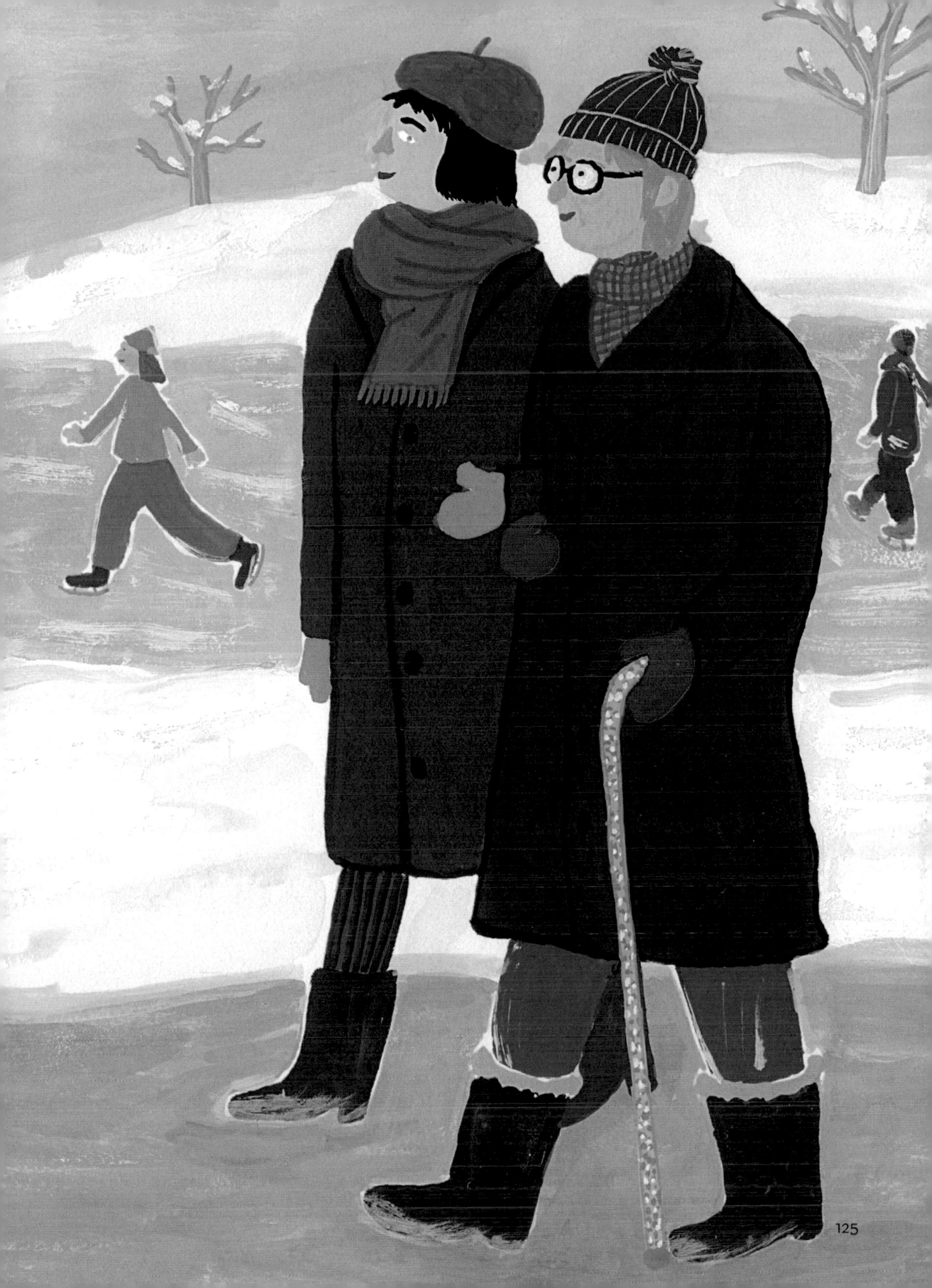

DAY 20,000: *Plan your dream death*

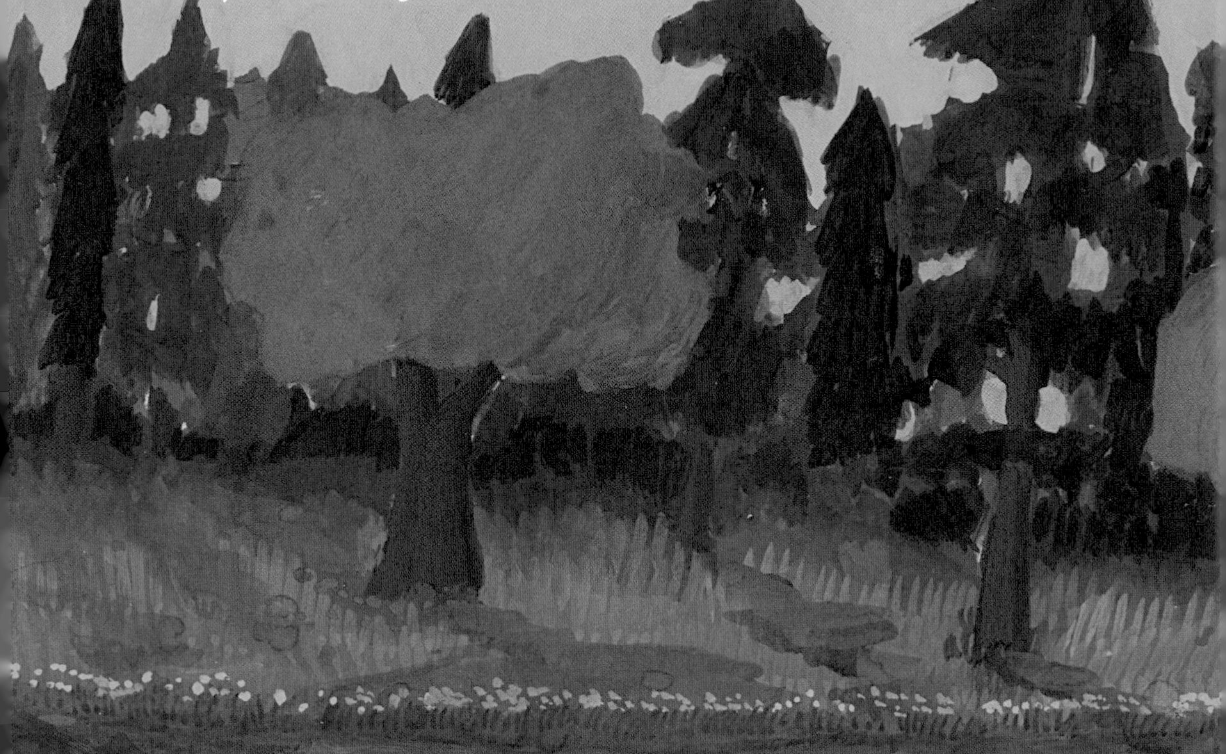

We spend our lives planning weddings, birthday parties, brunches, births, surprise parties, anniversaries, shopping trips, vacations, family reunions, romantic weekends. But why stop there? Spend some time thinking about how you'd really like to die.

Where are you? What are you wearing? Who are you with? Is there music? What happens next? What do you hope happens next?

Keep in mind that no matter how many people you're surrounded by, you die alone. This is really your show.

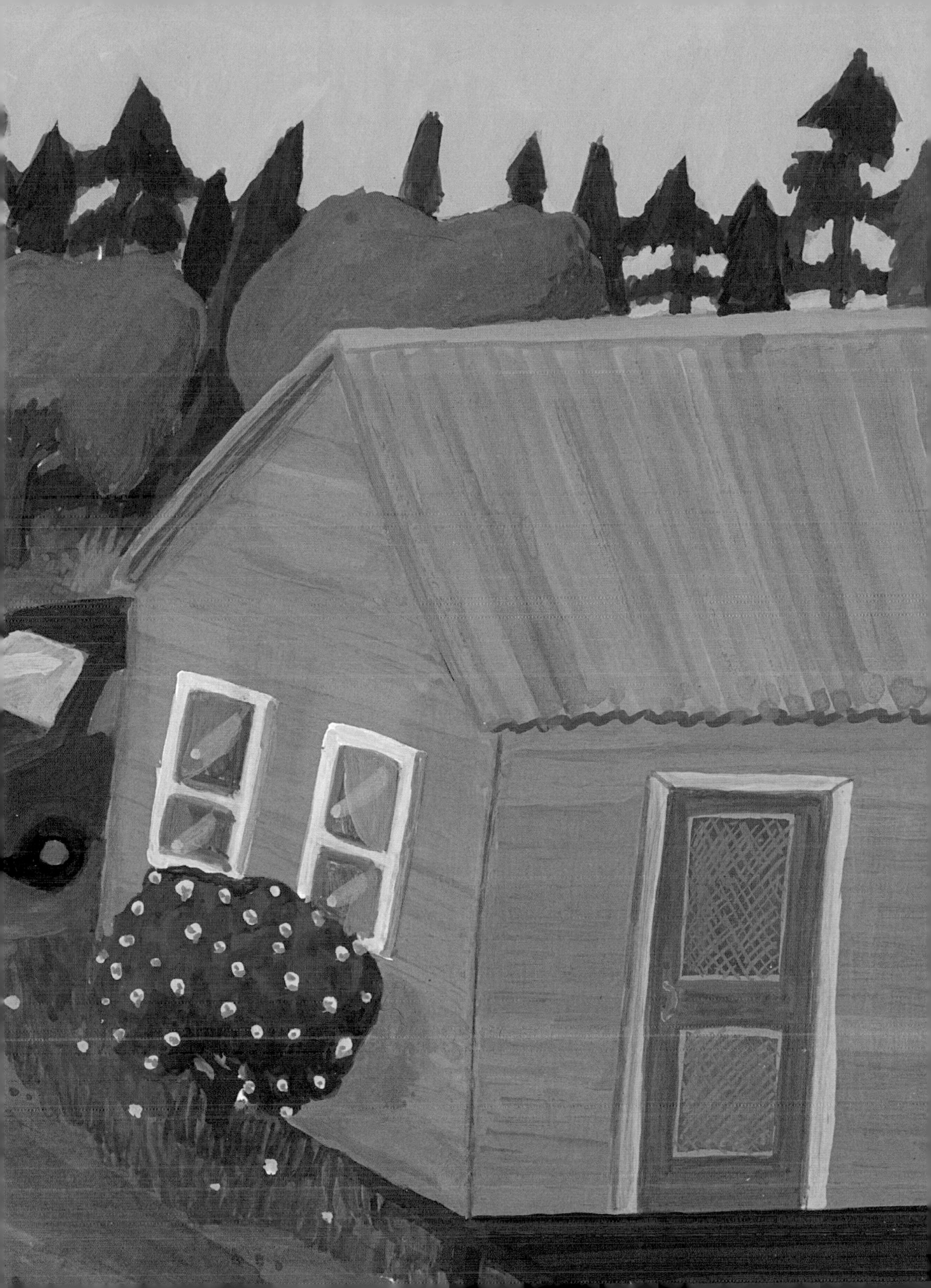

In fact, it has been your show all along, long before the day I died.

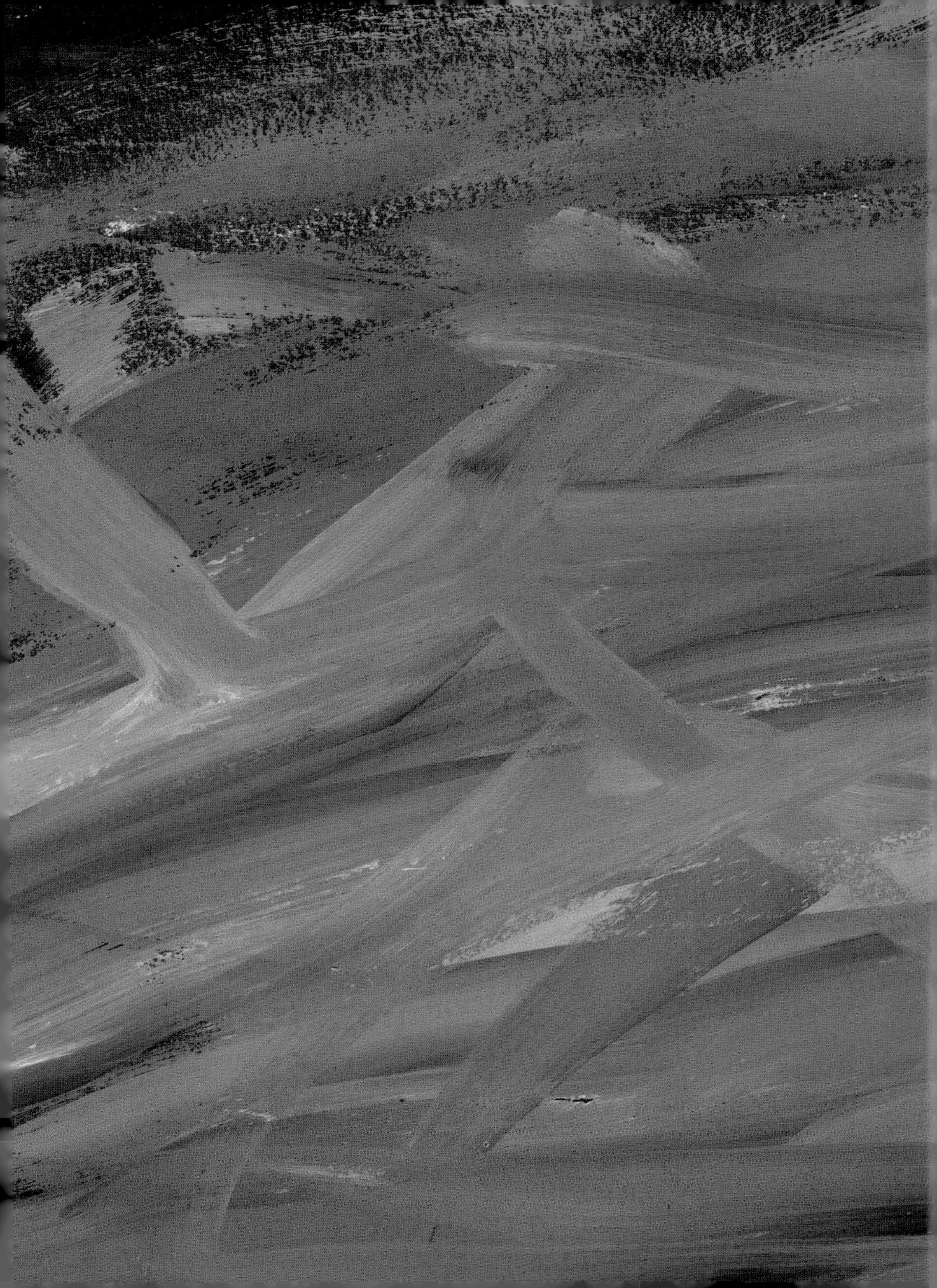

Even though it comforts you to get my advice—and trust me, I have no shortage of it—you already know all the answers. In fact, you don't really need this book.

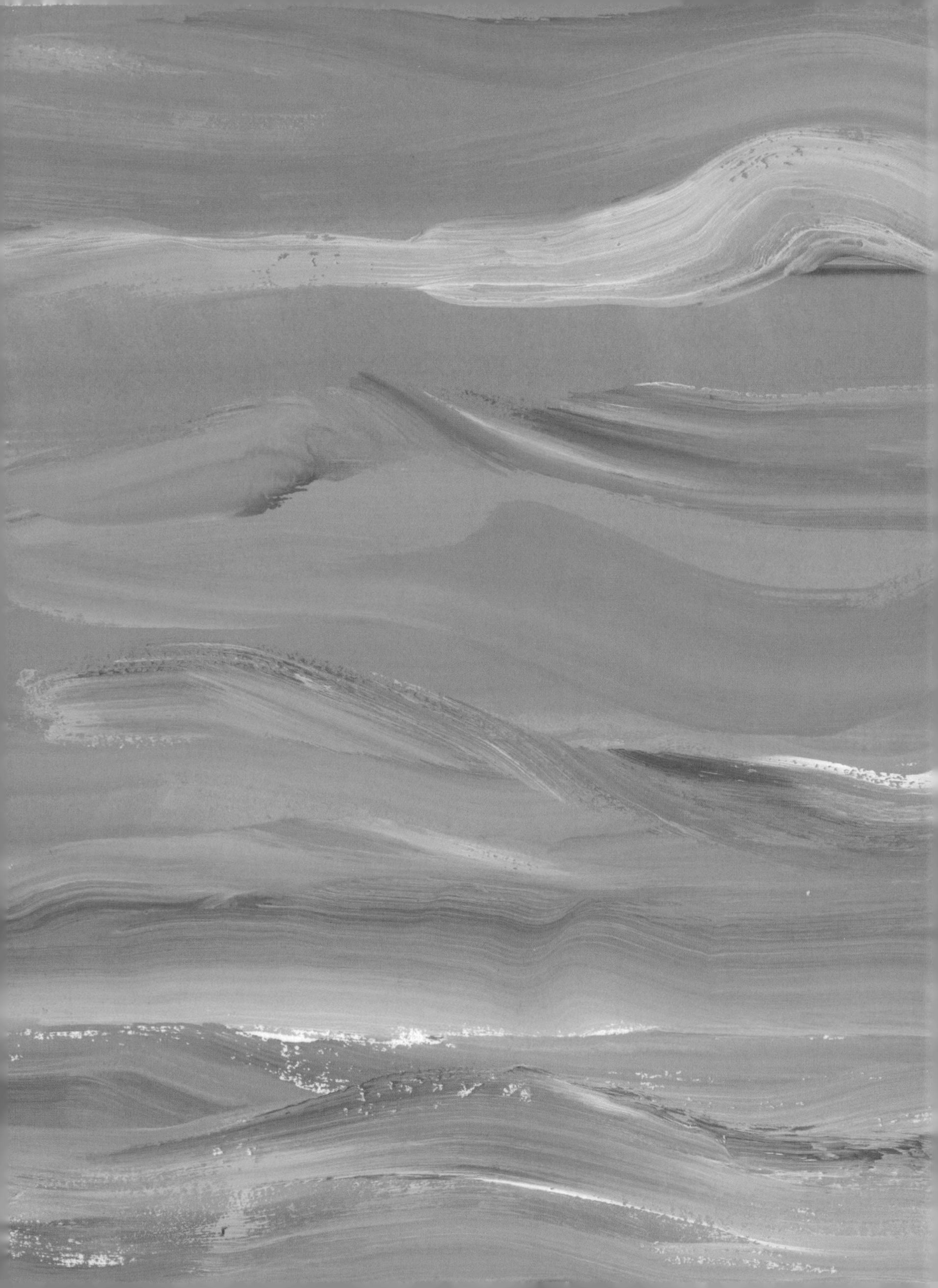

I was happy to write it with you, but you don't need it. You already have what it takes to carry on without me. You already have it within you to face what's ahead.

The infinite river of memories
we shared still connects us. Let that
river flow over you and through you,
carrying you forward and beyond.

Acknowledgments

Heartfelt thanks to our agent, Kate McKean, for her belief in this book, her support, and her encouragement. And much gratitude to Nancy Miller and her incredible staff at Bloomsbury for thoughtful editing, kind guidance, and for making this such a happy and memorable experience.

From Hallie

Many thanks to Jack Sjogren—your encouragement and hugs at the end of so many long workdays kept me going. To Alice Medland, for being my best friend and for bringing me joy and flowers on a regular basis. To Ariana Lenarsky, for pulling me away from the desk to hike each Sunday, always returning me more inspired and eager to work. To Nick and Ben for many long, life-sustaining phone calls and for always making me laugh. To my dad, Chris Bateman, for his humor, generosity, and for patiently waiting his turn. (Don't worry, Dad, I've got some ideas for how to immortalize your wisdom.)

And to my mom, for being utterly irreplaceable but willing to try to replace herself anyway.

From Suzy

I'm grateful to the many elders I've interviewed over the past decade for helping me understand the depth and duration of love and loss. To Ben, Hallie, and Nick, for three decades of action-packed training on being a mom. To my sister, Ann Gosman, for her friendship and insights during and after our mother's death. To Chris Bateman, the funniest writer I know, for reading draft after draft and still laughing out loud, and for joining me thirty years ago on this grand experiment called parenthood.

And to Hallie, again, for our long talks that are the heart of this book, and for illustrations that reach so far beyond words.

A Note on the Author and the Illustrator

 Hallie Bateman is an illustrator and writer whose work has appeared in the *New Yorker*, the *New York Times Magazine*, *Lenny*, *BuzzFeed*, the *Awl*, and elsewhere. Her creative journal, *Brave New Work*, was published by MoMA in 2017. She lives in Los Angeles.

 Suzy Hopkins is a former newspaper reporter who since 2008 has published a quarterly magazine (*Friends and Neighbors*, www.seniorfan.com) for boomers and seniors in California's Central Sierra. She is also Hallie's mom. She lives in Columbia, California.